# Juan Alvarado
# Governor of California
# 1836–1842

*Juan Bautista Alvarado, 1854.* Courtesy of the San Pablo Historical Society.

# Juan Alvarado Governor of California 1836–1842

Robert Ryal Miller

UNIVERSITY OF OKLAHOMA PRESS : NORMAN

Also by Robert Ryal Miller

*For Science and National Glory: The Spanish Scientific Expedition to America,
    1862–1866* (Norman, 1968)
*Arms across the Border: United States Aid to Juárez during the French Intervention in
    Mexico* (Philadelphia, 1973)
*Mexico: A History* (Norman, 1985)
*Shamrock and Sword: The Saint Patrick's Battalion in the U.S.-Mexican War*
    (Norman, 1989)
*Captain Richardson: Mariner, Ranchero, and Founder of San Francisco* (Berkeley,
    1995)

**Library of Congress Cataloging-in-Publication Data**

Miller, Robert Ryal.
    Juan Alvarado, governor of California, 1836–1842 / Robert Ryal
Miller.
        p.   cm.
    Includes bibliographical references and index.
    ISBN 0-8061-3077-6 (cloth   :   alk. paper)
    1. Alvarado, Juan Bautista, 1809–1882.   2. Governors—California—
Biography.   3. California—Politics and government—To 1846.
4. Mexican Americans—California—Biography.   I. Title.
F864.A484M55   1998
979.4′03′092—dc21
    [b]                                                                          98-17589
                                                                                       CIP

Copyright © 1998 by the University of Oklahoma Press, Norman, Publishing
Division of the University. All rights reserved. Manufactured in the U.S.A.

1   2   3   4   5   6   7   8   9   10

# Contents

| | |
|---|---|
| Illustrations | vii |
| Preface | ix |
| 1. Boyhood in Monterey, 1809–1827 | 3 |
| 2. Civil Servant and Legislator, 1827–1836 | 21 |
| 3. Revolutionary Governor, 1836–1839 | 45 |
| 4. Constitutional Governor, 1839–1842 | 63 |
| 5. Revolt against Micheltorena, 1843–1845 | 97 |
| 6. Colonel against the Yankees, 1846–1848 | 111 |
| 7. *Ranchero* at Rancho San Pablo, 1848–1882 | 130 |
| 8. The Great Land Case and Legacy, 1867–1894 | 161 |
| Appendix A: Typical Land Grant Awarded by Governor Alvarado | 179 |
| Appendix B: Children of Juan B. and Martina Castro de Alvarado | 181 |
| Appendix C: Children of Juan B. Alvardo and Juliana Castillo | 182 |
| Notes | 183 |
| Bibliography | 197 |
| Index | 209 |

# Illustrations

## Figures

| | |
|---|---|
| Photograph of Juan Bautista Alvarado, 1854 | *Frontispiece* |
| Signature and flourish of Juan Bautista Alvarado | 22 |
| Home of Alvarado's mistress on Dutra Street, Monterey | 33 |
| El Cuartel (government building) in Monterey | 66 |
| Martina Castro de Alvarado, 1854 | 68 |
| Alvarado's two-story adobe home in Monterey | 73 |
| Alvarado's adobe house at Rancho El Alisal | 86 |
| General Manuel Micheltorena | 98 |
| General José Castro | 113 |
| Castro-Alvarado home on Rancho San Pablo | 134 |
| Invitation to a patriotic ball in San Pablo, 1862 | 150 |
| Celinda Alvarado, c. 1867 | 156 |
| Juan Bautista Alvarado, 1881 | 159 |
| Delfina Alvarado, c. 1865 | 168 |
| Juan B. Cosme Alvarado, c. 1895 | 170 |
| Henry Alvarado, c. 1920 | 172 |
| Adelina Alvarado Tedford, c. 1887 | 174 |

## Map

| | |
|---|---|
| *Diseño* of Rancho San Pablo, 1830 | 132 |

# Preface

VICTOR HERBERT'S ROMANTIC OPERA *Natoma*, which premiered in 1911, is set in California during the Hispanic era and calls for a baritone to sing the principal role of Juan Bautista Alvarado. This imaginary Alvarado is a hot-headed Spaniard who aspires to marry a young woman and thus gain control of the estates left to her by her mother. Joseph Redding, the librettist, who was born and raised in California, may well have based his story on the real-life Don Juan Bautista Alvarado, an ambitious and talented Californio (son of California) who married Martina Castro, whose mother deeded to her most of the vast Rancho San Pablo, across the bay from San Francisco. Alvarado is also mentioned in all the standard histories of California as well as in western novels such as *The Californios*, by Louis L'Amour, and *The Saga of Andy Burnett*, by Stewart Edward White.

Although Juan Bautista Alvarado has been characterized in song, novels, and brief biographical sketches, until now there has not been a full biography of this fascinating person. Born in 1809, Don Juan lived the first half of his life in Monterey, the capital of Alta California. During those years, he twice witnessed a change of flags over the public buildings—from the red and gold Spanish ensign to the Mexican red, white, and green tricolor; and finally to the American Stars and Stripes. Alvarado's career was in the Mexican government civil service; he rose from legislative clerk and customhouse appraiser to president of the California territorial legislature.

Then, at the age of twenty-seven, he became the governor of California, gaining the executive office through a revolution he organized in 1836, which toppled the dictatorial military governor.

Alvarado was filled with great political ambition for himself and for California. He not only wanted to govern the province, but he also tested the idea of making the territory a free and independent country. Unlike most of his colleagues, he realized that California was in a precarious position—a target for acquisition by France, Great Britain, or the United States, yet neglected and unprotected by a weak Mexico. Thus, he believed that Californians would have to overthrow Mexican rule and establish control by native sons in order to protect the region from foreign encroachment.

Don Juan Alvarado was the youngest governor California has ever had and the only one in the Mexican era to serve his entire six-year term. But more important, as the first civilian governor—his predecessors had all been professional military officers—he emphasized such civil pursuits as education, cultural affairs, the court system, and private property rights. During his administration he transferred hundreds of thousands of acres of public property (former mission lands) to private individuals, awarding more ranch grants than any other governor. And unlike other chief executives, he did not give himself any land, either openly or through an intermediary. This vast transfer of land had a tremendous impact on California, transforming the poverty-stricken frontier garrison state, headed by a military elite, to a proud, pastoral civilization and prosperous economy based on widespread private ownership of ranches and farms.

The first years of Alvarado's governorship were marred by revolts of southern Californians who championed their own candidate for governor and who wanted the capital moved to Los Angeles; but when those uprisings were quelled, he adroitly tackled the major problems facing the region. For better administration of the area, he persuaded the legislature to divide California into districts, each placed under a prefect; and to improve the justice system, he promoted the establishment of a supreme court. Secularization (phasing out) of the missions had proceeded haphazardly until Alvarado issued comprehensive regulations for the administrators. He also sponsored erection of a new government headquarters building in Monterey, ordered repair of streets in the capital and other towns, gave assistance to presidial and private schools, and raised money for medals to be awarded to young scholars.

This study of Alvarado's life illuminates much of California's history during the Mexican period and the transition to American rule. It presents the Mexican interpretation of several incidents involving Americans in California—for example, the Graham affair of 1840, when a number of Americans were arrested; Commodore Jones's abortive takeover in 1842; John C. Frémont's role in the Bear Flag revolt; and California battles during the U.S.-Mexican War. The book also embraces social and cultural topics, including ranch life, censorship of books, multiculturalism, and weddings. The married children of Don Juan and his wife, Martina, all chose English-speaking, non-Hispanic spouses; so did hundreds of their contemporaries. Intermarriage and bilingualism have a long tradition in California.

After he left office and the Americans took over California, Alvarado moved his family to Rancho San Pablo, located on the eastern shore of San Pablo Bay about thirteen miles northeast of San Francisco. For more than thirty years Don Juan lived the life of a "land poor" rancher while engaged in litigation over ownership of the 17,000-acre spread. Meanwhile, the gold rush and continued immigration brought a flood of Anglo Americans to California, which made San Francisco the metropolis of the state. Because it was an exciting commercial and social center where many of his friends lived, Alvarado spent much time in the city. There, in 1876, the historian Hubert Howe Bancroft provided him with lodging, in exchange for which the former governor dictated to one of Bancroft's agents a remarkable five-volume manuscript, "Historia de California," totaling more than twelve hundred pages. That important unpublished source, as well as Alvarado's "Notes on California History" (written for his attorney, Theodore H. Hittell), have been invaluable for writing his biography. But in their published histories of California, neither Bancroft nor Hittell relied completely on Alvarado's version of past events. So too, this biography has tempered Don Juan's recollection of his life and accomplishments with observations by his contemporaries and interpretations of later writers.

Each chapter of this book contains excerpts from letters, reports, documents, or memoirs that were written by Alvarado or his contemporaries during the period under discussion. Those that were written in Spanish have been translated by the author of this biography. These firsthand accounts lend authenticity and give historical perspective to the era or subject being discussed; at the same time they expose readers to some of the vast literature and sources of California history. Because much of the action takes place in the Mexican period (1821–1846) and the chief characters were native Spanish-speakers, a number of Spanish terms, such as *alcalde, baile, diputación,* and *vaquero,* after being defined, have been printed in italics throughout the book to emphasize the Hispanic cultural environment in which the Alvarado family lived.

My research about Alvarado began when I was teaching university classes on the history of California and discovered that there was no biography of the former governor. After retirement, I continued the search and began to write the story of his life, utilizing the vast collection of books and manuscripts in the Bancroft Library at the University of California, Berkeley. I am grateful for the assistance of librarians and staff at the Bancroft and other research facilities: the California Historical Society, California State Library, Contra Costa County History Center, Huntington Library, Oakland Public Library, San Pablo Historical Society, Society of California Pioneers, and the Sutro Library. I am indebted to Earl and Frances Conley, who generously made available their extensive collection of genealogical records, photographs, and research notes about Don Juan Bautista Alvarado and his extended family. I would also like to thank Roger Rehm, who contributed material from his library, and Ann Roberts, long-time curator at the Alvarado Adobe Museum in San Pablo, who provided information, clues, and encouragement. I also appreciate the constructive criticism offered by Janet R. Fireman and David J. Langum, scholars of early California history, who read earlier versions of the manuscript. Thanks also to Sarah Iselin, of the University of Oklahoma Press, who did superb editorial work and prepared the manuscript for publication.

R.R.M.

*Santa Barbara, California*

Juan Alvarado
Governor of California
1836–1842

# Boyhood in Monterey
# 1809–1827

ALTA CALIFORNIA, THE SPANISH empire's northernmost colonial outpost, was sparsely settled by about two thousand *pobladores* (Spanish-speaking colonists) when Juan Bautista Alvarado was born there in 1809. During the previous forty years, Franciscan friars had established a string of twenty missions along the Pacific coast from San Diego to San Francisco Bay, where they indoctrinated numerous California Indians in Christian practices and taught them European cultural values and skills. By 1810 there were 18,770 *neophytes* (Christianized Indians) in the missions; the number of *gentiles* (non-Christianized Indians) who lived in the north and interior regions is unknown— perhaps there were as many as 200,000. Spanish infantry and cavalrymen were stationed at the four military presidios: San Francisco, Monterey, Santa Barbara, and San Diego. About one hundred active soldiers were attached to each presidio; the families of the married soldiers at least tripled the population of these military settlements. A squad of soldiers was assigned to guard duty at each of the missions, thus reducing the number in each presidio garrison. Retired soldiers and some civilian residents lived in three small Spanish *pueblos* (towns): Los Angeles, San Jose, and Branciforte (Santa Cruz), with a total "urban" population of 536 in 1810. A few ranchers and their families and *vaqueros* (cowboys) lived on ranches, where they raised livestock.[1]

Although it was not strictly observed, there was a social hierarchy in Alta California which was based somewhat on racial and cultural lines as well as on one's place of birth. During the Spanish era (1769–1821), the few *peninsulares* (persons born in Spain) were considered an elite; their numbers included virtually all of the missionaries and the commandants of the presidios. Ranking just below them were the limited number of *criollos* (creoles), those persons of all-Spanish ancestry who had been born in the New World; the Alvarados were creoles. But the great majority of the *pobladores* were *mestizos* (offspring of mixed Spanish and Indian ancestors), and there were also some blacks and mulattoes in the population. All of the above were considered *gente de razón* (rational or civilized people), as contrasted with the Native American Indians.[2]

The Spanish military governor and other government officials resided in Monterey, the capital of Alta California and birthplace and hometown of Juan Bautista Alvarado. Until 1820, all the residents of Monterey—military men and their dependents plus the few civil officials and their families—lived in the presidio. Built in the form of a quadrangle with an exterior perimeter of 481 by 352 feet, the compound was enclosed by an adobe wall five feet thick and twelve feet high with a large gate set in it, the keys to which were delivered to the governor each evening at sunset by the head of the guard. In the center of the enclosure was a large plaza, or parade ground, surrounded by tile-roofed adobe structures that had been built against the walls. These buildings, which had a continuous covered *portal* (corridor) fronting on the plaza, housed officers, enlisted men, and their families; workshops and storerooms; an armory; an infirmary; a guardhouse; and a jail. In addition, there was the Royal Chapel (still extant), which served the approximately three hundred residents, although occasionally the soldiers or their family members received religious solace and sacraments at Mission San Carlos Borromeo, familiarly called Mission Carmel, located three leagues (eight miles) away, near the mouth of the Carmel River.[3]

Juan Bautista Alvarado was born to the union of two military families of Spanish ancestry, the Alvarados and Vallejos, both with early connections to Monterey. His paternal grandfather and namesake had been a soldier in the Spanish army and had accompanied Gaspar de Portolá and Father Junípero Serra when they marched north from Baja California in 1769 to establish the first outposts in Alta California. After returning to Baja California, this ancestor was sent across the Gulf of California to the garrison at Sinaloa, a town in the northwestern part of New Spain (colonial Mexico). There, his son José Francisco Alvarado enlisted in the army and was posted to Loreto, Baja California, where he rose to the rank of sergeant. In 1805 Sergeant Alvarado was transferred to the cavalry company at the presidio of Monterey, traveling as an aide to Governor José Joaquín Arrillaga. Three years later he married fourteen-year-old María Josefa Vallejo, daughter of Don Ignacio Vallejo, a distinguished sergeant at Monterey.[4]

The Vallejo family history included conquistadors and many persons of education—notably, several priests, friars, and nuns of some prominence in colonial Mexico. Juan Bautista Alvarado's maternal grandfather, Ignacio Vallejo, had been destined by his parents for an ecclesiastical career, but in 1769, at the age of twenty-one, he fled the seminary in Guadalajara and enlisted in the Spanish army. Joining one of the companies recruited to go to Alta California, he accompanied Captain Fernando Rivera y Moncada to Monterey in 1773, and three years later he was present at the founding of the presidio and mission of San Francisco. During the subsequent half century, he served at various missions and presidios and was promoted to the rank of distinguished sergeant. In his enlistment papers Ignacio Vallejo was described as five feet five and one-half inches tall, with chestnut hair, gray eyes, short nose, full beard, and a fair complexion. In 1790 he married María Antonia Lugo, and they had thirteen children, one of the daughters being María Josefa, who married Juan Bautista Alvarado's father in 1808.[5]

Born on Saint Valentine's Day in 1809, Juan Bautista Valentín Alvarado y Vallejo was baptized the next day at the presidio chapel at Monterey. Just three months later, his father fell gravely ill with a fever at Mission San Luis Obispo, 150 miles south of Monterey, where he had stopped en route home from carrying a dispatch to San Diego. Josefa, with her baby in her arms, hurried down El Camino Real (the Royal Highway), but upon reaching Mission San Miguel, about three-fourths of the way to San Luis Obispo, she received the sad news that her husband had died and had been buried on May 29. Before dying, the sergeant left instructions for the Monterey paymaster to sell his horses and saddles, the proceeds to be divided between his wife and child. The items brought six hundred *pesos* (Mexican dollars), a substantial sum in those days.[6]

With her infant boy, the grieving young widow returned to Monterey and reluctantly moved back to her parents' quarters in the presidio. Three years later, when Josefa married army cadet Don Raymundo Estrada, she left her son in the care of his Vallejo grandparents. Subsequently she had nine children, who were half brothers and half sisters of Juan Bautista. Meanwhile, young "Juanito" grew up in the Vallejo home, where "obedience" and "respect" were the two watchwords of conduct. In this Monterey home Juanito was surrounded by five aunts and three uncles, plus two more of each born in the next seven years.[7] One of the uncles was Mariano Guadalupe Vallejo, only a year and a half older and a boyhood playmate. (He would become a noted military commander and one of the largest landholders in northern California.)

Alvarado later wrote down some of his memories of family life in the Vallejo household. In addition to celebrations in connection with religious holidays, there were numerous birthday parties as well as fiestas on each person's saint's day. Don Juanito celebrated his birthday in mid-February and his saint's (John the Baptist's), day on June 24. He also remembered a common punishment inflicted by his stern old grandfather on any child who misbehaved. The miscreant was not permitted to join the family at the well-set table for the main midday meal; instead, the child was forced to kneel in a corner of the dining room and eat his or her food with a wooden spoon from an earthenware dish and drink from a tin cup placed on a hide-covered wooden stool. "When I was young," he recalled, "I underwent this kind of punishment on two or three occasions, and I assure you that I would have preferred to receive ten hand slaps from Archuleta, the schoolmaster, or, indeed, a scolding sermon of reprimand from José el Cantor [the singing master], rather than endure the shame of remaining on my knees beside a stool while my uncle and fellow pupil, Mariano Guadalupe Vallejo, was seated at the table. I will say to their credit, however, that when I was 'doing penance,' neither he nor my brothers would laugh about it at the table."[8]

Alvarado and his playmates entertained themselves with various games, sometimes wagering bets and using buttons as counters. They played *vaquela*, which involved throwing pebbles at a mark drawn on the ground, and *tágamo* or *manica* (games of peg toss); they skipped stones on the surface of water in a game called *caña* (ducks and drakes); they rolled a hoop with a stick; they rode hobbyhorses in the nearby hills; and on moonlit nights they played *gallina ciega* (blindman's bluff). Both boys and girls played simple musical instruments such as drums, flutes, and Jew's harps. On rainy days they amused themselves with dolls, homemade toys, *naipes* (playing cards), and other indoor activities.[9]

Formal education was minimal and neglected in California during the Spanish and early Mexican eras—few people could even sign their names. One of the first teachers in Monterey was a retired corporal named Manuel Boronda, who instructed presidio boys in their first letters. Boronda and another teacher named Salvador Aspiroz were followed by Corporal Miguel Archuleta, who had a class of more than a dozen boys including Juan Alvarado and Mariano Vallejo. Don Juan remembered that two boys in rotation were assigned to sweep the classroom every morning; if it was not cleaned by seven o'clock in the summer and eight o'clock in the winter, the teachers were sure to punish them "with a good slapping." The pupils sat on rough benches facing the schoolmaster, who had a hemp scourge across his desk ever ready to punish offenses such as laughing or spilling ink. Besides learning to read, write, and cipher, they were instructed in the *doctrina*, which consisted of the sign of the cross; the acts of faith, hope, and charity; the ten commandments; six precepts; seven sacraments; the necessary points of faith; the four last things; and the prayers: Our Father, Hail Mary, the Creed, and the Confiteor. The boys also studied religious singing with José el Cantor, who taught them to chant the rosary and to sing a mass.[10]

Colonel Pablo Vicente Solá, who was appointed governor of California in 1815, was interested in education. Soon after his arrival, he ordered Corporal Archuleta to bring his pupils to the governor's office, along with the slates on which each one wrote and the books they were studying. When asked who were his most advanced students, the schoolmaster replied, "Young Alvarado and Vallejo." The books they read were Jerónimo de Ripalda's *Catechism*, the *Novena of the Most Holy Virgin*, and tracts about the lives of saints. After stating that the boys should be taught things other than religion, the governor distributed candy, nuts, and figs to the students. Before dismissing the group, he ordered the star pupils, Alvarado and Vallejo, to come to his office regularly. During subsequent sessions, the governor gave them a chance to improve their penmanship by copying documents and letters, and he explained the necessity and advantages of diligent study, accompanying this advice with gifts of newspapers published in Mexico City, a copy of the Spanish Constitution of 1812, and an edition of Cervantes' novel, *Don Quixote de la Mancha*.[11]

Mariano Vallejo later recalled an incident that occurred when he and Alvarado were schoolmates in Monterey. Hearing that a ship was about to anchor in the bay, Corporal Archuleta granted a recess to his pupils so they could watch the official welcome. Although ordered to cork their ink bottles and close the *gatera* (cat door), the pupils rushed to the beach without doing either. On their return they found the room full of chickens that had come in through the cat door and had scattered papers and spilled ink on the government documents the boys had been copying. The schoolmaster was furious and ordered all the boys into the adjacent "punishment room," but they rebelled, whereupon he locked them in the school and reported them to the governor. Sergeant Ignacio Vallejo, ordered by Solá to settle the matter, pardoned the boys "because it was the chickens that had done the damage," on condition that they rewrite the spoiled sheets.[12]

Through conversations with his grandfather and with the governor, Alvarado became aware of the Peninsular War and French invasion of Spain as well as the simultaneous independence wars being waged in Spain's American colonies. During those years, California was virtually abandoned by the Spanish government, which also discontinued sending the annual ship carrying the *Memoria del Rey* (memento of the king) payment for the troops, normally amounting to fifty thousand *pesos* in cash and a similar amount in goods. To make up for the loss, the governor requisitioned foodstuffs, clothing, and other products from the missions, paying with a draft on the government. Trade was also carried on with officers of the Russian American Company, which in 1812 had established bases at Fort Ross and Bodega Bay in northern California. The Spanish missions provided grain and furs in exchange for Russian and European manufactured goods. Although Spanish laws forbade foreign merchant ships from calling at colonial ports, the regulations were often overlooked, and smuggling became common, especially at out-of-the-way spots.

At the time of Don Juan's eighth birthday in 1817, an alien schooner that anchored in Monterey Bay caused some concern and excitement. Using a speaking trumpet, a presidio officer demanded the ship's name and business, but the visitors did not understand Spanish. Although the ship hoisted an American flag, the banner was not recognized by the Spanish shore party; nor did the Stars and Stripes appear in their official flag book, which dated from the previous century. Eventually, an English-speaking interpreter ordered the captain to come ashore, where he was marched to the governor's reception room. Dressed in a peculiar costume never seen before in Monterey—a black suit with swallow-tailed coat and a black stovepipe hat—the stranger was questioned by the governor and the presidio commandant, who were wearing their dress uniforms. Captain James Wilcox explained that his ship, the *Traveller*, was bound for Boston, loaded with a cargo of Chinese merchandise, some of which he was willing to sell or exchange in California. While an executive council discussed the matter, the visitor sat guarded in the presidio plaza, where Alvarado and the other school-boys dubbed him the "Red Captain" because he frequently wiped his brow with a large, red silk handkerchief. Finally, the captain was released, permitted to fill his fresh water kegs, and ordered to have his ship out of firing range within five hours.[13]

In November of 1818, privateers captured Monterey, a humiliating experience for the government officials and an event long remembered by Don Juan and other residents, who dubbed the invaders "pirates." Previously warned that revolutionaries from South America, fighting for their independence from Spain, had outfitted vessels for raiding Spanish ports on the Pacific, Governor Solá had taken preliminary precautions. Then, when an exhausted courier galloped into the presidio on November 20 with news that two hostile warships had attempted to attack the settlement across the bay at Santa Cruz and were headed toward Monterey, the governor put his plans into action. He ordered the soldiers and the militia to prepare for battle while the women and children were to retreat to the government-owned Rancho del Rey, about twenty miles away (site of the present city of Salinas), or to outlying missions. Ten-year-old Juanito joined his mother to help her care for his three young half brothers and half sister. After piling bedding, clothing, food, and children in ox-drawn *carretas*, the military dependents headed inland, annoyed by a constant drizzle.[14]

Some days later, Alvarado and other refugees heard about the shocking events that had taken place in Monterey. At dawn on November 21, one of the armed frigates, the *Santa Rosa*, had approached the shore and fired a broadside at the *castillo* (artillery fort) that was on a hillock overlooking Monterey Bay. Following two hours of artillery dueling, during which much damage was done to the frigate, the insurgents lowered their flag in token of surrender, but not before having sent six boatloads of men to the larger ship. In response to the demand that some responsible person be sent ashore, the second officer and two sailors landed and were questioned, but because of their "lies and frivolous excuses" the governor put them in the guardhouse. Then, Hipolito Bouchard, a French-born resident of Buenos Aires who commanded the larger frigate, the *Argentina*, sent an officer, under a flag of truce, bearing a formal demand for the surrender of the province. Governor Solá scorned the demand, saying that he and his men were loyal to Spain and would repel any attempt to take possession.[15]

Early the next morning, nine boats, four of them carrying small cannon, conveyed ashore an invading force of more than three hundred armed men. With a defense of only twenty-five cavalrymen and fifteen artillerymen, the governor was obliged to withdraw. After ordering the cannons spiked and the powder magazine blown up, Solá retreated to the Rancho del Rey with his soldiers, one cannon, two boxes of gunpowder, six thousand musket cartridges, and all the documents of the archives. The invaders stayed in Monterey for five days while they repaired their damaged ship, ransacked the dwellings for loot, destroyed the orchard and gardens, loaded beef and other supplies, and set fire to roof beams in the presidio before sailing to southern California.[16]

As soon as Don Juan's stepfather, Cadet Raymundo Estrada, arrived at Rancho del Rey, the family moved north to Mission San Juan Bautista, from where they were invited to stay temporarily at Rancho San Ysidro (near the present city of Gilroy). For more than six months they lived in a small house adjacent to the principal one occupied by Don Ignacio Ortega; his wife, María Gertrudis; their married son, José; and two daughters, Clara and Antonia, then about ten and twelve years old. Ranch life was a new experience for Juan—he learned to ride horseback and rope cattle, and he helped with the chore of milking cows. He later wrote about his association with the Ortega girls, recalling that they were "beautiful, fair-skinned, with hair that reached almost to their knees": "I used to stay in Don Ignacio's house a good part of the night telling stories to the girls, because I remembered many stories that the boys used to tell in school. Most of them were tales from *The Arabian Nights*, which they greatly enjoyed hearing and to which I used to make some additions of my own; and they would beg me to be sure to come every night, because, apart from the story-telling, they wanted me to give them lessons in reading and writing, since at that age I could already write a good letter and knew some arithmetic."[17]

At the ranch, Don Juan also learned how to kill bears, which were very numerous and were destroying the livestock. In an autobiographical account, he told how his stepfather constructed an observation platform in an oak tree, placed a dead mare under it, and shot the maurading bears. One night Juan stayed in the platform with his stepfather, who shot a female bear and her two cubs. During their stay at Rancho San Ysidro, Estrada shot forty bears, skinned them, and eventually sold the bearskins to a trader for two hundred *pesos.*[18]

In addition to what he learned about ranch life during this period, Don Juan acquired some possessions there. Ignacio Ortega gave young Alvarado several yards of Spanish woolen cloth, from which Alvarado's mother made him a fine suit of clothes. A nearby rancher, Mariano Castro, who previously had been aided by Juan's father in a land dispute, gave him one hundred *pesos* and two fine colts, and another acquaintance presented him with a handsome tooled-leather saddle decorated with some silver ornaments. Don Juan later wrote, "With this saddle and with my thoroughbreds I expected to make my appearance in the capital, Monterey, as though I were the son of a rich landowner."[19]

Reconstruction of the Monterey presidio took about six months. The nearby missions provided Indian laborers, tools, oxen, wagons, and provisions. Don Juan's grandfather, Sergeant Ignacio Vallejo, was in charge of the rebuilding project and supervised the various crews—carpenters, adobe makers, masons, painters, and so on. When the viceroy of Mexico heard about the raid on Monterey, he sent munitions and two hundred soldiers—infantry, cavalry, and artillery—to California as reinforcements. Much later, in their histories of California, Alvarado and Antonio María Osio both described the arrivals as *cholo* (mixed-blood, disreputable) soldiers who committed numerous robberies, stabbings, and other crimes. As soon as the presidio walls and houses had been rebuilt, the scattered Spanish families returned to the capital. Beginning in 1820, a number of residents erected houses between the presidio and the fortified *castillo* near the landing place. Don Juan stayed in the presidio with his mother and stepfather for about a year.[20]

When Alvarado's stepfather was transferred to the Presidio of San Francisco, Don Juan sold his horses, which required feeding and stabling, and moved back with his Vallejo grandparents, where he remained for more than a decade. In 1821 he was able to make a short visit to his parents at the northern presidio, but the trip involved riding on the *anquera* (leather apron) behind Cadet José Joaquín Estudillo. They covered the fifty leagues (130 miles) northward in twenty-two hours, changing horses at missions and various ranchos. After returning to the capital with a military escort, he went to the governor's office daily for lessons and for practice in writing by copying official dispatches. In addition, he was able to browse through some of the government books, including the compilation of Spanish laws entitled *Novísima Recopilación de Leyes.* For several years William Hartnell, a well-educated English trader who resided in Monterey and who had an extensive library of books in English, German, French, and Spanish, tutored young Alvarado and his uncle Mariano Vallejo.[21]

In March 1822, Don Juan and other residents of California were stunned by news from Mexico City. They learned that, after a decade of struggle, the colony of New Spain had won its independence from Spain and would henceforth be known as Mexico. Following a special mass, there were shouts of "*viva*" for independence, cannonades, a grand ball, and fireworks at night. Along with the change of flags from the Spanish lion and castle to the Mexican eagle and cactus, all military and civil officials in California had to take an oath to

support the new empire. Then, in September Don Juan witnessed impressive ceremonies in Monterey when an imperial
commissioner arrived to oversee the transition; the visiting
dignitary was Agustín Fernández de San Vicente, a canon of
the cathedral of Durango who had been decorated by Mexican Emperor Agustín Iturbide with the Order of the Virgin of
Guadalupe.[22]

Because the Mexican government permitted foreign ships
to anchor in its ports, unlike the previous Spanish regime,
Don Juan and other residents of the province began to have
more contact with foreigners. All ships were supposed to stop
first in Monterey, where their captains were obliged to pay
customs duties ranging from 24 to 42 percent on goods they
wished to sell or barter. Revenue from the customs fees
became the major source of income for the California government. This international commerce was the beginning of the
"hide and tallow trade," which lasted for a quarter century,
during which Yankee and British sailing ships loaded with
manufactured goods arrived on the California coast, where
they traded their cargo for cowhides and tallow (beef or
mutton fat) and occasionally for salted beef, cow horns,
wheat, furs, and other produce. Most of the hides went to
Boston for leather; the tallow was taken to South America and
the East Coast for candles and soap. Profits for the seaborne
merchants came from a customary markup of 200 to 300
percent on the New England or European finished goods.
Imported items included textiles (cotton, linen, flannel, wool),
ready-made clothing, boots and shoes, furniture, carpeting,
hardware, tools, crockery, cutlery, cooking utensils, glassware,
clocks, flour, rice, tea and coffee, ale, rum, coffee, cocoa, and
tobacco.[23] California life became more luxurious under the
Mexican flag than it had been under the Spanish.

After Mexico became independent, the new central government authorized California to have its own legislature, or
*diputación*, made up of seven *vocales* (deputies or members),

one from each presidio and pueblo district, and a secretary. Fulfilling their first task to select a governor to succeed Solá, the members chose Lieutenant Luis Antonio Argüello as the first California-born governor of the province, and they selected Solá to represent the province in the Mexican Congress.[24] As a confidant of the governor and a habitué of his office, Alvarado was privy to some of the correspondence and witnessed many of the stirring events that occurred in this transitional period.

Don Juan's growing liberalism, stimulated by reading works of the liberal philosophers of the late eighteenth century, such as Rousseau and Voltaire, as well as by conversations with English and American residents of Monterey and other foreigners, induced him to favor local rule and to oppose authoritarianism. Thus, he was pleased when the Mexican empire was overthrown and replaced by a republic, thereafter called the United States of Mexico. Although the Mexican Constitution of 1824 gave a certain amount of freedom to the newly created states, California was not a state—it was considered a territory, the governors of which would be appointed by officials in Mexico City. However, the great distance from the national capital and the difficulty of communication would make the governors subject to the will of the native-born Californios who served in the territorial *diputación*. Alvarado's enthusiasm for the central government was dampened when a ship arrived in Monterey bearing several officers and soldiers in charge of sixty civilian convicts who had been sent to California to be given their liberty. He later ironically wrote, "This shipment of criminals was the first proof offered to the Californians that the general government had not entirely forgotten them. Oh, what generosity! What magnanimity!"[25]

In May 1825 the arrival in Monterey harbor of two Spanish warships, the *Asia* and the *Constante*, created a sensation, especially because Spain had not officially recognized the independence of Mexico. At first it was feared they were hostile, but when the commander, Captain José Martínez, landed, he explained that he wished to transfer the ships and the 660 men aboard them to the Mexican navy. After an agreement was signed ensuring the liberty of the men and payment of their salaries, the officers and sailors came ashore, pitched tents on the beach, and swore allegiance to the federal constitution of Mexico. Don Juan was impressed when the entire crew walked barefoot to the presidio chapel in order to render thanks to the Virgin for having protected them during a great storm in the Pacific. For three weeks Montereyans sponsored dances, picnics, and other social events involving the visitors; finally, except for a dozen men who remained in California, the strangers set sail for Acapulco under command of a Mexican officer. Given the state of the Mexican treasury, it is unlikely the men ever received their back pay, which amounted to ninety thousand *pesos.*[26]

Not all residents of California applauded the newly created Mexican republic. Some royalists and conservatives, mainly those who had been born in Spain, were opposed to the change, especially after laws were passed (but not entirely enforced) requiring Spaniards to leave the country. A number of the Franciscan missionaries, most of whom had been born in Spain, were displeased with the new government and its leaders, who talked about secularizing or terminating the missions, freeing the neophytes, and distributing the mission lands and livestock. Indeed, the prefect, Padre Vicente Sarría, and the president, Padre Narciso Durán, as well as Fray Luis Martínez and others refused to take the oath of allegiance to the new government, maintaining that they had sworn allegiance to the king of Spain and could not break that oath. Alvarado, who favored the separation of church and state and was somewhat anticlerical, faulted the missionaries for their intransigence.[27]

Don Juan also thought that the church prelates were prudish and stupid when they condemned the waltz, which had been introduced into California about 1824 and had become popular. The bishop of Sonora, whose jurisdiction extended to California, ruled that the dance was immoral and published an edict of anathema, accompanied by excommunication of anyone who danced the waltz. A week after the edict had been read in all the churches and publicly posted, Governor Argüello gave a ball during which one of the young men lamented that the waltz had been banned. The governor replied that he was "neither a bishop nor an archbishop," nor was it within his province to examine the conscience of each one, but if the waltz was pleasing to those assembled there, they might dance it, as he was master of the house. Alvarado noted, "I think it is superfluous to say that the waltz was danced in the parlor of that place that very night to the great pleasure of those in attendance. A few days later it was also danced in other private homes, as the example given by his Excellency proved contagious throughout the entire territory."[28]

Don Juan later recalled that entertainment in Monterey intensified at the end of the 1820s, but his observation may have stemmed from his awareness of such things as he was "coming of age." As a young man Alvarado was fine-looking, well proportioned, strong, and athletic. An old military document made at Loreto in 1797 described his father, José Francisco Alvarado, then twenty years of age, as "a little over five feet one inch in height, hair chestnut, eyes gray, color white, nose sharp and inclined to aquiline, face without beard or scar."[29] This description, increasing the height a few inches and darkening the hair and eyes, would apply also to the son.

Don Juan attended a number of weddings, including three at Mission San Carlos (Carmel) for his Vallejo aunts: Magdelana, Prudencia, and Encarnación. In 1827 the latter married an English-born American, John Rogers Cooper, who had arrived in Monterey in 1823 and boarded with the Vallejo family; thus he was very well known to Alvarado. Wedding celebrations often lasted for two or three days, according to Esteban de la Torre, who grew up in the presidio. He recalled that wedding guests were served large dinners, typically served in courses: soup, lamb or chicken stew, stuffed turkey, fruit, cheese, various kinds of desserts, all accompanied by wine and brandy. For wedding *bailes* (balls) at ranchos or in the pueblos, some families erected outdoor arbors of boughs lined inside with cloth or coverlets to keep out the wind. The dance floor was pounded earth that had previously been well watered and leveled; benches or seats were placed around the edges; and the music consisted of one or more violins, guitars, and singers. Besides waltzes, favorite dances included the *jota*, *jarabe*, *burro*, and *son* (rumba). When a woman was a particularly graceful dancer, the men placed their *sombreros* on her head; then, when she returned to her seat, the hats had to be redeemed with a coin or a poem.[30]

One of Don Juan's acquaintances was a young woman about his age named Brígida Cañes (de Briones), who later wrote a short account about social life in Monterey in that decade. Noting that women wore plain clothes when they attended mass, she added, "For home wear and company we had many expensive dresses, some of silk, or of velvet, others of laces, often of our own making, which were much liked. . . . The rivalry between beauties of high rank was as great as it could be in any country, and much of it turned upon attire, so that those who had small means often underwent many privations in order to equal the splendor of the rich. . . . One of the gallants of the time said that 'dancing, music, religion, and amiability' were the orthodox occupations of the ladies of Alta California."[31]

Señorita Cañes also described the *carnaval* festivities held each year before the beginning of Lent. One year, when the *fandango* (dance) took place on a ranch near Monterey, the guests rode to the party on horseback, the young men showing off their dexterity by picking up a leaf or a flower as they galloped past. On arrival, most people had a supply of *cascarones*—eggshells filled with colored paper or colored earth and cologne—which they broke over the heads of other guests with much laughter. Then everyone cleaned up and sat down to a banquet before the dancing began. "The wild revel of the earlier part of the ball was succeeded by the most courtly behavior."[32] Dances, fireworks, bullfights, and barbecues were held in Monterey on religious holidays and when new governors arrived.

Soon after the Mexican republic was created, its president replaced the California-born governor, Luis Argüello, with Colonel José María Echeandía, an officer from the engineer branch of the army. The new governor traveled overland from Loreto, Baja California, to San Diego, where he arrived in late October 1825 accompanied by a retinue that included his private secretary, Lieutenant Agustín Zamorano, and Lieutenant Romualdo Pacheco, who held the post of aide-de-camp. Residents of Monterey were disappointed when Echeandía decided to establish his residence at San Diego rather than the capital—he gave as reasons: ill health and the fact that the southern presidio was more centrally located for a governor of both Californias. In April 1828, Echeandía began an inspection tour of all the missions, *pueblos*, and presidios of Alta California, arriving two months later in Monterey, where he was greeted with a fiesta, a bullfight, fireworks, and a grand *baile*. At that time, Don Juan first met the new governor, as will be explained in the next chapter.[33]

# 2

# Civil Servant and Legislator
# 1827–1836

THE CHAOTIC POLITICAL SCENE in California, in which Don Juan Bautista Alvarado became intimately and professionally involved, reflected the political instability and revolutionary disturbances in central Mexico during that republic's early history. The vacillation in Mexico City revolved around the struggle between liberals, who favored federalism (states' rights) and an egalitarian society, and conservatives, who preferred preservation of privileges of the elite and a strong chief executive with centralized control over the entire nation. During the republic's first quarter century, the executive power changed hands forty times; political turbulence in California caused a number of governors to be ousted by conspiracies or outright military revolts, sometimes supported by the territorial *diputación*.[1]

Don Juan Bautista Alvarado's first public service and regular employment began in June 1827 when, at the age of eighteen, he was chosen secretary of the territorial *diputación*. This civil service position had a salary of twenty-five *pesos* a month, but as was the case for the military branch of government, the salaries were often in arrears. When the seven deputies met in Monterey, Don Juan recorded that Governor Echeandía addressed their opening session with a long speech in which he explained various policies of the Mexican government and the situation of the territory of California. Echeandía told the delegates that he had been sent to enforce the republican regime and to carry out the laws of Mexico,

*Signature and flourish of Juan Bautista Alvarado.* Courtesy of the San Pablo Historical Society.

including an important policy that called for gradual secularization of the missions. This process embraced three aspects: The mission Indians were to be freed from religious control and encouraged to form their own towns; mission lands and herds were to be divided, with a portion set aside for the mission Indians and the rest for the government, which could then grant parcels of land to deserving citizens; and the Franciscan missionaries were to be replaced by secular parish priests, whereupon the old mission chapels would become parish churches.[2]

The members of the *diputación* met intermittently for three months, during which they considered various subjects, especially foreign commerce, customs duties, and financial matters. They also drafted a petition begging the central government to suspend shipping convicts to California and, instead, to encourage the immigration of honorable citizens. Acting on the governor's recommendation, they voted to change the name of California to "Moctezuma," sending this proposal to Mexico City along with a suggested coat-of-arms for the territory: an Indian with a plume, bow, and quiver in the act of crossing a strait, all within an oval surrounded by olive and oak leaves. Officials in the Mexican capital did not ratify those proposals, nor the one to change the name of the *pueblo* of Los Angeles from "Nuestra Señora la Reina de Los Angeles" to "Victoria de la Reina de Los Angeles."[3]

When the legislative sessions ended in September, Don Juan accompanied Governor Echeandía and his staff on a visit to San Francisco Bay. Lieutenant Ignacio Martínez, commandant of the Presidio of San Francisco, led them on a tour of the fortifications, Point Lobos, and the cove of Yerba Buena. As an engineering officer, the governor speculated on the effectiveness of fortifying Alcatraz and Angel Island as well as the opposite shore to protect the entrance of the bay. Alvarado reminisced, "We climbed the high hill known today as Telegraph Hill, and Echeandía uttered those remarkable words: 'This is marvelous! Mexico is not aware of what she possesses.' Both Echeandía and his secretary Zamorano spoke in loud praise of the beautiful situation of the great bay and the fertility of the land lying thereabout."[4]

At the end of 1827 Echeandía headed back to his residence at the Presidio of San Diego, accompanied by his military escort. When he stopped in Santa Barbara he received a warm reception, which Alvarado later characterized as "concealing a plot." While the governor was being entertained, two Franciscan priests, José Altimira and Antonio Ripoll, secretly embarked on an American brig, the *Harbinger*, and put to sea, leaving California forever. Echeandía was angry and sent for their superior, Father Vicente Sarría, who declared that he had not covered up the escape and that the two friars had taken no great quantity of gold with them, contrary to rumor. Doubtless, the missionaries left because they were royalist sympathizers who objected to the Mexican republic and its various laws that discriminated against citizens who had been born in Spain and threatened to deport them. A related factor was Spain's continued refusal to recognize the independence of Mexico. (Diplomatic recognition was not extended until 1839.)[5]

Echeandía continued to administer territorial affairs from San Diego, where he convoked the *diputación* in 1829. When Alvarado, as secretary, and the members assembled there in January, they objected to meeting so far from their homes. The deputies passed a resolution against further functioning outside the capital, whereupon the miffed governor told them they should return home, which they did. However, for some months Don Juan remained in San Diego, where he became friendly with the presidio chaplain, Fray José Antonio Menéndez, a Dominican who had come from Baja California. Alvarado often dined with the chaplain, sharing a fondness for conversation along with wine and brandy. Sometimes he helped the chaplain copy his religious tracts, and once he wrote a sermon for him "about the depths of hell, painted with all its horrors." The friendship broke up after Alvarado spoke harshly about the Vatican, accusing its agents of "taking money from the Mexicans and milking them."[6]

Don Juan was acquainted with the principal characters, including Chaplain Menéndez, who were involved in San Diego's celebrated "Fitch romance." Henry Fitch, an American ship captain, had fallen in love with Josefa Carrillo, daughter of a retired presidio soldier, and the two were to be married by Chaplain Menéndez. The marriage ceremony had just begun when it was interrupted by an aide to Governor Echeandía, who ordered the padre to desist under the pain of incurring the wrath of civil, military, and ecclesiastical authorities. Echeandía had several reasons for preventing the marriage: Some formalities had been overlooked, such as the requisite banns (i.e., proclamation of an intended marriage); but that was a church, not a state, matter. The real reason for his involvement was jealousy—for two years the governor had tried to court Josefa Carrillo. In her memoirs, Josefa wrote that "his persecution of me . . . was only incited by the spite which possessed his soul when he realized that I preferred a rival whom he detested."[7] The love-smitten couple secretly eloped to Chile, where they were married in July 1829 before returning to California.

Later that year, Alvarado was unintentionally involved in the beginning of a military revolt in Monterey. Some of the soldiers, disgruntled because they had not received their full pay and rations for many years, took over the presidio during the night of November 12–13 by forcing their way into the houses of the officers and then locking them in the *calabozo* (jail). Alvarado and his friend José Castro happened to be staying that night in the quarters of Alférez (Ensign) Mariano Vallejo, acting commandant of the presidio; thus, they were temporarily arrested along with Vallejo. The rebels chose Joaquín Solís, an ex-convict and former soldier, as commanding general of the troops, and they enlisted the aid of José María Herrera, formerly the officer in charge of territorial finances whom the governor had suspended from his office. Herrera drew up a long manifesto of grievances addressed to the governor. Rebels from the presidio of San Francisco also joined Solís and his men; they then headed south, where they met Echeandía's military force at Santa Barbara and were defeated and dispersed. Alvarado aided in retaking Monterey from the insurgents left there. Most of the rebels were pardoned and reincorporated into the army, but fifteen of the ringleaders, including Solís and Herrera, were court-martialed and sent as prisoners to San Blas, Mexico, where they seem to have been released. Padre Luis Martínez of Mission San Luis Obispo was also exiled for his alleged collusion with the rebels in conspiring to bring back the Spanish regime. Thus ended what Don Juan called "California's first revolution."[8]

When the revolt ended, the governor went to Monterey, where he was met by Alvarado and a welcoming committee. Three days of fiestas, fireworks, horse races, and bullfights celebrated the reestablishment of public order. A typical bullfight of that era was described by Carlos N. Híjar:

The manner of bull fighting was the following: they put a spirited bull with full horns in the ring, then the Californios would begin to go in on horseback and turn him around with their cloaks. At the beginning of the fight they would be timid, but afterwards they would play with him, now embracing him when he was not on guard, now petting his cheeks or pulling out his eyebrows, now mounting him or pulling his tail. They would keep playing with him until both were on very good terms, they they would chase him out of the corral, giving him the plain to go wherever he wished. . . . In the afternoon they fought four or five bulls, as many as time permitted.[9]

In July of 1830 Echeandía convoked the *diputación*, which met for several months to consider various problems. The legislature also approved some land grants to individuals, particularly to retired soldiers who needed land to support their families. This action was in accord with previous Mexican government legislation: the Colonization Law of 1824, which provided for the granting of lands to those who would live on them and cultivate them, and the more specific Naturalization Law and *Reglamento* (Regulation) of 1828. The procedure for obtaining a land grant involved several steps. First, the applicant had to petition the governor, offering proof of his citizenship and membership in the Roman Catholic Church, the reason for his need of land, and information about the land sought, including a *diseño*, or rough sketch showing its boundaries. After the governor tentatively approved the petition, it had to be submitted to the territorial *diputación* for its approval, and then local authorities had to certify that the land was available and not claimed by others. Neighbors and an official rode around the perimeter of the grant, marking a few boundaries. There was a requirement that the property be occupied and livestock introduced within one year. The procedure normally took years rather than months to complete.[10]

After Mexico became independent from Spain, the Spanish-speaking residents of the frontier province began to refer to themselves as Californios rather than Mexicans—indeed, as time went by, many developed a hostility to Mexicans of *la otra banda* (central or mainland Mexico). This discontent was fueled by the central government's failure to provide money or other resources; its inability to protect the region from foreign encroachment; the appointment of Mexican governors, rather than choosing Californios; and its sending of convicts as soldiers and settlers.[11]

In the summer of 1830, Don Juan and other Californios drew up resolutions addressed to officials in Mexico, protesting the continued sending of convicts to California and requesting that only "good and useful families" be sent as settlers. Sixty criminals had been sent in 1825, eighty arrived in February 1830, and fifty additional convicts landed in July. The protestors stated that many of the convict-settlers had committed new offenses, and because there were no adequate jails, the local authorities could not protect the community from these criminals. Mexican officials justified the use of California as a penal colony by saying it would improve the morals of the convicts and, at the same time, colonize the sparsely settled territory.[12]

The convict issue embittered the already-negative feeling between Californios and Mexicans, especially at Monterey. On September 16, 1830, during a dance celebrating Mexican independence, a fight erupted between native-born young men and those from Mexico. According to Alvarado, it began during some toasts when Lieutenant Rodrigo del Pliego "pronounced several phrases or words defaming the feelings of Californians." Don Juan replied to this perceived insult with the following toast, "I drink to all persons of all classes, origin, or nationality, who may know how to appreciate the frank hospitality with which the Californians are accustomed to treat them, and here in front of all present, I demonstrate that I loathe every man who, forgetting his education and good taste, might insult them, as just happened in this room." Pliego then threw his glass of liquor on Alvarado's chest, which spurred Don Juan to strike the lieutenant so hard that it knocked him to the floor. After the governor heard what had happened, he sided with Alvarado and punished Pliego.[13]

Secularization of the missions proved to be the most controversial matter dealt with by the *diputación* in the 1830s. In accordance with Mexican laws, ten years after founding a mission the missionaries were supposed to turn over their possessions to secular authorities and move on to another mission field. Thus, the central government that appointed Echeandía desired to phase out the missions, replace the friars with secular priests under a bishop, create *pueblos,* emancipate the Indians, and redistribute mission lands. It was a difficult procedure for several reasons: first, because the missionaries resisted the change. Alvarado's cynical anticlericalism was evident when he wrote, "The friars here among us had a real flowing breast to suck; they had found the Golden Calf and it was hard for them to let go of its teats." Another problem was that there were no priests available to take over new parishes. At first most Hispanic residents opposed secularization because they realized that the friars were able to control the Indians and make them work, but freeing them might bring the economy to a standstill. However, when Californios learned that they could be beneficiaries of redistributed mission land, they supported the scheme. In 1826 Echeandía had decreed that married Indians who had been Christians for fifteen years and had some means of support could leave the missions. In 1830 his more extensive plan for secularization was approved by the territorial legislature and sent on to Mexico City for approval.[14]

Lieutenant Colonel José María Padrés, who arrived in Alta California in the summer of 1830, was a keen promoter of secularization and other liberal ideas. His official role was as military inspector and aide to Echeandía. A brilliant radical who justified secularization with "idealistic oratory about the rights of man, the wrongs of the neophytes, and the tyranny of the missionaries," Padrés influenced many Californians, including Juan Alvarado, Mariano Vallejo, and José Castro. The historian Hubert H. Bancroft wrote that "Padrés was a man of remarkable energy, intelligence, and magnetism, a most radical republican . . . and one whose influence was long felt in California through his teachings to the young men who later controlled the country."[15]

At the end of 1830 news arrived that Mexico's president and administration had changed from liberal to conservative and that Manuel Victoria, a pro-clerical lieutenant colonel, had been appointed governor and commanding general of Alta California. In January 1831, Echeandía, persuaded by Padrés that the new central government would not support his plans, decided to issue his secularization decree without ratification. The missions were to be immediately organized into *pueblos*, and the surplus property, after some distribution to *neophytes*, would pass to secular administrators appointed for each former mission. The governor appointed Padrés civil administrator of Mission San Carlos, José Castro was sent to Mission San Antonio, and Juan Alvarado became administrator of Mission San Miguel, about one hundred miles south of Monterey.[16]

Don Juan's tenure as administrator of Mission San Miguel lasted less than a month, and the results were very disappointing to him. Early in January 1831, after Spanish-born Father Juan Cabot gathered the *neophytes* in the courtyard, Alvarado carefully explained the secularization plan and his role. Then, he told them, "Those who want to continue living with Father Cabot step to the left of me; those that prefer to be free men and become owners of their own land, step to my right." All of the Indians went to the left, shouting that they wanted to remain with the missionary. Administrator José Castro had the same experience at Mission San Antonio, where the missionary was Pedro Cabot, a brother of Father Juan.[17]

When Alvarado and Castro heard that the new governor was fanatically religious, that he had countermanded Echeandía's secularization decree, and that he had abolished the positions of mission administrators, they both abandoned their posts and hurried to the capital. There they learned that Governor Victoria had ordered criminal proceedings against them "because they had tried to arouse the neophytes." The two young men secretly fled by horseback to Mission Santa Clara, where they had friends. Meanwhile, Victoria, whom Alvarado called "the friar-loving black governor," took over the reins of government on the last day of January 1831.[18]

Alvarado and Castro, out of employment and out of favor in Monterey, successfully petitioned the new governor for a permit to hunt sea otters, which would be sold and sent to the market in China. The average price for a pelt at that time was twenty-five to thirty *pesos* in California and fifty-five in China. As neither of them knew anything about the otter business, they had asked for permission to hire skilled Aleuts from Kodiak Island. Their license specified that only one-third of the crews might be Kodiaks and that the rest must be California natives; they would have to pay duty on the skins; their time was limited to April and May of 1831; and they could hunt only from San Francisco Bay, to the north. The two entrepreneurs made an arrangement with the Russian manager of Fort Ross, Peter Kostromitinov, who agreed to furnish Aleut hunters and *bidarkas* (skin-covered kayaks) for a share of the pelts. Based at Yerba Buena Cove and on an island in San Francisco Bay, the company of hunters, consisting of thirty Indian neophytes and fifteen Aleut hunters with eighteen kayaks, harvested sea otters for two months until the contract expired. Alvarado and Castro spent this time at the Presidio of San Francisco as guests of Alvarado's uncle, Lieutenant Mariano Guadalupe Vallejo, adjutant at that post. In his "History of California," Alvarado mentioned the otter hunting and noted, "We made money, but we were two gay young men, and whenever we were in funds we gave a grand ball, to which the whole world was invited; so the money did not last long."[19]

The three friends—Alvarado, Vallejo, and Castro—were about the same age, had gone to school together, and were interested in reading and collecting books. Besides a copy of *Don Quixote*, Alvarado possessed, among others, the following books: *Obras escogidas de Miguel de Cervantes; Historia del reinado del Emperador Carlos Quinto*, a Spanish version of Sir Walter Scott's *Rob Roy* in three volumes; *Dios es el amor más puro*; and *Memorias para servir a la historia del Jacobinismo*. His library was increased in 1831 when Vallejo acquired several large boxes of books and shared them with his two friends. After a sailor had reported to the padre at San Francisco that these books, some of which were on the Catholic Index of prohibited works, were aboard the merchant vessel *Leonor* but not on the manifest, Vallejo heard of the problem, boarded the vessel at midnight, and purchased the books for four hundred cowhides and ten casks of tallow, valued at $815. By five o'clock in the morning the boxes had been delivered clandestinely to his quarters.[20]

Possession of the books acquired from the *Leonor* led to a problem for Don Juan and his two friends. José Castro's sweetheart in Monterey told her confessor that her lover had shown her books by Rousseau and Voltaire, as well as other works he said were banned, and that he and Alvarado had enjoyed reading them. She also reported that Vallejo had many other books of the same kind. When the missionary subsequently discovered that Vallejo had a copy of *Telemaque*, a condemned work by François Fenelon, he informed the president of the missions, Fray Narciso Durán, who issued a writ of excommunication against the three young men. That ecclesiastical anathema, which was announced in the churches, meant that all the sacraments, including marriage, were denied the offenders and that similar punishment awaited any person who had any dealings with them. The mothers, sisters, and female friends of the outcasts were especially intimidated by the decree. Three weeks later, Alvarado returned from a trip to Los Angeles with several thousand *pesos* that had been entrusted to him to give to Father Durán; but before offering to turn over the money, he reminded the prelate that he had excommunicated him and thus could not have any relations with him. Seeing that Alvarado was about to leave with the money, Father Durán said that he would would lift the ban resting on Alvarado and his two friends, and he gave them permission to read prohibited books, "provided they would not allow them to fall into the hands of persons of little intelligence."[21]

While becoming more worldly through reading, Don Juan also developed an interest in earthly pursuits, including amorous ones. In 1831 he had a modest, one-story, three-room adobe house built on Dutra Street in Monterey for a beautiful young woman with whom he maintained a liaison. Alvarado's mistress was Juliana Francisca Ramona Castillo, nicknamed "Raymunda"; she was the daughter of José Castillo, the local *sangrador* (bloodletter), and his wife, Serafina. Raymunda lived in this house for a decade and bore five illegitimate children fathered by Juan Bautista Alvarado; the first, named Josefa, was born on December 6, 1831. He acknowledged the five daughters and gave them his surname. Perhaps Alvarado did not marry Raymunda because of her family's social status, but one of the granddaughters later said that her grandmother refused matrimony because of Don Juan's addiction to liquor.[22]

Alvarado later wrote that his use of alcoholic beverages began as a cure for stomach pains. Stephen Anderson, a Scottish physicican aboard the trading ship *Ayacucho*, recommended that if he wanted to live for many years and enjoy good health, he should surrender himself to Bacchus at least once every six months. After following that advice, Alvarado said that he felt better, so he shortened the time to a spree every five months, then monthly, and finally daily. When he was sixty-five years old and ill, Don Juan joked about his addiction, claiming, "It is to this cause, more than to any other, that

*Home of Alvarado's mistress on Dutra Street.* Courtesy of the Bancroft Library.

I owe the excellent state of health I have enjoyed."[23] His drink of preference was *pisco,* a white brandy imported in small jugs from Peru, but he also enjoyed the *aguardiente* (brandy) produced at San Gabriel and other missions.

Besides his daily social drinking, Don Juan was an episodic drinker who went on several sprees a year with intervening periods of relative sobriety. During these alcoholic binges, he was not able to perform his work, carry out any responsibilities, or even have sustained dialogue with family members or friends. His alcoholism seriously undermined his career and wreaked havoc in his domestic relations. Juan Espejo, a Chilean acquaintance who lived near the Alvarados for two years, testified,

Generally speaking, Alvarado was sober, taciturn, sensible, without affection, generous and gentlemanly in his behavior, but occasionally he drank spiritous liquors, which affected his nervous system to such a degree that they rendered him unfit to attend to anything. When he had the weakness to drink a glass of liquor, he was transformed; he lost all judgment and no power could keep him within bounds. He continued drinking day and night and destroyed everything he could lay his hands on—not until after the excess prostrated him did he recover his senses—he then, ashamed of himself, remained for a long time secluded in his house, thinking over his business and attending to his family. . . . Alvarado was more an unfortunate man than a vicious one.[24]

In Monterey one source of Don Juan's liquor was the store operated by the Yankee merchant Nathan Spear. Because the governor did not convene the *diputación* or authorize payment of Alvarado's salary as its secretary, Don Juan earned some money by clerking at the store, where he was able to purchase brandy and other liquors at wholesale prices. Spear's nephew, William Heath Davis, who knew Alvarado, later wrote, "I have frequently heard Spear speak in terms of the warmest admiration of his honesty and great ability. Spear himself was well-read and intelligent, and I have heard him say that he took such an interest in young Alvarado, as he called him, that he was in the habit of imparting to him when in his employ a good deal of information about other countries and governments. Alvarado, who had a thirst for knowledge, was an eager listener and received it gratefully; for a considerable portion of his acquirements he was indebted to Spear."[25]

Alvarado, Spear, and others were unhappy with the reactionary and dictatorial rule of Governor Victoria. The executive suspended the territorial *diputación*, recommended the abolishment of elected city councils and the restoration of military rule, and governed by harsh, high-handed methods. He had several people shot, among them an Indian boy who stood accused of only theft, and he had others imprisoned. With no trial or specification of charges, he banished several men, including Lieutenant Colonel Padrés, José Antonio Carrillo, Juan Bandini, and Abel Stearns. The governor's repressive regime soon provoked a revolution that overwhelmed him. Those whom he had exiled went from Baja California to San Diego, where they joined former Governor Echeandía in a revolutionary movement. When a military force under Victoria met the rebels north of Cahuenga Pass, near Los Angeles, on December 4, 1831, the governor was wounded. Soon thereafter he gave up his office and fled to Mexico.[26]

Pending the appointment of a new governor, California's chief political power was exercised at first by Pío Pico, the senior voting member of the *diputación*. Don Juan, Mariano G. Vallejo, and Antonio M. Osio went to Los Angeles to attend the legislative meeting. Pico later recalled the ceremony in front of the parish church in the Los Angeles *pueblo*: "For the act of taking the oath, it was necessary to have on hand the Book of the Gospels and other sacramental objects of the church. The Padre Ministro [father minister] refused to lend us the keys to the church so that they could be taken out. Then, Juan Bautista Alvarado crawled through a skylight, opened the door from the inside and took out the necessary things."[27]

During 1832 the military power was divided, with Echeandía commanding in the south, and Captain Agustín Zamorano in the north. This north-south split, which sputtered for more than a decade, was not just a matter of city prestige and rivalry—it involved the control of political offices, custom house revenues, and distribution of public funds.

To pacify the rebellious Californians, the Mexican government appointed Brevet Brigadier General José Figueroa as *comandante general* and *jefe político* (civil governor) of Alta California. He had a fine military reputation and good administrative abilities, and he was skillful at making himself popular. Of mixed Spanish and Indian ancestry, he was short and thickset, with a swarthy complexion, black hair, piercing eyes, and large, prominent teeth. Although he reportedly had a family in Mexico, he kept a mistress and left a natural daughter in California. In mid-January 1833, soon after his arrival in Monterey by ship, he met Don Juan and members of the *diputación*, to whom he relayed the priority items in his instructions. According to Alvarado, the governor was ordered to promote colonization of the territory between San Francisco Bay and the Russian establishments and to strengthen fortifications in that area. In addition, he was to formulate a plan for secularization and distribute to *neophytes* such mission lands as they might be capable of cultivating.[28] Although Figueroa was probably the best governor ever sent by Mexico to rule the territory, he faced an almost impossible task in phasing out the mission system and transferring mission lands to private ownership in a way that would be satisfactory to the various factions.

Besides Alvarado, other Californios praised Governor Figueroa. The veteran soldier José María Amador stated, "California never had an executive so generally appreciated by its inhabitants." Another contemporary, José de Jesús Pico, related the following in his memoirs: "Señor Figueroa was a man of ability and of honorable intentions. His prudence and good judgment kept the country in peace—he maintained excellent friendship with the *diputación* and the municipal government. And he made himself exceedingly popular through his assiduous attention to the duties of his office, and through the refinement of his manners and the goodness of his heart. . . . With equal goodness and benevolence he treated the poor Indian and the highest official of the government."[29]

Governor Figueroa was accompanied on his trip to California by ten Franciscan friars, all Mexican-born, who were reinforcements for the dwindling numbers of padres at the missions. Because they came from the monastery of Our Lady of Guadalupe at Zacatecas, they were called Zacatecanos; the earlier friars, mostly Spanish-born, had been known as Fernandinos, from the name of their college of San Fernando in Mexico City. Upon arrival, the Zacatecanos were put in charge of the seven northernmost missions, while the Fernandinos remained in control of the fourteen missions to the south. Historian Bancroft observed, "The Zacatecanos were as a class by no means equal morally or intellectually to their predecessors . . . and besides this inferiority, there were naturally many difficulties to be encountered by them at the first, arising from their inexperience and a certain degree of prejudice felt against them by neophytes and others."[30]

The problem of secularizing the missions was the most difficult one facing the new governor, who was convinced that the change must be gradual. Then, in August 1833, the Mexican Congress enacted a law requiring immediate secularization of all the California missions. This law was promoted by Juan Bandini, California's representative in Mexico, and by José María Padrés, who had been in California before and who persuaded Vice-President Valentín Gómez Farías and the government to approve a related scheme for colonization of the territory. A few months later, when word reached Mexico City that Figueroa was ill and wished to resign, Padrés was appointed military commander of California, and his close associate, José María Híjar, was appointed civil governor as well as director of colonization. Híjar was ordered to take possession of all mission property, distribute some of it to the colonists, and establish towns where settlers and Indians would live. He and the vice-president recruited more than two hundred colonists, including farmers, lawyers, teachers, barbers, shoemakers, carpenters, printers, and other artisans, and put them aboard two vessels bound for California. Twenty-one of the colonists were designated as administrators of the missions.[31]

When Figueroa and the Californians learned of the plan to distribute mission lands and livestock to a colony of strangers, they preempted the scheme. The *diputación* and the governor issued their own plan of secularization, under which the missions were to be converted to *pueblos* and half of the mission livestock and some land were to be given to the Indians, who were enjoined from selling it. Figueroa appointed Californios as *comisionados* (administrators) for the missions. Then, before the arrival of the colonists, a special courier came overland bearing dispatches from the new conservative government in Mexico City and revocation of Híjar's orders—Figueroa was to remain governor.[32]

By mid-October 1834, when a majority of the colonists had arrived in Monterey, the governor sent them to the northern frontier of the Sonoma Valley, where Lieutenant Mariano G. Vallejo was phasing out Mission San Francisco Solano. Settlement there would serve as a buffer to Russian advance. Alvarado later wrote that Figueroa alleviated the destitute condition of the colonists by ordering them to be supplied with food and clothing, but the recipients repaid these kind attentions with treachery. He added, "Experience has taught that Mexicans repay good with evil." Five months later, after an abortive revolt in Los Angeles that involved one of the colonists and the discovery of a cache of munitions in Sonoma, Híjar and Padrés were arrested, charged with plotting a revolt, and sent back to Mexico. Figueroa's 189-page account of the controversy was printed in Monterey on the first press in the territory, imported in 1834. Figueroa's account was entitled *Manifiesto a la República Mejicana*; it was the earliest substantial book published in California. The Mexican colonists were subsequently dispersed, but most of them remained in California, where they made up a very respectable element of the population.[33]

During the time the governor was involved with the Híjar-Padrés colony, Don Juan's professional career and financial position improved. In 1834 he ceased being secretary of the *diputación* when he was elected for a two-year term as a member of that elite body of legislators. He also was appointed *vista* (customs inspector) and commander of the revenue guards in the Monterey customhouse. On September 30, 1834, Governor Figueroa granted him Rancho El Sur, a property of two square leagues (8,856 acres) along the Pacific Ocean about thirty miles south of Monterey. The following March, Alvarado purchased a residential lot in Monterey that measured 139 feet wide by 149 feet deep. The property, adjacent to the home of his uncle, Juan R. Cooper, had walls around it, a flowing well, and unfinished foundations (thirty-three by eighty feet) on which he had a two-story adobe house built.[34]

While his residence was under construction, Alvarado lived in the household of Angel Ramírez, administrator of customs. Because their mother was ill, Don Juan's twelve-year-old half brother, Rafael Estrada, and his half sister, ten-year-old Rita Estrada, also lived in Ramírez's house, along with two boarders, Agustín Janssens and Eugenio Montenegro. A census of the population of Monterey in the mid-1830s gave a total of 701 persons for the capital.[35]

After the death of her second husband, Raymundo Estrada, in 1830, Don Juan's mother lived in Monterey with her nine Estrada children. In May 1831 she married Bonifacio Madariaga, a clerk and minor government official, with whom she had four additional children. By 1835 she was living apart from her husband, who had been ordered by the *alcalde* (mayor) to pay half of his monthly salary for his wife's maintenance, to provide her with a cook, and "to take her clothes out of pawn." Josefa died on December 27, 1836, at the age of forty-two.[36] Don Juan was only twenty-seven, but he had attended quite a few funerals for family members, acquaintances, and dignitaries.

The previous year, in September 1835, when Governor Figueroa died from an apoplectic stroke, Monterey residents held elaborate mourning ceremonies. Military honors included cannonades on the day of the funeral and the firing of a gun each half hour during the following week. After the religious last rites, the governor's body was taken by ship to Mission Santa Barbara, where it was interred. The *diputación* met and heard a moving oration by Don Juan, who proposed that Figueroa's portrait, with the inscription "Benefactor of the Territory of California," should be hung in the legislative hall. He also suggested that a suitable monument should be erected at Monterey, but it was never done. Alvarado noted, "My proposal was adopted unanimously, and this was the last time the memory of this great man was honored publicly."[37]

Alvarado's eulogy of the late governor, delivered to the *diputación* on October 9, 1835, was printed in Monterey. Part of it follows:

Our chief is dead! . . . The Californians weep for a beneficent father, who has given an incalculable impulse to their prosperity, and with unexampled diligence, with constant and unparalleled exertions, contributed largely to the public weal. . . . The name of General Figueroa is repeated everywhere; his merits are spoken of, his political prudence, his zeal for the public good, and the gift which he possessed to captivate the will; his honor, his probity, were acknowledged by the people, who proclaimed him an eminent patriot and well-deserved son of the fatherland. . . . Let us immortalize his glory and our gratitude, and encircle his brow with a crown of eternal life.[38]

Before his death, Figueroa had separated the political and military commands of the territory, naming José Castro, senior member of the *diputación*, as political head, and Lieutenant-Colonel Nicolás Gutiérrez as military commandant. In January 1836, in obedience to an order from Mexico, the two offices were again combined and held by Gutiérrez. Alvarado noted that officials in Mexico City preferred Gutiérrez, even though he had been born in Spain, over Castro because the latter had been born in California. The new governor served for only four months, during which he carried out routine duties and proclaimed that Los Angeles would henceforth be the capital. In this matter, he followed a Mexican congressional decree of the previous May that had elevated Los Angeles to the status of a city and declared it was to be the future territorial capital. But the capital remained in Monterey, mainly because of inertia and the lack of rent-free quarters for government officials in the south.[39]

Dramatic changes in the government in Mexico City in 1835 and 1836 had repercussions in California and other frontier regions. Conservative leaders, unhappy with the liberal regime, goaded President Santa Anna into action. He ousted his liberal vice-president, replaced liberal governors, and secured a conservative Congress that eliminated the state legislatures and did away with the federal system, replacing it with a centralized one whereby the states became military departments headed by military officers appointed by the president. After abolishing the federal Constitution of 1824, the Congress enacted various laws that eventually were incorporated into the Constitution of 1836 (Las Siete Leyes). Opposition to this centralization erupted into revolts in Zacatecas, Yucatan, Texas, and California.[40]

On May 1, 1836, the acting governor of California, Colonel Gutiérrez, turned over his office to Colonel Mariano Chico, who had been appointed by the new conservative, centralist government in Mexico. Alvarado, as the senior member of the *diputación*, was among the committee that rode out a mile from Monterey to welcome the executive. Don Juan's friend, José de Jesús Pico, described the governor: "Señor Chico was tall, slender, blond, handsome, and had good manners. He was about fifty to sixty years old, was toothless, and he wore green eyeglasses. He was a man of very bad temper and he arrived like someone who comes to conquer a lawless country."[41]

In the evening there were dances and other festivities in honor of Governor Chico, who had not come alone but was accompanied by a woman named Doña Cruz, whom he introduced to everyone as his niece. Alvarado noted, "We probably would have believed the story if José Antonio Carrillo, who was in Mexico City representing the territory of the Californias, had not written to friends in Monterey. He said that Doña Cruz was not Chico's relative, but was a married woman, wife of an honest artisan, from whom Chico had stolen her, and that she was nothing else but his concubine. The ladies of Monterey abstained from visiting her."[42]

Chico, who was pompous, censorious, and, according to Alvarado, mentally unbalanced, lasted only three months as governor. Antonio María Osio, who had met the governor in Los Angeles, remarked, "he could have been a distant relative of Don Quixote." Citing the new basic Mexican laws, the governor announced that states and territories were now to be called departments, and that the *diputación* would henceforth be known as the departmental *junta*. Alvarado and others continued to use the old term for their legislature. Chico summarily suspended the *alcalde* of Monterey and the *asesor* (legal advisor). Although the governor wished to have the missions reinstated to their former position, he offended the padres by his officious decrees and by ordering the arrest of Father Durán for refusing to swear allegiance to the new conservative Mexican constitution. Chico mistrusted and molested foreign residents, exiling some and ordering all of them to report to the authorities, giving their nationality, age, religion, and information about how they made a living. He prohibited retail trade aboard foreign vessels, heretofore a common practice, and required the landing of all cargoes at Monterey. Chico was unpopular with Hispanic Californians for several reasons: Besides being a Mexican, he was a centralist and opposed by a party of young men who claimed to be ardent federalists. Alvarado and Vallejo later stated that they, along with José Castro and a few other friends, had planned a revolution but that Chico's own actions obviated the plan.[43]

Having heard rumors that a revolution was being plotted against him, Chico convened the *diputación* near the end of July 1836. As president of that body, Alvarado read a letter from the governor in which Chico asked whether it would be convenient for him to go to Mexico to secure troops and bring them back in order to assert his authority. After some debate, the members voted to permit the governor to leave, and they delegated Alvarado to deliver the reply to the governor. When he heard about the decision, Chico was furious that they had not begged him to stay; nevertheless, he announced publicly his plan to recruit soldiers in Mexico and return. Meanwhile, Alvarado had compiled a series of charges against Chico and forwarded them to the central government, hoping the charges would prevent Chico's return. Before sailing away with his "niece" on July 31, Chico appointed Lieutenant Colonel Gutiérrez to take interim charge of the civil and military power of the department. In Mexico, Chico was not given troops; instead, he was reprimanded for leaving his post without orders to do so.[44]

Political discontent in Monterey and Los Angeles continued during the second rule of Gutiérrez, leading to his ouster after three months in office. There was general agreement that he was an immoral bachelor, unduly addicted to wine and women. Don Juan noted that Gutiérrez arrived in Monterey from Mission San Gabriel, where he had recently been administrator, with a seraglio of Indian girls whom he installed in the governor's palace. "He gave one the title of mistress of the key, another was keeper of the wardrobe, another the chambermaid, another the laundress, another the cook, and so on until all had a title."[45] Contemporaries complained that the governor proceeded to carry out the arbitrary measures initiated by Chico, and Padre Ramón Abella stated that he interfered in mission affairs and "intended to cause the friars all possible annoyance." The incompetent governors imposed by Mexico deepened the Californios' distrust of Mexican authority and strengthened their demands for home rule. When Gutiérrez disparaged the *diputación* and attempted to disperse it by force, a group led by Alvarado rose up against him and drove him from office. The next period in California's political history would be dominated by Don Juan.

# 3

# Revolutionary Governor
# 1836–1839

BY 1836 THE CALIFORNIOS had developed a strong prejudice
against Mexico and Mexicans who arrived from *la otra banda*.
For a quarter of a century the government in Mexico City had
failed to provide adequate funds to pay the miliary and civil
servants; yet at the same time, Mexican officials had been sent
to oversee and draw off customs revenues. The territorial residents resented the despotic military governors and inexper-
ienced Mexican officers who were sent to command native-
born veterans, and they especially objected to the sending of
convict settlers and *cholo* soldiers. Although the central government held out the promise of benefits from republicanism, it
had begrudgingly granted only limited self-government; and
finally, it had abolished the federal Constitution of 1824 and
substituted a centralist dictatorship. Foreign residents, traders, and the missionaries also added their voices to these
complaints.[1]

As instigator of the revolt against Governor Nicolás
Gutiérrez, Don Juan Bautista Alvarado had much to lose—or
to gain. In the event of a battle, he could be wounded or
killed, and if the uprising failed, he could be ousted as
second-in-command at the customhouse or be accused of
plotting a revolt and imprisoned or exiled. Grievances of
Alvarado and others against Gutiérrez were multiple: The
governor was typical of the haughty military officers sent from
Mexico to govern the department; he was not only a Mexican,
but a Mexican of Spanish birth, and the Californians wanted

the departmental government to be headed by someone born in the territory; he arbitrarily imprisoned the *síndico* (attorney) of Monterey and ordered the arrest of other persons on flimsy grounds; he had a weakness for alcohol; he kept a harem of Indian servants; and he would not relinquish any civil power to the *diputación*, of which Alvarado was president.[2]

The outbreak against Gutiérrez began in October 1836 after the governor moved to arrest Alvarado and to dissolve the *diputación* by force, claiming that the legislative body had met without his approval. Gutiérrez had also quarrelled with Angel Ramírez, administrator of customs, and with Alvarado about management irregularities and the stationing of revenue guards on recently arrived vessels. To avoid arrest, Alvarado and key members of the *diputación* fled to the former Mission San Juan Bautista, twelve leagues from the capital. They were joined by two foreign residents of Monterey: David Spence, a Scottish merchant, and Esteban Munrás, a Spanish trader, both recent members of the legislature. The rebels condemned the conservative dictatorship in Mexico City, and they declared that Governor Gutiérrez did not have the right to exercise civil power, vowing that if he refused to surrender that power to the *diputación*, the Californians would take up arms and force him into exile. A revolutionary plan was now instigated; it called for Alvarado to head the revolt and José Castro to lead the armed citizens. Alvarado was delegated to visit Sonoma and request cooperation from his uncle, Lieutenant Mariano G. Vallejo, commandant of the northern frontier.[3]

Before going to Sonoma, Alvarado made a secret, nighttime visit to Monterey in order to consult with friends and potential supporters. His friend and erstwhile customs supervisor, Angel Ramírez, provided funds and said he would use his influence to protect the families of the conspirators. At Tía Boronda's shop, Alvarado sent for Isaac Graham, a Kentucky-born mountain man and distillery operator, who agreed to gather a band of his acquaintences, mostly foreigners, to help. At about dawn, Alvarado looked out the door and saw Captain Juan Antonio Muñoz and a squad of soldiers approaching, whereupon he rushed out, mounted Graham's horse, and headed north at full speed. He later wrote, "When Captain Muñoz realized his victim was escaping, he ordered his men to fire on me. Bullets whistled all around, but not a single one reached me."[4]

Don Juan proceeded toward Sonoma, gaining adherents along the way at San Jose, Rancho San Pablo, and San Rafael. In Sonoma, he conferred with the commandant about events in Mexico City and Monterey and about the burgeoning movement against the governor. Vallejo promised that his services and his soldiers would be at the disposition of the *diputación*. The two men then rode to Napa Valley, where Chief Solano of the Suisun tribe had made great preparations for a ceremonial visit and had assembled about a thousand warriors armed with bows and wearing colorful feather head-dresses. Directing Alvarado to the center of a large circle formed by the most valiant braves, Solano made a speech in his language, the gist of which was, "Behold this man, know him well, examine his face and all his features. He has worked for the liberty of the mission Indians, now he is laboring so that the whites may not be slaves of other men that come from other lands wishing to rule them as if they were children. He is the great leader of the whites and Indians who live from the other side of Carquinez Strait [mouth of the Sacramento River] to San Diego. We must be prepared to go with him and fight whenever he needs us."[5]

Embarking the next day on a launch, Don Juan sailed to San Jose, where he met with José Castro and other associates. After hearing that Vallejo was willing to support them but could not send troops immediately, the leaders decided to move on toward Monterey with the dozen men recruited locally—they called themselves "the Vanguard of the Division of Operations." The next rendezvous was at the Pájaro River ranch of another of Don Juan's uncles, José de Jesús Vallejo, where they were joined by more than seventy-five mounted Californians armed with lances and old muskets. A loyal supporter, José de Jesús Pico, arrived with some cowboys driving three hundred horses taken from the Rancho Nacional. Another contingent was Isaac Graham's company of about twenty-five or thirty foreign *rifleros* (riflemen), who were important to the operation because of the superiority of their guns and supposed marksmanship. Two English residents, William Garner and John Coppinger, had aided Graham in recruiting sailors, trappers, and hunters, all of whom were reputed to be "crack shots." The rebel forces carried a Mexican flag and had drums and bugles obtained at Mission San Juan Bautista.[6]

The attackers approached Monterey under the cover of darkness and a heavy fog on the night of November 3, 1836. After splitting their forces, with Castro moving toward the fortified *castillo* near the beach and Alvarado and his followers taking the heights, they soon surrounded the presidio, which housed the governor, his troops, and a few civil officials. At dawn, Alvarado sent a dispatch to Gutiérrez, asking him to surrender with all his officers, his troops, and the convicts he had armed. After several hours, when the governor had not replied, the rebels loaded a cannon with the only ball they could find, aimed it toward the presidio, and fired. The ball crashed through the tile roof and fell in the inner hall of the commandant's quarters, near where Gutiérrez and his officers were discussing the situation. Soon, under a flag of truce, one of the Mexican officers met with Alvarado and Castro and, after many hours of debate, agreed to surrender terms: The lives of all military and civil personnel would be guaranteed, the presidio would be evacuated, officers were permitted to retain their side arms, soldiers would be disarmed, and an inventory would be made of all munitions surrendered.[7]

On Saturday, November 5, after Gutiérrez and his forces had abandoned the garrison, Don Juan and his followers made a triumphant entry into the presidio plaza. Rebel infantrymen with their musical band led the procession, followed by members of the *diputación* on horseback and dressed in formal clothes. Next came the company of foreign *rifleros* under Captain Graham and Lieutenant Coppinger, who were accompanied by musicians from foreign ships anchored in the port. With their bugler giving commands, the cavalry brought up the rear of the parade. That evening there was a fiesta and ball celebrating the occasion. An honored guest was William Hinckley, the American captain of the *Don Quixote*, who had contributed arms and men to the rebel cause. Alvarado summarized the victory in the following words: "Without shedding a single drop of blood, we overcame that veteran soldier, Gutiérrez, and his forces. On the one hand they were experienced men in the art of war. On the other hand, the only thing we had on our side was the justification of our cause; commandant Vallejo's prestige, whose name we used to our greatest advantage; and a few firearms that perhaps were useful."[8]

After deporting Gutiérrez and a number of his officers to Cape San Lucas, Baja California, the leaders of the revolution proceeded to organize their own government. There was some discussion of absolute independence—Californians were aware that Texas had won its independence from Mexico earlier in the year. American supporters had even prepared a white flag with one red star and proposed raising it over the presidio, but Don Juan and others who feared foreign influence opted for a less drastic plan that would keep them partially under the Mexican flag but give them considerable autonomy.[9]

In a decree written by Alvarado, signed by members of the *diputación*, and printed in Monterey, California was proclaimed "a free and sovereign state" until Mexico should repudiate centralism and readopt the federal Constitution of 1824. The new officials also transformed the *diputación* into a congress. An English translation of the articles of this "Declaration of Independence" follows:

1. Alta California is declared independent of Mexico until the federal system of 1824 shall be reestablished.
2. California is erected into a free and sovereign state, establishing a congress that shall pass all the particular laws of the country, also the other necessary supreme powers, the present most excellent deputation declaring itself constituent.
3. The religion will be the apostolic Roman Catholic, without admitting the public worship of any other; but the government will molest no one for his private religious opinions.
4. A constitution shall regulate all branches of the administration provisionally, so far as possible in accordance with the said [1824 federal] constitution.
5. While the provisions of the preceding articles are being carried out, Don Mariano Guadalupe Vallejo will be called to the military command. (He was promoted to the rank of colonel.)
6. The necessary communications will be made to the municipalities of the territory by the president of the deputation.[10]

José Castro, president of the deputation, served as chief executive until December 7, when Don Juan Alvarado became interim governor. Alvarado's annual salary was $1,500, and he was authorized a secretary at $1,000, and a clerk at $375. The governor's powers were to appoint officials in accordance with the constitution and laws; to oversee the security and tranquility of the state; to command the militia; to enforce the constitution and laws and issue the necessary decrees to that end; to see that justice was promptly and fully executed; to appoint and remove administrators of missions and report to

congress on mission matters; to fine corporations, subordinate authorities, and private individuals for disrespect to the
government or for failure to comply with duties; and to suspend officials, immediately reporting such action to congress.
Because Alvarado was suffering from a bout of heavy drinking,
he was too hungover to attend his inauguration, but he
achieved the highest possible honor in the state. And at the
age of twenty-seven, he was the youngest governor California
would ever know.[11]

At the end of 1836, Governor Alvarado and his associates
issued a series of decrees and laws on a variety of subjects.
Revenue from the customhouse was henceforth to be under
the control of a collector, whose salary would be $1,000, and a
clerk at $360. Restrictions on foreign trade imposed by Chico
were abolished, and import duties were fixed at forty percent,
with tonnage duties at eight *reales* per ton (there were eight
*reales* in a *peso,* or dollar). The government organized a civic
militia, naming Alvarado and Castro as colonels. Two towns in
northern California were honored with additions to their
names: San José de Alvarado, and San Juan de Castro, formerly San Juan Bautista. (These name changes did not last.) A
decree that divided the state into two districts, with regional
headquarters at Monterey and Los Angeles, was never put into
effect because of troubles that developed in southern
California. In fact, evidence of opposition to the *arribeños*
(northern Californians) and their new regime, orchestrated
by *abajeños* (southern Californians) Antonio María Osio,
attorney for Los Angeles, and Juan Bandini, a rancher and
erstwhile customs official of San Diego, led Don Juan to give
his civil authority temporarily to General Vallejo while he
visited the south in person.[12]

Antonio María Osio, a member of the *ayuntamiento* (city
council) of Los Angeles, listed three reasons that body
opposed Alvarado's government and its decrees. First, they
thought it was absurd to create a state from a territory of

fewer than nine thousand inhabitants, of whom not even three hundred were educated. Second, attempts at annexation by foreign governments, especially the United States, abetted by foreign residents, were becoming apparent. Third, by issuing a decree of religious tolerance, the Monterey faction had exceeded the power of the Mexican Congress and offended Osio and other staunch Roman Catholics.[13]

On Christmas Day of 1836, Alvarado started southward with fifty mounted soldiers and Isaac Graham's riflemen, a part of his force being sent by sea. Along the way, Don Juan and his men stopped at former missions, arriving at Mission Santa Inés early in January 1837 for a rendezvous with the men who had come by sea. The next stop was Mission Santa Barbara, where Father Durán welcomed the men with a Te Deum chanted in honor of Don Juan. Alvarado later wrote, "The fact of my being received by the president of the southern missions, with all the honors which were only accorded to the governor, was more to my advantage than a victory won on the battlefield, for the southerners, being profoundly religious, began to be inclined in my favor when they saw that Father Durán was treating me as the governor."[14] In the adjacent presidio settlement, regional leaders took an oath to support the regime and conferred with Don Juan on ways to unite all of Alta California.

In mid-January 1837, Don Juan continued toward Los Angeles, where the city government officials had assumed a hostile attitude, declared their city the capital, and assembled a military force under Lieutenant Juan Rocha. Marching with Alvarado was a band of thirty Indian musicians recruited at Mission Santa Barbara. As the two armed groups moved toward each other, both sent envoys to discuss peace, and finally, Rocha's forces retreated southward. Don Juan then rode on to Los Angeles, where he was joined by Castro and his reinforcements.[15]

Alvarado asked the Los Angeles *ayuntamiento* to hold an open meeting in which north-south grievances could be discussed and the future decided. Representatives from San Diego, Los Angeles, and Monterey finally agreed to a number of points, including the following: Alta California would adhere to the federal system promulgated in 1824; Californians would not recognize governors appointed from Mexico until that republic reestablished the Constitution of 1824, and they insisted on a native-born ruler; and Alvarado should call for the election of statewide deputies to meet in Santa Barbara. While in Los Angeles, Don Juan had a romantic affair with a young local woman and rented a house for their use. On observing him enter the house, Castro ordered artillery salvos during the visit, saying they were "in honor of the act of the governor." About nine months later, when this young woman bore her first baby, there was a public fiesta for the governor's bastard child.[16]

Don Juan was in Santa Barbara for more than three months, beginning in February 1837. With the threat of civil war seemingly over, he disbanded Captain Graham's rifle company, paid the men, thanked them, and sent them back north along with the Monterey militia. He also interviewed a French-born Mexican citizen named Victor Prudon (or Prudhomme), who had come to California two years earlier with the Híjar-Padrés colony. Prudon, about twenty-eight years old, was considered a learned man—he was conversant in English as well as French and Spanish and was an excellent extemporaneous orator. Alvarado later wrote, "I offered him the post of private secretary, which he accepted, and he was an ardent sympathizer with the principles which my following had espoused."[17] Alvarado also commissioned Prudon as a captain in the militia.

Although deputies were elected at the end of February, they did not assemble at Santa Barbara until April. The harmonious discussions concluded with eight resolutions that confirmed in substance all that had been done by Alvarado's government. Two of the propositions called for petitioning the national government to restore the federal system, "it being understood that California is an integral part of the Mexican republic," and to permit California to govern herself as a free and sovereign state. Regarding the triumph of his cause as complete, on May 10 Alvarado issued a grandiloquent manifesto of congratulations to the people of California, copies of which were printed in Monterey and signed by him as "Interim Governor of the Free and Sovereign State of California." Before leaving for the capital, Don Juan signed officers' commissions for a few southern supporters and granted land to others. He arrived back in Monterey on May 30, 1837.[18]

No sooner had Alvarado arrived at Monterey than he heard of new troubles and armed resistance in the south. Juan Bandini, with the help of Captain Zamorano (who styled himself "commandant general and governor ad interim") had proclaimed the Plan of San Diego, which disavowed Alvarado's acts and his government and recognized the full authority of Mexico. After getting the approval of the town council of San Diego, they went to Los Angeles, where the majority of the city council concurred. By mid-June they had gathered an army at Los Angeles and prepared for a showdown with forces from the north. Meanwhile, Don Juan sailed from Monterey to Santa Barbara, having sent Castro overland with sixty men to the south.[19]

The situation was complicated by the arrival in southern California of Captain Andrés Castillero, commissioner of the Mexican government, who came to proclaim the new constitutional laws of 1836, "Las Siete Leyes," and to exact an oath of allegiance to the new centralist administration. Leaders in San Diego and Los Angeles approved of the new constitution and sent Castillero to meet with Alvarado in Santa Barbara. Although Don Juan had won the governorship as an advocate of federalism (states' rights), he recognized some merit in the new basic laws, which united the territories of Alta and Baja California into one department and specified that the governor would be "a Mexican by birth and native or resident of the respective department." Faced by rebellion in the south, some disaffection in the north, and rumors that Mexico planned to send an army to subdue California, Alvarado seems to have made a deal with Castillero: Alvarado would support the constitution if the agent would return to Mexico and use his influence to secure official confirmation of Alvarado's title as governor.[20]

On July 9, in a carefully worded proclamation to the people, Don Juan declared that the new regime and laws passed by the Congress of Mexico "guarantee to us our rights, and even extend them beyond our moderate desires. . . . Our votes may be cast in favor of the citizen whom we deem worthy to fill the supreme magistracy of the nation—and what more do you wish? . . . *Viva la Constitución del año de '36!* . . . *Viva la Union!*" This declaration bore the heading "Department of Alta California," confirming the abandonment of the region's status as an independent, sovereign state and restoration of loyalty to the central Mexican government. Alvarado's position now appeared to be secure, and he returned to Monterey.[21]

In August Don Juan sent the agent Castillero to Acapulco aboard the *California,* a schooner the governor had just acquired for the regional government. This eighty-three-ton vessel, previously named the *Clarion,* was purchased for $9,000, of which $6,424 was the duty charged on her cargo, the balance to be paid in hides and tallow within two months. Alvarado employed the vessel to take government officials, mail, prisoners, and surplus products between California and San Blas, Mazatlán, and Acapulco, the ports on Mexico's west coast that connected most directly with Mexico City.[22]

Monterey social life was enlivened in the autumn of 1837 when the *Venus,* a French vessel on a globe-circling voyage for scientific purposes, anchored in the roadstead for almost a month. Captain Abel Dupetit-Thouars went ashore on October 19 and rented a house for the sick crewmen and as a place for his cooks to bake a supply of sea biscuits. In his published account of the visit, the captain said that there were thirty or forty scattered houses between the presidio and the fortified *castillo*, the latter having eight cannon mounted in an earthworks. He received a warm welcome from Don Juan, who authorized the visitors to make maritime observations, cut timber and wood, and purchase foodstuffs. On a political note, the captain wrote, "Alvarado appeared to feel keenly the precarious and unfortunate position of California, too weak by itself to be independent and too backward in civilization to administer itself. He understood the deplorable necessity for foreign support and that meantime experience seemed to have demonstrated to him that the government in Mexico, too unstable and too preoccupied with interests nearer at home, was not in a position to help California to get out of the state of anarchy and unrest in which she found herself."[23]

While Dupetit-Thouars was still in Monterey, Don Juan received the disheartening news that the Mexican government had appointed Carlos Antonio Carrillo as governor of Alta California. This nomination had been secured by José Antonio Carrillo, California's representative in the Mexican Congress and a younger brother of the newly named official. Carlos Carrillo (whom Alvarado called "uncle," although he was actually a cousin to an aunt by marriage) had originally favored Alvarado, but his appointment won him over to the southern California faction, and he took office in the presence of the Los Angeles *ayuntamiento* on December 6, 1837.

Two southern Californians who were well acquainted with Carlos Carrillo strongly disapproved of his appointment as governor. Agustín Janssens gave his opinion that the government of Mexico could not have made a worse choice "at a time when the need was for a man of energy, courage, and at least average talent—qualities which poor Carrillo almost completely lacked." Pío Pico characterized the appointee as follows: "Carlos Antonio Carrillo was a man of great height and bulk—of handsome appearance and truly a fine looking man; bushy beard and with very curly, black hair; fair, rosy complexion and large black eyes. He was in the habit of always keeping his head covered with a black handkerchief, tied with a knot in front and his hat way back of his head. He was a man of strong and capricious temperament. Some days he conducted himself as if he were a lunatic."[24]

Thus, there were two governors in Alta California—Alvarado in the north and Carrillo in the south—and the situation led to civil war. Within a month of taking office, Carrillo ordered the ports of Monterey and San Francisco to be closed to foreign trade and the principal customhouse to be established at San Diego. Although favored in the south, this action united northern Californians in support of Alvarado, who refused to acknowledge Carrillo's authority.

In order to enforce his authority in the south, Don Juan ordered José Castro to lead a contingent of soldiers to southern California. Toward the end of March, the northern force met the southern army at San Buenaventura, where the *norteños* defeated the *sureño* troops. Castro sent a group of important prisoners under guard to Don Juan, who was not far away at Mission Santa Inés. In addition to José Antonio Carrillo, a prime mover of the insurrection, the captives included Andrés Pico; Ignacio del Valle; José Ramírez; Ignacio Palomares, a member of the Los Angeles city council; and Gil Ybarra, *alcalde* of that city. Alvarado, who was reportedly drunk at the time, ordered the prisoners to be conducted north to Sonoma, where they would be under the supervision of Comandante General Mariano Guadalupe Vallejo. Osio, a member of the Los Angeles *ayuntamiento* and an opponent of Alvarado, later reported that Alvarado eloquently reprimanded the prisoners, saying "that if he were to send them to hell, their crime would remain unpunished, and he would receive very little satisfaction. He was sending them to Sonoma instead, entrusting them to the commanding general. There they would receive the punishment he desired."[25]

Early in April, Don Juan, himself, set out to quell the continued southern opposition to his regime. After rendezvousing with Castro in the San Fernando Valley, the united northern army of about two hundred men, including a contingent under militia Captain Salvador Vallejo, moved southeastward to Mission San Juan Capistrano, about sixty miles from Los Angeles. At the nearby rancho of Las Flores, Alvarado's forces faced those of the "pretender" governor, Carlos Carrillo. Positioning his troops on a hill overlooking the enemy, Don Juan opened fire with his cannon, and after three days of siege and conferences, an agreement was signed. The Treaty of Las Flores, dated April 23, 1838, specified that the armies of the opposing forces would for the most part be disbanded and that Carrillo would accompany Alvarado to Mission San Fernando, where an arrangement was to be made respecting the governorship. The treaty was virtually a surrender by Don Carlos to Don Juan. At San Fernando the two governors discussed their claims, during which Alvarado got his opponent to admit that during the year since his appointment, Carrillo had received no official communication from the central government. Finally, Don Juan went to Santa Barbara and Don Carlos went to Los Angeles.[26]

Supporters of Carlos Carrillo were plotting a third revolt in Los Angeles in mid-May 1838, when seven of them were surprised and arrested by Alvarado's men. After the captives (including the Carrillo brothers and Pío Pico) were taken to Santa Barbara, Alvarado released Carlos Carrillo on parole with a promise that the latter would not leave his sister's nearby ranch home and would stay out of politics. Except for Pío Pico, who was ill, Don Juan sent the others under escort to Sonoma, where they were kept under confinement for four months. In late June Alvarado went to Los Angeles to address the *ayuntamiento* and try to pacify recalcitrant citizens. While there, he learned of a conspiracy to attack him and take his life; the warning came from a mysterious woman who, according to Alvarado, "seemed to have been Doña Concepción Argüello," the heroine of the 1806 romance involving the Russian count Nikolai Rezanov.[27]

Don Juan was back in Santa Barbara in early August, when Don Carlos Carrillo broke his parole and escaped in a boat, along with his son and a friend. In a farewell letter to Don Juan, Carrillo claimed that he was leaving for fear of being executed by Alvarado or his men. Forced by weather to beach their boat near Los Angeles, Don Carlos and his partners made their way overland to Mission San Luis Rey, north of San Diego, where they joined fellow conspirators who still favored Carrillo as governor. However, when news from Mexico arrived there indicating that Alvarado had been confirmed as governor, Don Carlos wrote to Alvarado begging for amnesty.[28]

Alvarado's disappointment over the flight of Carlos Carrillo was compounded when he learned of the partial defection of General Vallejo. During the period when José Antonio Carrillo had been imprisoned at Sonoma, he had apparently held long discussions with Vallejo and convinced him of the genuineness of his brother's appointment as governor. Furthermore, this crafty and eloquent speaker promised that his brother would, when recognized as governor, reorganize the presidial companies, a project dear to the heart of the commandant general. On August 10 and 11, Vallejo sent letters to Alvarado, Castro, and another officer, advising the recognition of Don Carlos as governor "in deference to peace and tranquility." Points made in the letter to Alvarado were the following: Experience indicated that there was little hope of ending the sectional troubles; the focus on quelling revolts had precluded the introduction of needed reforms; Carrillo's title being valid, it would be necessary to yield sooner or later;

it would be noble and generous for Alvarado to yield while he was enjoying success and military triumphs; voluntary surrender of the office would make a good impression in Mexico and might check dissention at home; and if Don Carlos were recognized as governor, he would doubtless establish his government in Monterey, where Alvarado and his friends could control public affairs in their own way. In a forceful reply to Vallejo, Don Juan stated that he was determined not to give up his authority unless compelled to do so by force. Upon receipt of Alvarado's letter, Vallejo issued a proclamation saying that he approved of Don Juan's policies.[29]

In mid-August 1838, good news arrived from Mexico for Don Juan: The agent Castillero wrote that he had been successful in getting approval of the continuation of Alvarado's regime. Castillero had planned to sail to Monterey aboard the *California* with letters and commissions from the president, but his return was delayed on account of a war between Mexico and France, dubbed the "Pastry War" because of the claims of a French baker whose shop had been damaged by Mexican troops. Meanwhile, Alvarado remained in the Santa Barbara area, awaiting the arrival of official communications from the central government.

During his prolonged stay in Santa Barbara in 1838, Don Juan participated in the christening of a baby that undoubtedly was one of his illegitimate children. Although Pío Pico was under house arrest by order of Alvarado, the governor invited him to be *padrino* (godfather) of the child. Pico later wrote about the event: "Alvarado, himself, came in the carriage of [Franciscan] Father President Narciso Durán to take me to the mission. Upon arrival, we were met by a force lined up on one side of the church, and while we were getting out of the carriage, the troops fired a volley in salute. Alvarado conducted me to a room in the house of the padres, where the officers were. There he presented me with about two hundred dollars in silver for my service as godfather. I accepted it and then we went together to the church where the baptismal ceremony was performed. This concluded, the governor returned me to my sister's home."[30]

Finally, on November 15, 1838, the schooner *California* anchored at Santa Barbara, bringing Castillero and a cargo of military supplies, including munitions and uniforms. The new decrees from Mexico were the following:

1. The republic was divided into twenty-four departments, one of them the Californias, with capitals as before.
2. The central government thanked the department of California for its gift of the schooner *California*.
3. Amnesty was granted for all political acts and opinions during the past troubles.
4. Carlos Carrillo was officially informed that the senior member of the territorial legislature (Alvarado) should be the provisional governor.
5. The governor was ordered to grant land on the coastal islands to Mexicans who might request them, giving preference to José Antonio and Carlos Carrillo, who were to have the exclusive right to one of the islands for their patriotic services.
6. Mariano Guadalupe Vallejo was promoted to the permanent rank of captain of the San Francisco presidial company (he held a brevet rank of colonel).
7. In consideration of his distinguished services, Mariano Guadalupe Vallejo was confirmed as *comandante general*.
8. President Anastasio Bustamante sent letters to Alvarado and Vallejo, expressing his high esteem for them and his confidence in their patriotism and ability to direct the affairs of California in the future.[31]

By these decrees, officials of the Mexican government put the stamp of approval on Alvarado, who had brought California back to Mexican allegiance and quelled the subsequent uprisings. Don Juan and his uncle, Don Mariano Guadalupe, elated with the news that confirmed them in offices they had previously held only by revolutionary title, issued printed announcements to the people informing them of the Mexican decrees. Alvarado's proclamation, dated November 21, 1838, congratulated the citizens on the happy ending of all the dissentions, announced his own purpose to sacrifice everything for his country, and advised all to forget their resentments and get ready for the coming elections.[32]

In December 1838 there was another spurt of revolutionary activity in San Diego. Hearing of the plot, Alvarado sent Lieutenant Colonel Castro southward with twenty-five men to arrest the ringleaders. At midnight, Castro's men surrounded Juan Bandini's house, where a Christmas pageant was in progress, and captured the Carrillo brothers and the Pico brothers; Bandini was not at home at the time. Conducted to Santa Barbara, the prisoners were interrogated by Alvarado and General Vallejo—the latter had come south to consolidate the victory and make plans for the future. Alvarado paroled Carlos Carrillo, but Vallejo sent the others to vessels in the harbor with orders to the captains that there should be no communications between the prisoners and persons on shore. About January 19, 1839, the prisoners were released, and Carlos Carrillo wrote a letter in which he formally recognized Alvarado as the legitimate governor, relinquished his own claims, and promised to give up all official documents in his possession. Don Juan ordered this letter to be printed and circulated throughout California, along with a notice about elections of representatives for a new departmental *diputación*.[33]

At the end of January 1839, Alvarado and Castro boarded the *California* and sailed back to Monterey, where they were welcomed with three days of fiestas, dances, and nightly fireworks. With an end to organized southern opposition to his government, Don Juan now could concentrate on government problems that had been neglected during the previous two years.

# 4

# Constitutional Governor
# 1839–1842

DURING THE LAST FOUR YEARS of his governorship, Don Juan devoted himself diligently to administrative duties and government reorganization. It was a very productive period highlighted by reforms in the collection of duties on imports, an expansion of education, new regulations for mission management as secularization wound down, the issuance of a great number of land grants to Californios and foreigners, and an attempt to deal with the increasing number of foreign immigrants, some of whom arrived without passports or permits to settle.

To help him manage the territorial government, Alvarado appointed several trustworthy individuals to key positions. Because his former secretary, Victor Prudon, had left Monterey, Don Juan named Manuel Jimeno (Casarín) to this important post, which was sometimes referred to as secretary of state. Jimeno was a man of good character and abilities, well fitted for the position. As treasurer in charge of the territorial finances, Don Juan chose José Abrego, an intelligent and honest citizen who was also a relative, since he was married to the governor's half sister, Josefa Estrada. A third official appointed by the governor was Antonio María Osio, who became administrator of customs. In his *History of Alta California*, written in 1851, Osio characterized the governor's work habits: "He usually would work by lamplight from four in the morning until seven. At that time, he would eat breakfast as he waited for his secretary to arrive so they could determine which matters needed attention on that day. Then he would read and sign papers that were ready to be dispatched.[1] Alvarado displayed the same energy and spirit in the cabinet and *diputación* meetings.

When the old *diputación* members met on February 25, 1839, Don Juan addressed the group, declared the body legally installed as a temporary departmental *junta*, and explained the recent Mexican congressional measures affecting California. During the eleven-day session, the members took action on several important matters, among them a ruling that the forthcoming elections for members of the departmental *junta* and the congressional delegate would be considered legal, even if a representative from Baja California had not arrived. They also compiled a *terna* (list of three candidates) for permanent governor, from which the central government in Mexico would select one; in order of preference the names were Juan B. Alvarado, José Castro, and Pío Pico.[2]

Following new regulations from Mexico, and with the advice of the *junta*, Alvarado issued a decree dividing the department of the Californias into three districts. The first extended south from the Sonoma frontier to the former mission of San Luis Obispo, with its capital or head town at San Juan de Castro (San Juan Bautista); the second extended from there to Santo Domingo, south of San Diego, with Los Angeles the head town; and the third covered virtually all of Baja California, with La Paz as its capital. Each district had a prefect, appointed by the governor and subject to final approval by the central government, and each district was further subdivided into two areas, each headed by subprefect appointed by the prefect with approval by the governor. The old *ayuntamientos* were abolished, except at Monterey, each to be replaced by a justice of the peace. Primary elections took place in March, and on May 1 the electors met at Monterey. They adjourned after choosing Andrés Castillero as congressman and electing seven members of the new departmental *junta,* with the governor's secretary, Manuel Jimeno, as president, or first *vocal.*[3]

Meanwhile, the customs administrator, Antonio María Osio, had urged Don Juan to change the policy regarding duties on imported merchandise. Pointing out that the practice of accepting goods from merchant ships as payment of duties had led to corruption and a shortage of funds, he recommended and drafted a new regulation. Thus, in April 1839 Governor Alvarado issued a decree on the subject: "If the duty totaled 3,000 pesos or less, it had to be paid in silver; for duties between 3,000 and 6,000 pesos, two-thirds must be in silver; for duties between 6,000 and 12,000 pesos, one-half must be silver; for duties of more than 12,000 pesos, one-third must be in silver."[4]

During the summer of 1839, Don Juan initiated civic improvements for the capital. He ordered a wall to be built around the cemetery, had two bridges constructed over *arroyos* (stream beds), and authorized construction of a government building outside the walls of the old presidio. Called El Cuartel (the Barracks), the new structure provided space for some government offices as well as housing for soldiers. The two-story building was made of adobe bricks and had a tile roof, sixteen windows on each side, and four fireplaces. It cost nine thousand *pesos* and was completed in one year. A team of experts, hired by the governor to determine the feasability of bringing water from the Carmel River to Monterey, estimated that project would cost forty thousand *pesos,* an amount far more than the treasury could afford.[5]

Don Juan next turned his attention to the new *pueblo* of Yerba Buena on San Francisco Bay, where foreign traders who wanted to acquire property and set up branch offices in the *pueblo* persuaded him to order a survey of the place. This was carried out in 1839 by Jean Jacques Vioget, a Swiss-born Frenchman who had settled in that town. Alvarado also decreed improvement of the public roads, putting soldiers in

*El Cuartel (government building) in Monterey.* Courtesy of the Bancroft Library.

charge of the project. Since the treasury was almost empty, he obliged all citizens to contribute three days of labor for the enterprise; the wealthy could send persons in their service whom they paid their regular wages. Because ox carts were needed to carry stones and gravel, those who brought a *carreta* drawn by four oxen had to work only one day.[6]

Alvarado fostered education, giving encouragement and assistance to the presidial, *pueblo,* and private schools of the department. He established a new school at Monterey, providing the location, furniture, and necessary equipment as well as monthly salaries for the teachers: French-born Henri Cambuston and José Campina, a Cuban, both of whom came from Mexico at the request of Alvarado. After a few weeks nearly sixty pupils were receiving elementary education free of charge. Owing to the lack of textbooks, those pupils who could write were put to work making manuscript copies of the few books in the school. In addition to the traditional courses of reading, writing, arithmetic, geography, history, and drawing, the governor directed that instruction be given in typesetting and printing, presumably to provide literate and competent printers for the government printing press, which had been operating in California since 1834. Don Juan also ordered money to be appropriated for medals to be given to the most proficient scholars.[7]

On July 4, 1839, Don Juan's neighbor, Thomas Oliver Larkin, a successful American merchant in Monterey, invited the governor to a dinner party at his residence. Larkin had come to California seven years earlier to join his half brother, Juan R. Cooper, who was Alvarado's uncle by marriage. Unlike many other foreign settlers, Larkin had not married a California woman—he married an American widow, Rachel Holmes—nor did he become a naturalized Mexican citizen. However, he had quietly supported Alvarado's revolution of 1836 and continued to be a friend. At that Independence Day party, Don Juan met John Augustus Sutter (Johann August Suter), a German-Swiss adventurer who had arrived in California by way of the Sandwich Islands. The next day, Sutter conferred with Alvarado, presenting letters of recommendation and stating that he wanted to start a colony in California. The governor told him that if he declared his intention of becoming a Mexican citizen and then chose the unoccupied land he considered necessary for his plan, eventually he would be given legal title to the land.[8] Two years later, Alvarado granted Sutter a large tract near the junction of the Sacramento and American Rivers. One reason that Don Juan favored Sutter's plan was that it would constrain Mariano Vallejo's power in the area north of San Francisco Bay.

Alvarado's two-story home, which served as his office and private residence as well as a place to entertain foreign visitors, was the scene of increased social activity after his marriage in August 1839. His bride was Doña Martina Castro,

*Martina Castro de Alvarado, c. 1854.* Courtesy of the San Pablo
Historical Society.

daughter of Francisco Castro and Gabriela Berreyessa de Castro. Her family had early roots in northern California—all four of Martina's grandparents had been in the party of settlers conducted to California in 1776 by Colonel Juan Bautista de Anza. Recruited in the northwestern Mexican provinces of Sinaloa and Sonora, the soldier-colonists and their families traveled sixteen hundred miles to San Francisco Bay, where they helped to establish a new presidio and mission. Martina's paternal grandfather and father both served in the Spanish army at the presidio. After his retirement, her father received a large land grant to Rancho San Pablo on the northeast shore of San Francisco Bay, where he raised a large family.

Don Juan and Doña Martina had been acquainted for eight years before they were married, although they saw each other only a few times during that period. They first met at Rancho San Pablo when Alvarado visited there in 1831—she was then sixteen. They later met in Monterey, in Santa Clara (where Martina's married sister lived), and at the San Pablo ranch when Don Juan stopped there on his way to Sonoma to solicit military aid from Mariano Vallejo. In February 1839, when their marriage was contracted, Martina was almost twenty-five years old—an advanced age for a California bride of that era—and Governor Alvarado was thirty. They chose August 24 as the date for the ceremony and Mission Santa Clara as the wedding site. Situated between Monterey and San Pablo, Santa Clara had been one of the richest of the missions, and the administrator there was José Ramón Estrada, an old school chum of Don Juan who had married Doña Martina's sister, María Gregoria. Those two were selected as *padrino* (best man) and *madrina* (bridesmaid). As the wedding day approached, family and friends of the bride-to-be gathered at the mission, awaiting the arrival of the groom and his attendants.

Encarnación Pinedo, an early resident of Santa Clara, described the wedding-day scene: "The entrance to the church was decorated for the occasion with arches of white muslin, artificial flowers, ribbons, flags and streamers. When the bridal party was nearing the church, musicians playing on different instruments met and joined it, marching at its head to the church. The soldiers fired salutes with cannon, the bells sent up joyful peals, and the people exploded firecrackers and cheered lustily."[9]

But, as will be explained later, Don Juan did not appear for his own wedding—instead he sent his half brother as proxy, who went through the ceremony, as recorded by the officiating priest, Fray José María de Jesús de Gonzalez: "On August 24, 1839, as specified in the file formed regarding the liberty and unmarried state of the Señor Don Juan B. Alvarado and of the Señorita Doña Martina Castro, there having been found no canonical impediment whatever that would obstruct the marriage . . . I joined their hands, and on the following 27th, I veiled at a nuptial mass the forementioned Doña Martina Castro with Don Juan B. Alvarado, a citizen residing at Monterey, who concurred with this act having been present, not physically but morally through his proxy Don José Antonio Estrada."[10]

Besides gifts for the bride, Don Juan had sent a silver box containing the *arras* (thirteen gold coins), a symbolic dowry of the groom's pledge to provide for the couple's material needs, and the two wedding rings of California gold used in the ceremony. (Although there were substantial discoveries of gold in 1842 and 1848, native gold nuggets and flakes were recovered earlier.) He also arranged for the priest to receive a beautiful silver chalice and two hundred pounds of candles. Although Doña Martina must have been devastated when her betrothed did not appear, she participated in the postnuptial celebrations at the mission, which lasted for a week. Then she and her small entourage traveled to Monterey, where there was a reception, a great banquet, and additional festivities.[11]

Two reasons have been suggested for the failure of Don Juan to show up at his own wedding. First, and most likely, one of his periodic bouts of drinking had rendered him unable to function; in fact, he had been ill during much of July and had turned the government over to his secretary, Jimeno. And undoubtedly he had participated in various bachelor parties in the days before the wedding. Years later, however, Alvarado offered another explanation: that affairs of state suddenly demanded his attention in Monterey. According to Don Juan, he and his party had actually started for Santa Clara, and after they had stopped for the night at a rancho twelve leagues from the capital, a special messenger brought a letter from his secretary begging the governor to return to Monterey. The reason was the arrival of the French frigate *l'Artemise*, commanded by Captain Cyrille Pierre Laplace, who wanted to discuss important matters about the future of California. Alvarado later wrote, "After due consideration, I gave up my trip to Santa Clara and, moved by considerations of delicacy, honor, and dignity, decided to return to the capital at once."[12] One problem with this explanation is that Alvarado had earlier signed the power of attorney with his half brother; but perhaps he was so ill that he did not know whether he would make it to Mission Santa Clara. His excuse was also belied by the fact that Laplace first anchored at Monterey on August 27, which was three days after Alvarado's wedding.

While the wedding festivities were under way at Mission Santa Clara, Don Juan was in Monterey, where he invited principal merchants and residents to a reception in honor of the French naval officer's visit. Captain Laplace, who spoke good Spanish, presented his staff of officers, and Alvarado introduced his guests; then refreshments were served. When the visitor indicated that he wished to speak to Don Juan alone, he was led to the second floor; there, he assured his host that France, though not at liberty to take the initiative, would favorably receive a proposition for a protectorate. He also confided, "I am making a trip around the world on a scientific expedition and at some of the points I have touched, I have learned from authentic sources that the government of the United States is trying to find some way of taking possession of Your Excellency's country, and above all, the beautiful San Francisco Bay. My desire is limited to informing Your Excellency what has been told to me, that, being advised beforehand, you may plan whatever is best for your fellow countrymen."[13]

The next night, after a state visit aboard *l'Artémise*, Alvarado became dangerously ill; his life was probably saved by the ship's surgeon, who diagnosed the problem as an angina attack and administered medication. During the following week, Don Juan met with Laplace several times. In a book published a few years later, the French captain described the California governor as "a man with a distinguished air, carriage and manners; dark skinned; a lively and intelligent expression; Andalusian appearance; one who expressed himself with charm and facility."[14]

Captain Laplace was favorably impressed with Alvarado, who doubtless gave him a glowing account of his accomplishments as governor. This was reflected in the visitor's report to the the French Minister of Marine:

Under his active administration order is slowly being reestablished, agriculture is being revived and the missions are better cared for. Through his efforts the deserting Christian indigenes are returning to their labors; indeed more, he has succeeded in forming the boldest among them into a corps of infantry disciplined in the European manner, by means of which he holds in check both the savages on the frontier and the trouble makers at home. Finally, laws have been made in favor of foreigners, so that at present merchants may trade in all ports of the province without exception, and immigrants receive gratuitously lands and livestock.[15]

Captain Laplace was one of the guests that Don Juan invited to a formal reception and banquet in honor of his new

*Alvarado's two-story home in Monterey.* Courtesy of the Bancroft Library.

wife, Martina, who had arrived in the capital. She was delighted with her lovely home, with its second-story balcony overlooking the town and beautiful bay, and which, like many of the better houses in Monterey, contained furnishings from China: inlaid tables, lamps, camphorwood chests, and embroidered silk bedspreads. Martina enjoyed the active social life of Monterey, which centered on their home since it was the governor's mansion. Her mother and younger sister, María Luisa, lived with them for two years, providing companionship and support, especially when Don Juan gave himself over to the pleasures of *aguardiente*. The Alvarados had a cook and a housemaid as well a servant who did various chores and took care of their riding horses.

A talented French cook named Raoul presided over the kitchen of the Alvarado house. One day Raoul, who wished to be addressed as "Señor Professor," told the governor that he could no longer remain in his service because there was a curse upon the house that meant everyone who lived there was going to die very soon. As proof, he took Alvarado outside and pointed to the flagpole, at the top of which a human skull had been tied to the halyard. Don Juan lowered the skull, but his entreaties to Raoul were unsuccessful—the cook left immediately, sailing to southern California. After keeping the skull in his study for a week, during which he had no luck in determining its origin or who had put it on the flagpole, Don Juan deferred to the religious beliefs of the Monterey women and had it borne to the church in a religious procession, after which it was buried in the Catholic cemetery.[16]

Within a year Martina bore her first child, a boy named María Alvino. When the baby was baptized on July 7, 1840, friends of the governor strewed rose petals all the way from the governor's home to the presidio chapel. But the baby lived less than two months. We can only try to imagine how Martina felt, when six months later, her husband's mistress, "Raymunda," who lived just up the street, gave birth to a healthy little girl, the fourth daughter she had borne to Don Juan. A few years later Raymunda married Mariano de Jesús Soberanes (Alvarado's uncle by marriage), a widower with seven children, and she lived out her days on Rancho Los Ojitos, which had been granted to her husband by Alvarado. In 1842, Don Juan sold Raymunda's house to Manuel Dutra de Vargas for one hundred silver dollars.[17]

Soon after Don Juan's marriage, the schooner *California* brought dispatches from Mexico with new appointments for the governor and the military commandant. Alvarado, who a year earlier had been approved as provisional or ad interim governor, was now named as the constitutional governor of the Californias. Mariano Vallejo was promoted to the permanent rank of colonel, with his office of commandant general confirmed. News of Alvarado's appointment was celebrated throughout the department, especially at Los Angeles, where the flag was raised, salvos were fired, and the houses were illuminated at night. Due to his illness, induced by overindulgence in alcohol, Don Juan was not able to participate in the noisy festivities in his honor at Monterey, and he was not sworn into office until November 24, 1839.[18]

Don Juan presided over the departmental *junta* meetings held at Monterey between mid-February and the end of May 1840. At the opening session, he sketched the conditions of the country, pointing out branches of public affairs that needed special attention. These were enumerated as the demarcation of public lands, the encouragement of agriculture and commerce, measures to aid public education, police and municipal regulations, the creation of a supreme court, and the organization of the public finances. Alvarado concluded his address with the following charge: "It is for you as a body to shower the most abundant benefits on the country you represent, reaping as the fruit of your tasks the eternal gratitude of its dearest sons."[19]

Two accomplishments of the *junta* deserve mention here. A *tribunal de justicia* (supreme court) was established and the four justices, a *fiscal* (government attorney), and a secretary appointed. When Juan Bandini, an old political enemy, was proposed as one of the justices, Alvardo consented to the appointment only because Vallejo favored it and he felt he owed something to the commandant for the aid he had given in the past. Jimeno introduced the other interesting resolution: that Monterey be declared the official capital. In the discussion that followed, Pío Pico bitterly opposed this proposal, insisting on obedience to the law of 1835 that had made Los Angeles the seat of government; however, other members pointed out that the decree had not been officially received and that a later law authorized the departmental government to designate the capital. The resolution was adopted, whereupon Pico stormed out of the hall, receiving thereby an official rebuke and orders to pay a fine. He later apologized and retracted his protest.[20]

The *junta* and the governor had to consider the problem of financing regular government operations as well as any new programs. Since Mexican independence in 1821, the principal source of revenue had been customs duties, augmented by goods and services provided by the missions. In addition, some funds were secured through licences, fees, and fines. But for the past decade, and especially during the three years of sectional warfare, revenues had declined considerably. And with the phasing out of the missions, that source of financial support was disappearing.

Secularization of the California missions in the 1830s had proceeded unevenly, with mixed results. Freed from mission discipline and guidance, a majority of the Indians refused to work in the fields; they slaughtered the herds of cattle, and they rapidly sold the properties that had been given them. At the same time, a number of Hispanic Californios profited by the arrangement, securing positions as administrators or obtaining grants of former mission land. Many of these administrators enriched themselves and their friends with mission booty; others proved to be incompetent rather than dishonest; and some were honest, faithful, and efficient. The Franciscan friars were disillusioned as they saw decades of patient work destroyed and church attendance fall off dramatically. Furthermore, no secular replacements were sent to take over their religious duties, so they remained as curates or parish priests.

Most of the missions had been plundered and were in decline before Don Juan came to power, but because he presided over the final secularization efforts and appointed a number of administrators, some writers, such as Father

William Gleeson in his *History of the Catholic Church in California*, have blamed him for the pillage. Alvarado did not profit personally by the spoilation—he got no mission live-stock or land—and it is to his credit that he endeavored to restrain within bounds the shameless proceedings of admin-istrators who had been appointed in 1833. The historian Bancroft concluded, "The most extravagant and sweeping charges are made of a deliberate plunder and distribution of the spoils by Alvarado among his friends; but no proofs are presented, the charges have always been denied by Alvarado and urged mainly by his enemies, and they are probably false. . . . The disastrous result was due more to circum-stances beyond the control of the governor than to any lack of wisdom or honesty on his part."[21]

Don Juan made some earnest efforts to improve the general condition of the mission establishments. On January 17, 1839, he issued government regulations for mission management—there had been none previously. These regu-lations prohibited the administrators from contracting debts on account of the missions; from slaughtering mission cattle, except for consumption; and from trading mission horses and mules for clothing for the Indians. They also prohibited the settlement of white persons in the establishments, "as long as Indians remained in the community." Each administrator was required to prepare a census of his establishment, stating the class and age of all residents, as well as listing emancipated Indians who were living on mission lands. Likewise, each had to submit a list of all employees, stating their monthly wages and including the wages of the priests. To examine the accounts and the fulfillment of the administrators' trust, the government would appoint an inspector.[22]

Two days later, Don Juan appointed William Hartnell to the post of *visitador*, or inspector of missions, at an annual salary of two thousand *pesos*, to be paid by fifteen of the missions. It was an excellent choice; Hartnell was an Englishman who had come to California in 1822, where he became a naturalized citizen and married a daughter of Captain José de la Guerra. First a trader at Monterey and later a schoolmaster, he was an intelligent and well-educated man with a reputation for honesty. He was also owner of Rancho Alisal, adjacent to Alvarado's Rancho El Alisal. Don Juan issued instructions to Hartnell, requiring him to make a tour of inspection of all the missions and authorizing him to hear complaints and introduce minor reforms.[23]

Between May and September 1839, Hartnell visited, inspected, and took inventories at missions from San Diego to San Francisco. Generally, the mission records and accounts, if kept at all, were incomplete and jumbled. Almost everywhere, the Indians complained about the treatment received at the hands of administrators, and at two missions the inspector ordered the expenditure of money to properly clothe the Indians and the slaughter of cattle to feed them. Hartnell's depressing report showed that secularization was not accomplishing the several goals anticipated; yet, neither he nor Alvarado wholly despaired.[24]

One problem was the hiring-out of mission Indians to *rancheros*. Mission administrators, who received a part of the fees, and *rancheros* and farmers were in favor of the practice, but the Franciscans and the Indians naturally complained. The issue was made explicit in August 1839, when an old Indian from San Juan Capistrano who had been "rented" to a *ranchero*, stole a horse and rode more than three hundred miles to Monterey to complain of ill treatment. He asked to be either released from his forced service or to be shot. Alvarado recalled, "I ordered Don Manuel Jimeno, whom I had left in charge of the government, to order William Hartnell, then inspector general of the missions, to forbid the administrators of the missions to rent out Indians."[25] The acting governor immediately issued an order forbidding the practice.

In March 1840 Don Juan issued a new set of regulations for the missions, under which the administrators were replaced by majordomos at reduced salaries and the authority of the friars was increased somewhat. Hartnell then made a second tour of the missions, after which he resigned his post in disgust. Lack of cooperation from those in charge of the missions was a principal reason; for example, General Vallejo would not permit him to take charge of San Rafael, as the governor had ordered, and briefly arrested him for having ventured to interfere in matters concerning the northern frontier without his consent. Hartnell's wife, María Teresa de la Guerra, later said, "No person can have even an approximate idea of the sufferings this post brought to Don Guillermo Hartnell."[26]

The controversy with Hartnell was just one incident in the strained relationship between Don Juan and his uncle, the military commandant. Conflict over military matters was another cause of the estrangement—Vallejo thought that the military branch was all important, whereas Alvarado believed that in a republican form of government, the military should be subordinate to the civil authorities. In one case, Don Juan had given orders to the militia without first having consulted the commandant, who bitterly protested the action. When the department treasurer wrote to Vallejo that he could supply the soldiers of the four presidios with clothing and shoes but could not pay the salaries due them, the commandant was angered, believing that Alvarado ordered the treasurer to give preference to the civil employees. The quarrel culminated when Vallejo resigned his post in January 1842 and sent his secretary, Prudon, as a commissioner to the president of Mexico with a strong recommendation that a new military governor be appointed to assume both the military and civil commands of California. Reflecting on the years 1840 through 1842, Don Juan later wrote, "Although official relations between the military headquarters and that of the governor's office were not cordial, as a nephew, I never ceased

to have great affection for the uncle for whom all of my compatriots had a certain regard."[27]

Don Juan and Don Mariano did cooperate in the "Graham
affair" when a number of foreign residents were arrested and
deported. On the third day of April 1840, Padre José Suárez
del Real, pastor of the presidio chapel of San Carlos in
Monterey, wrote a note to Governor Alvarado informing him
that a foreigner had revealed a plot to take over the government. Two days later, William Garner, a former English sailor
who had settled in California in 1824 and married a local
*señorita*, confirmed the plot and denounced Isaac Graham as
head of the conspiracy, which involved capturing Alvarado
and José Castro, who were to be deprived of life if they could
not be taken prisoners. Graham was a Tennessee backwoods-
man who had trapped in New Mexico before moving on to
California, where he set up a whiskey distillery and drinking
place at Natividad, about twenty miles northeast of Monterey.
In 1836 he had raised a company of *rifleros*, composed mostly
of loafers and deserting sailors, who had aided Alvarado in his
revolt against Gutiérrez, but subsequently Graham and his
rude followers created disturbances, especially when they had
been drinking. Alvarado was quoted as saying, "I was insulted
at every turn by the drunken followers of Graham; and when
walking in my garden, they would come to its wall and call
upon me in terms of the greatest familiarity, 'Ho Bautista,
come here, I want to speak to you'—'Bautista here'—
'Bautista there'— 'Bautista everywhere!' "[28]

Persuaded that Graham and other Anglo foreigners were
plotting to take over California, and aware that a similar class
of what he termed *malditos extranjeros* (wicked foreigners) had
carried out a successful revolution in Texas, Don Juan took
action. Soon after hearing of the plot, he issued orders to
California military and civil officials to arrest all foreigners
who had entered the country unlawfully, except those who
were married to native women or were well known and had

some honorable occupation. Every *alcalde* from Sonoma to San Diego received identical orders. In the Monterey district Colonel Castro dispatched a party of soldiers, who arrested Graham and others at his house, and in Sonoma, General Vallejo sent squads to arrest foreigners in northern California. Vallejo, himself, with about seventy cavalrymen, rode to Monterey. About one hundred foreigners were arrested, most of whom were taken to the capital; more than half of them were soon released, but the others were put in the *calabozo* (jail). William Garner, suspected by Graham and others to have revealed the plot, was detained for a time in Governor Alvarado's house and pressured to give evidence.[29]

After conferring with a judge and an advisory council, who pointed out that the majority of the prisoners had come into the country without passports and thus could be deported legally, Alvardo determined to send the men to Mexico for trial. Forty-five prisoners, about half of whom were Americans and the others English-born, were shackled, put aboard a Mexican bark, and shipped off under a military guard headed by José Castro. After anchoring at Santa Barbara in order to pick up additional prisoners, the ship sailed to the Mexican west coast port of San Blas, from where the prisoners were marched to Tepic to stand formal trial.[30]

Meanwhile, on April 23 Don Juan sent a long report of the Graham affair to the Mexican government, and the next day he informed the council in Monterey that his efforts to ensure the public peace had been successful and the troublemakers embarked. A few days later the governor issued a printed, informative proclamation:

Fellow-citizens! A sordid and mercenary faction, incited by some ungrateful foreigners whom you had received to your hospitable land, purposed to deprive you of the richest of treasures, your lives and country, and sacrifice to their ungovernable desires the highest authorities. The departmental government, with the assistance of its subalterns and the honorable military garrison, was enabled to smother the conspiracy at its commencement. The necessary proceedings were taken, but for want of a competent tribunal the villains were sent to the supreme government, together with the leaders of the faction and a multitude of other foreigners who were illegally introduced into the country. . . . Fellow-citizens! I can assure you that the country has been saved from imminent danger.[31]

At Tepic, the British vice-consul, Eustace Barron, intervened on the prisoners' behalf, as did a vociferous American lawyer and journalist named Thomas Jefferson Farnham. About twenty-eight of the men—those who had not become naturalized or married in California and who lacked any papers to show they had complied with the laws—were freed from prison but banished from Mexico. Graham and eighteen others were held for further hearings, which lasted for more than five months. Finally, in June 1841 the nineteen prisoners were found not guilty of the charges against them and were to receive compensation for the loss of property and time. Sent back to Monterey at government expense, they were given valid passports and documents listing their claims against the government in California. Alfred Robinson, who saw them land, wrote, "They came ashore, dressed neatly, armed with rifles and swords, and looking in infinitely better condition than when they departed, thanks to the energetic measures of the British consul."[32]

The Mexican minister of the interior, Alvarado's superior, generally approved of the governor's zeal in preventing a revolt. In a communiqué, he ordered Don Juan to make sure that henceforth foreigners would be permitted to enter California only in accordance with the laws. If necessity arose again to expel foreigners, he should be careful to gather proof of their guilt in order to avoid reclamations by those arrested. Meanwhile José Castro, who had conducted the prisoners to Tepic, went to Mexico City, where he was tried by a court-martial on charges brought by the British and American ministers. Ably defended by Brigadier General Manuel Micheltorena (a future governor of California), Castro was acquitted, and he returned to Monterey.[33]

The Graham affair had international repercussions that haunted Alvarado for several years. After the prisoners had been sent to Mexico, warships of three nations anchored at Monterey, where their captains made anxious inquiries about treatment of their citizens. In mid-June 1840, Captain Joseph de Rosamel, commander of the French warship *Danaïde*, informed government officials that he had heard that foreigners had been arrested and that he had come to protect French citizens. He was delighted to learn that no Frenchman had been sent to San Blas. The same month, Captain French Forrest arrived aboard the United States corvette *St. Louis* and, in a letter to the governor, demanded an explanation for the deportation of Americans. He was assured that certain foreigners had been sent away according to law, either for offences against the public peace or for having entered the country illegally. Before departing, he gathered some testimony. In 1841 Captain Jones of the Royal Navy's man-of-war *Curaçao* put in at Monterey for the purpose of assisting the British subjects in collecting indemnity for their arrest and loss of property. Apparently he had some success. In November of that same year Captain J. H. Aulick anchored the USS *Yorktown* at Monterey and attempted to collect testimony concerning American losses, but he soon sailed away, frustrated by the lack of cooperation of Graham and his friends.[34]

Graham's followers and other foreigners in California, as well as many Spanish-surnamed residents, wanted above all to acquire ranch land; consequently they appealed to Governor Alvarado for land grants. In that era, land ownership not only provided an important way to earn a living, it also conferred social status and prestige. Don Juan freely disposed of former mission property, approving more land grants to individuals than had any other governor. He justified his liberality by citing an action of the Mexican Congress, dated August 17, 1837, ordering the immediate distribution of surplus mission property. Furthermore, the amount of livestock belonging to the former missions had dwindled, reducing the need for vast pasturage, and because the number of Indian *neophytes* had plummeted while the white inhabitants had increased, "it was a simple act of justice, made imperative by the circumstances, to take away lands from those who had too much and grant them to industrious persons who needed them for their horses and cattle."[35]

Don Juan endorsed more than two hundred land grants to applicants who lived in various parts of the department. Besides fostering ranching and agriculture, the judicious awarding of land grants was an important factor in maintaining his hold on the governorship. Most of the grants were to Californios, many of them members of well-known families such as Alviso, Amador, Armijo, Bandini, Berryesa, Castro, Estrada, Estudillo, Galindo, Hernández, Martínez, Moraga, Pico, Sánchez, and Vallejo. Alvarado granted several islands to qualified applicants: Santa Rosa Island to Carlos and José Antonio Carrillo; Santa Cruz Island to Andrés Castillero; Angel Island to Antonio M. Osio; and Mare Island in San Pablo Bay to his brother-in-law Victor Castro.[36]

The legal text of the land grant issued to Victor Castro is similar to others awarded by Governor Alvarado:

Inasmuch as Don Victor Castro, Mexican by birth, has solicited from this government ownership of Mare Island, situated near Carquinez Strait, for which a tentative permit was previously given by Don Manuel Jimeno Casarín, interim head of government, and in virtue of the solicitor having newly resubmitted his petition proving that the said island is not the property of any individual, town, or corporation, in conformity with the powers conferred on me by the Supreme National Government, I have resolved in a decree of this date to declare Don Victor Castro owner in possession of the referred island in all of its extension. Therefore, deliver this to the concerned party to serve as his title and for security and other pertinent purposes. Dated at Monterey, capital of the Department, May 29, 1841.[37]

Don Juan did not set aside any land for himself or his wife, an oversight he doubtless regretted later. But he already had property: Rancho El Sur, a nine-thousand-acre spread along the Pacific Ocean south of Monterey, granted him by Governor Figueroa, which he traded in 1840 to his uncle, Juan Rogers Cooper, for the smaller but more accessible Rancho Bolsa del Potrero, along the lower Salinas River. (Three years later Cooper reacquired the Bolsa ranch from Alvarado for one thousand dollars in coin.) In January 1841 Alvarado purchased Rancho El Alisal, about seventy-four hundred acres with a tiled-roof adobe house, for thirty-five hundred *pesos* from Feliciano Soberanes. There, only twenty-five miles east of the capital (near the present city of Salinas), he often retreated from the cares of office, especially when he suffered from periodic bouts of drinking. Soon after acquiring this land, Don Juan appointed Soberanes administrator of Mission Soledad and granted him the 21,884-acre Rancho San Lorenzo on the east side of the Salinas River.[38]

Alvarado also awarded property to men with Anglo American surnames who had become naturalized Mexican citizens and had married California women. Surnames of principal recipients were the following: Bale, Bowen, Chapman, Cooper, Coppinger, Den, Fitch, Forbes, Leese, Majors, Martin, Spence, Reid, West, and White. And a few Americans, such as Isaac Graham and John Marsh, acquired property in those years by purchasing it from Hispanic grantees. As a barrier to Russian expansion from their bases at Bodega Bay

*Alvarado's adobe house at Rancho El Alisal.* Courtesy of the Bancroft Library.

and Fort Ross, the governor encouraged land applicants to settle north of San Francisco Bay, coordinating the grants with the approval of his uncle, General Vallejo, commander of the northern frontier.

To block operations of Hudson's Bay Company trappers in the Sacramento Valley and to check American overland immigrants, in 1839 Alvarado gave John Sutter permission to settle in the interior valley. The German-Swiss entrepreneur founded his colony of New Helvetia near the junction of the Sacramento and American Rivers, and the following year he became a naturalized Mexican citizen. On September 1, 1840, Alvarado wrote to Sutter that because the maintainance of order on that frontier was of great importance, he was authorized to administer justice in the region. He could pursue and arrest robbers and horse thieves, warn off unlicensed hunters and trappers, and, with permission of the government, wage war on raiding Indians. In 1841 Don Juan granted eleven square leagues (48,708 acres) of land to Sutter. At the end of that year Captain Sutter acquired a large quantity of material goods—livestock, grain, buildings, tools, a launch, eight brass cannon, and other items—on credit from the Russian commander at Fort Ross.[39]

After twenty-nine years in California, officials of the Russian American Company (not the Russian government) decided to abandon their foothold at Bodega Bay and Fort Ross. During their occupation they had successfully hunted marine mammals for their pelts and had been good customers for California wheat, beef, suet and fat, dried meat, and salt. But when seals and otters became scarce, and New England merchants opened new markets for California products, the Russians found that their outpost was no longer remunerative. At first the Russian commandant tried to sell the improvements and livestock for thirty thousand *pesos* on credit to General Vallejo, who attempted to interest Don Juan in the proposal. But Alvarado, worried that the Mexican government might oppose the sale and wary of extending more power to his uncle, thwarted the deal. Negotiations with Vallejo were broken off, and the Russian property was sold to Captain Sutter for the same figure quoted to Vallejo. On January 2, 1842, Alvarado gleefully wrote to the Mexican minister of the interior, reporting the Russian departure from California.[40]

Don Juan also sent a report to the Mexican government regarding the discovery of gold in southern California. In March 1842 a *vaquero* (cowboy) named Francisco López, having found some particles that looked like copper or gold, took them to Los Angeles, where they were verified as *pepitas de oro* (gold nuggets). Within a few days a number of gold seekers went to the discovery site—Placerita Canyon in the San Fernando Hills, about forty miles northwest of Los Angeles— and a few prospectors also arrived from Sonora, Mexico. A limited amount of the precious metal was found—Don Juan estimated the total recovery as two thousand ounces—

although a Los Angeles merchant sent nuggets and gold dust from the area to the U.S. Mint at Philadelphia for several years. Someone gave Governor Alvarado about one ounce of the gold dust, which he had made into earrings for his wife and a ring for his eldest daughter. When the governor forwarded his report to Mexico City along with a sample of the gold, he requested the government to send a scientific mining team to explore possibilities of additional gold-bearing deposits. The minister of the interior's reply noted that Mexico had an immense wealth of minerals and implied that the California discovery seemed to be an insignificant matter. Alvarado later commented, "Perhaps Providence had decided to reserve for the United States the vast mineral wealth of California."[41]

Some of the California gold, along with surplus ranch and agricultural products, was taken away in foreign ships, the number of which increased each year. The list of vessels that arrived during Don Juan's governorship totals 141, with an average of twenty-three per year. There were whalers, barks, schooners, merchant ships, and men-of-war, flying flags of Chile, Colombia, France, Great Britain, Hawaii, Mexico, Russia, and the United States.[42] When these foreign ships anchored in Monterey, there were usually dinners and balls for the visiting officers and elite government officials.

Captain William Phelps of the *Alert* recalled a *cena* and *baile* (dinner ball) given ashore on July 4, 1842, at which ship officers and principal residents were present. The government hall was decorated with American flags and portraits of Washington and Lafayette, and an excellent supper was prepared by cooks and stewards of the ships. Phelps, a Boston teetotaler, disapproved of the *fandango*: "A large quantity of liquors and wines disgraced the occasion and the Governor got drunk before midnight and most of the natives followed his example before morning. About 4 in the morning I was desirous of leaving but found soldiers stationed at the door by order of the Gov. with orders to let no person pass out. He said the Americans invited him hither to celebrate the 4th of July and he should keep it up untill [*sic*] he was tired and no person should leave before he did, and in fact the dancing was not discontinued untill [*sic*] 9 AM."[43]

British officers of the Hudson's Bay Company also made official visits to Monterey during Don Juan's governorship. On New Year's Day, 1841, James Douglas, chief factor of the company's operation at Fort Vancouver, arrived aboard the English bark *Columbia*. Two days later, when he went to the governor's office to request an interview, Alvarado invited him to return in the afternoon and suggested that David Spence, a Scottish trader who lived in Monterey, accompany him as interpreter. After the meeting, Douglas recalled that the governor was "a middle sized man, rather stout, good looking, with a harrassed jaded air. He received us with a sort of reserved courtesy . . . in the course of conversation this stiffness wore off and he insensibly entered with great spirit into the matters under discussion."[44]

Douglas reported that several topics were considered. First, Alvarado wanted the company's trapping parties withdrawn from the Sacramento Valley. The governor granted permission for the company to carry on trading business in certain California ports but noted that all merchandise first had to be landed and duties paid on it. Alvarado gave his consent for the company to establish a trading post at Yerba Buena on San Francisco Bay. When Douglas asked about the possibility of purchasing live cattle and sheep to be driven to the Oregon country, Don Juan said that private citizens were not permitted to sell livestock for that purpose but that the government would furnish the required number at six *pesos* for choice cows and two *pesos* for ewes of the same quality. A few days after the interview, Douglas entertained Alvarado "and a party of gentlemen" aboard the *Columbia*.[45]

A year later, in January 1842, Sir George Simpson, governor of the Hudson's Bay Company, anchored at Monterey in the course of a trip around the world. In his book, published later that year in London, he described the California capital and estimated its population as about seven hundred. He despised the crooked streets, the "cheerless" adobe dwellings with a paucity of windows because of the exhorbitant cost of glass, the illiteracy of the residents, flea-filled mattresses in the homes, and the defense battery of "eight or ten rusty and honey-combed guns." Accompanied by David Spence, Simpson visited Governor Alvarado at home:

We were ushered into his excellency's best apartment, which contained a host of common chairs, a paltry table, a kind of sofa, a large Dutch clock, and four or five cheap mirrors, boasting, however, the unique feature of three large windows that reached to the floor, and communicated with a balcony overlooking the town and bay.

We found the governor lame. . . . About a month ago Alvarado, who had been entertaining the priest and some other friends in honor of the saint of the day,—probably the very saint who had been forced to contribute the wine,—managed, by means of his windows and his balcony, to fall to the ground and dislocate his ankle. . . . He has not allowed the cares of government to prey on his vitals, for the revolution of 1836, amid its other changes, has metamorphosed its champion from a thin and spare conspirator into a plump and punchy lover of singing and dancing and feasting.[46]

Alvarado had a greater opportunity to become acquainted with Eugène Duflot de Mofras, an attaché to the French legation in Mexico, who spent almost six months in California in 1841. Duflot was sent to study at close range the geography, economy, and politics of the country as well as the character of the inhabitants and how they managed Indians. He seemed to be spying out the possibility of French acquisition of all or part of California; indeed, he proposed such a course to the minister of foreign affairs in Paris. Duflot de Mofras published his well-written report in two volumes plus atlases in Paris in 1844. Although the Frenchman claimed that Governor Alvarado had proposed granting him "a large tract of land on which to settle a colony of 500 French," it is clear that both Don Juan and General Vallejo took a dislike to Duflot, partly because of his haughty attitude and remarks intimating that he was better than the inhabitants. Don Juan characterized the visitor as "a young man of great literary reputation, of fiery disposition and generous impulses, but who, unfortunately for him, came among us imbued with very false ideas as to our character."[47]

Besides the French and British, Americans were also interested in California, a concern that increased during Alvarado's governorship. Because of the Monroe Doctrine, U.S. officials did not want a European power to acquire the territory; but they also coveted land on the Pacific coast. More than once, American diplomatic agents in Mexico City had offered to purchase part or all of California, but these proposals were not accepted by the Mexican government. In 1841 four American warships, part of Charles Wilkes's exploring expedition, entered San Francisco Bay. The *Vincennes* under Lieutenant Ringgold was anchored for two and a half months, August 14 to November 1, while the ship's personnel used six small boats to explore and map the bay and the Sacramento River as far as the mouth of the Feather River. Meanwhile, Wilkes had sent a party under Lieutenant Emmons to examine the overland route from the Columbia River to Sutter's Fort on the Sacramento. Alarmed by this American penetration but unable to stop it, General Vallejo went to San Jose to confer with Lieutenant Colonel José Castro about the danger of foreign intervention. After the conference, the two military leaders reported their fears to Governor Alvarado and appealed to the Mexican government for aid.[48]

In January 1842, Don Juan wrote to officials in Mexico City about the growing number of Americans who were coming to California and the inability of the department to stop the flow. By 1840 the number of foreigners had reached 380, most of them Anglo American males, of whom about fifty trappers and traders had come overland. (The Hispanic population was 5,580.) Then in 1841 a new type of immigrant began to arrive—companies of pioneers who came overland with their families, planning to settle down and farm. They preferred the inland, unsettled areas, such as the Napa, Sonoma, and upper Sacramento valleys, and they did not mingle with the Californios. Generally without passports or permits to enter Mexican territory, some followed the Oregon trail and crossed the Sierra Nevada; others came via New Mexico. Both Alvarado and Vallejo sent emissaries to the supreme government in Mexico to explain the defenseless condition of their department, the arrival of Americans, and the danger of the country experiencing the fate of Texas. In reply to notification about the foreign influx, the Mexican government urged the governor and the commandant to enforce the laws against foreigners, but it sent no aid in the way of military or customs reinforcements.[49]

Responding to requests from Alvarado and Vallejo, on January 22, 1842, President Antonio López de Santa Anna appointed Brigadier General Manuel Micheltorena, who had been with him in the Texas campaign, as governor, commanding general, and inspector of California. After gathering a force of about three hundred men, at least half of whom were *cholos* recruited from prisons, the newly appointed governor embarked his followers on four vessels at Mazatlan in late July. A month later the men landed at San Diego, where the general spent several weeks organizing and drilling his convict recruits before marching northward.[50]

On hearing of General Micheltorena's arrival in California, Alvarado issued a printed proclamation on September 24, announcing that he had asked to be relieved from office and expressing satisfaction with the appointment of a successor who came with a reputation for military ability and nobility of character. In late September, Micheltorena and his force reached Los Angeles, where they stayed for almost a month, during which the resident civilians complained about the thievish soldiers. Resuming his march northward, Micheltorena was twenty miles beyond the former mission of San Fernando when he received the startling news that two American warships had anchored at Monterey and their commander had demanded surrender of the place.[51]

This international incident occurred because Commodore Thomas ap Catesby Jones, who was commander of the American naval forces in the Pacific and had been officially warned of strained relations between Mexico and the United States, heard a report that war had broken out. Indeed, Richard T. Maxwell, a surgeon aboard Jones's flagship, wrote that when the American ships were in Peru, their officers had been shown a Mexican newspaper stating that Mexico had declared war on the United States. Commodore Jones was aware of British and French interests in California, and when he learned that warships from those nations had left Peru for an unknown destination, he decided to act. Considering it his duty to occupy California before other naval forces might do the same, he sailed north aboard his flagship, the *United States*, accompanied by the *Cyane*, and anchored in Monterey Bay.[52]

At four in the afternoon of October 19, 1842, Commodore Jones sent ashore his secretary and Captain James Armstrong under a flag of truce with a demand that the capital be surrendered to the United States. Addressed to the governor and military commandant, the demand was delivered to Alvarado, who was given until nine the following morning to respond. Don Juan called a meeting of officers to consider the situation. The customs administrator, Osio, described the governor's response to the surrender demand: "Señor Alvarado was in shock as he read the note, which was written in Spanish. After a period of silence his face suddenly became pale and then immediately turned red, as if blood was about to burst from his eyes. In a voice choked with emotion he told the commodore's secretary, who was a Spaniard, that if he had only half the number of men in the commodore's force he would consider their forces equal. . . . It would bring him pleasure as well as honor to fight him in defense of his country. However, since he could not do this, he would comply."[53]

Late in the evening, Thomas O. Larkin, an American trader and neighbor of Alvarado, went to the governor's residence, where he learned that Alvarado was sending a dispatch to the new governor, telling him of the surrender demand and other developments. Don Juan protested to those in the room that he no longer had authority because his successor was already in California and said he wanted to leave Monterey at once. But the Mexican officers would not agree, and about midnight two commissioners appointed by Alvarado, accompanied by Larkin as interpreter, boarded the American flagship to negotiate the surrender. In two hours, terms were agreed upon and scheduled to be signed at nine in the morning. A final clause of the treaty, inserted to protect the reputation of Alvarado, stated that the governor had been induced to capitulate from motives of humanity, his small force being no match for the invaders.[54]

After his guests left, Don Juan went on a drinking binge. Before sunrise he sent an urgent message to Larkin, asking him to take charge of his property "because he had no other friends." When Larkin arrived at Alvarado's house, he found that Don Juan's family had left town and the governor was "at the billiard table, almost crazy, none the better or clearer for wine or brandy. He fairly raved. . . . He forgot his country & all under his command."[55] Alvarado then asked Larkin to go aboard the American flagship and request a special passport for himself and his family, but the commodore would not issue such a document. This episode shows Don Juan's weak character at a time of stress. Indeed, this pathetic man got drunk on many of the significant occasions of his life: his inauguration as governor, his wedding, and when his country was about to be invaded by a foreign military force at the time when he was the chief executive officer in the capital.

At eleven in the morning of October 20, a contingent of 150 American marines and sailors landed, took possession of the Monterey presidio, lowered the Mexican flag, and ran up the Stars and Stripes while a naval band played "The Star Spangled Banner" and "Yankee Doodle." Governor Alvarado signed the surrender treaty and then retired to Rancho El Alisal, accompanied by a bodyguard of forty cavalrymen. When Commodore Jones went ashore the next day, he found letters and newspapers from Mexico that clearly showed that the two nations were at peace, so he admitted his mistake, restored the presidio to Mexican officers, and raised the Mexican tricolor to the accompaniment of a salute from the American men-of-war. The commodore invited Alvarado to return to Monterey, but Don Juan declined, referring all matters to Micheltorena.[56]

During the following ten weeks, while their ships were anchored in the bay, many of the American sailors and officers spent time ashore riding horseback, hunting game, and dancing. The flagship's band provided music for the weekly balls, one of which was described by Doctor Maxwell: "On the night of the First of January [1843], we gave them a ball at the Government House. . . . The stewards of our messes were set to work making all kinds of delicacies in the shape of cakes and pies for the supper at the ball. Our wine from Madeira was all expended, so we were obliged to depend on whisky toddy, which the ladies thought was very fine, and indulged in rather too freely. . . . These people had the most extraordinary customs. They came on board the ship and danced all day, and we would go on shore and dance all night."[57]

While in Monterey, Commodore Jones attempted to settle the question of indemnity for Americans who had been exiled with Isaac Graham. The claimants were slow to collect evidence, however, so the naval officer departed with nothing more than a few sworn statements, and apparently Graham and his followers received no indemnification. Early in January 1843, Jones sailed south and met with Governor Micheltorena in Los Angeles.[58]

Meanwhile, in early December Don Juan had returned to the capital, but he soon indulged in another alcoholic binge and again withdrew to Rancho El Alisal, leaving affairs at Monterey in the hands of his secretary, Manuel Jimeno. When the new governor asked Alvarado to go to Los Angeles and surrender the command, Don Juan authorized Jimeno, the senior member of the *diputación*, to represent him. Accompanied by several important civil and military officers, Jimeno proceeded to Los Angeles, where on the last day of 1842 Micheltorena took the oath of office in the presence of the *ayuntamiento* and prominent citizens.[59] Thus ended the regime of Governor Alvarado, which had lasted six years, a tenure longer than that of any other governor in the Mexican era.

# 5

# Revolt against Micheltorena
# 1843–1845

OFFICIALS WHO RETURNED FROM Los Angeles early in 1843 told
Don Juan something about the new governor, Brigadier
General Manuel Micheltorena. In physical stature he was tall,
slender, and straight; he was clean-shaven and had agreeable
features, a light complexion, and brown hair. He was forty-two
years old, was a gentleman of considerable culture, and spoke
grammatically correct Spanish, sometimes embellished with
literary quotations. Soon after taking office, he ordered primary schools to be established in the principal towns under
the patronage of Our Lady of Guadalupe, and he aided California's first bishop, Francisco García Diego y Moreno, in
founding a seminary at Santa Inés. Micheltorena brought with
him his mistress, Josefa Fuentes, an intelligent and pleasing
woman, whom he later married at the urging of the bishop.[1]

The new governor and his soldiers spent the first seven
months of 1843 in Los Angeles. The local citizens, who were
forced to put up the officers in their homes, were appalled by
the conduct of the battalion members. Antonio María Osio
commented on the situation: "Micheltorena's apathy in
restraining the criminal activity of his soldiers, who committed
robberies and stabbings daily, simply exacerbated the problem
and increased the number of citizen complaints. . . . With one
or two exceptions, his officers were worse than the soldiers.
These officers would encourage the other men to commit
robberies and insist that they treat them as knights by giving

*General Manuel Micheltorena.* Courtesy of the Bancroft Library.

them a share of the loot. They would also borrow money with no intention of paying it back."[2]

A principal reason that Governor Micheltorena did not proceed to the capital at Monterey was lack of money—his government not having sent the promised funds, he had no way to obtain subsistence, nor could he pay the troops of his command. His *cholo* soldiers, whom Osio called former members of "chain gangs, made up primarily of thieves and assassins from different jails," generally foraged for their food. In midyear, Colonel Mariano Vallejo sent a schooner loaded with provisions valued at eleven thousand *pesos* (in return, he was later granted Rancho Suscol). Alvarado remembered, "When the *cholos* who had accompanied General Michel-torena, had stolen and eaten all the pigs and chickens in Los Angeles, His Excellency began his journey to the capital, where he was received with some show of welcome on the part of the citizens."[3]

Residents of Monterey were soon disillusioned with the new administration when the governor quartered his officers in private homes, a custom not previously known there, and when it became clear that he could not control the depre-dations of his men. Alvarado noted that it was not safe to walk on the streets after sunset because the soldiers, bad enough when sober, were intolerable when drunk. A few incidents are recorded in contemporary records: A servant of Thomas Larkin was assaulted, wounded, and robbed by a soldier; Pierre Attilan, a French resident of Monterey, was terribly cut and crippled for life by a party of soldiers to whom he had refused liquor; and another group of uniformed men com-mitted "a beastly outrage" on an Indian woman on the streets of the capital. Some believed that these attacks were related to the shortage of money in the department's treasury, a condi-tion keenly felt by those whose salaries were not paid, as well as by citizens and merchants. Virtually all of the departmental income came from import duties; in 1843 these amounted to

$52,504, but the salaries for civil and military officials totaled well over double that amount.[4]

Seeking to find out about the expenses and income of the department and to devise means of financial relief, Micheltorena had a series of meetings with military and civil officials, including Alvarado and Vallejo. In October Don Juan's committee made a number of recommendations that were ultimately adopted by the governor. These included abolishing the offices of prefect and subprefect; suppressing three of the five judgeships; putting military officers on half pay; and stopping the pay of the general and his secretary, the post surgeon, and auxiliary officers. The measures produced a budget saving of forty-nine thousand *pesos*. But Alvarado insisted that shortage of funds was not the most serious problem; in a speech he declared that it was useless to talk of reforms as long as the defense of California homes and families was entrusted to convicts.[5]

Rumors of a revolution against the governor and his *cholo* soldiers occurred several times in 1844, finally proving to be true. In January the governor ordered the arrest of Alvarado, an incident not mentioned by Don Juan when he later wrote his "Historia." Florencio Serrano's manuscript narrative and other accounts give details of the affair. It seems that Governor Micheltorena, being informed that Alvarado was plotting a revolt, ordered Captain José Mejía to arrest him. But Don Juan refused to be arrested by an officer of lower rank, so he donned his colonel's uniform, sent Mejía away, and went voluntarily to Monterey. Very soon, the governor, responding to the appeals of several prominent individuals, permitted him to return home. This affair did not affect Alvarado's petition for land, for in February the governor granted Don Juan the large tract of Las Mariposas in the Sierra Nevada foothills, eventually measured as 44,386 acres.[6]

In addition to rumors about local revolts, Micheltorena was troubled by reports of an impending foreign war. In July his government informed him that the projected annexation of Texas by the United States might precipitate a war and that he should prepare for the defense of California. The governor immediately ordered enrollment in the militia of all able-bodied males between the ages of fifteen and sixty; this decree included naturalized foreigners but not ecclesiastics or government officials. Formed into regiments and companies, they were to be drilled every Sunday and be ready for active duty as "Defensores de la Patria" (Defenders of the Nation). Alvarado, having been commissioned a militia colonel in 1842, headed the First Regiment; Colonel Mariano G. Vallejo commanded the Second Regiment. For security, the governor moved his headquarters inland to San Juan Bautista and had all the serviceable cannon and munitions moved there. Thomas Larkin, who had recently been notified of his appointment as consul of the United States, wrote to his government that in the event of war, Micheltorena could depend only on his 280 Mexican troops because the 150 to 200 California soldiers and the militia were not disposed to fight for a government in which they took little interest. By September the war alarm had passed and the governor returned to Monterey, but the cannon and munitions were left in San Juan Bautista.[7]

Although a foreign threat did not materialize, Governor Micheltorena worried about the growing domestic discontent and indignation expressed by many citizens. The governor, who was kindhearted and somewhat popular personally, was an indolent ruler who rarely appeared before noon and left his office early. Furthermore, his policies had not produced notable benefits for the country. Some Californios, including a few with a personal ambition to govern and handle the revenues, opposed him because he was not a native Californian; others objected because he would not move the capital to Los Angeles. Certainly, a great many residents felt insulted and threatened by his little army of hardened criminals and Mexican convicts. Alvarado and other prominent northern Californians who headed the opposition wanted to delay any confrontation until they could determine how much support they might receive from residents in the south and from foreign settlers. But events overtook their caution.

Don Juan came to the front in the revolution that erupted on November 14, 1844, which proved to be the last one of Californios against Mexicans of *la otra banda*. It began when a party of about fifty young Californios, led by Lieutenant Manuel Castro, Jesús Pico, and Antonio Chávez, drove off all the government horses from Monterey to the Salinas Valley, seized government munitions in San Juan Bautista, and appealed for popular support of their movement. Their goal was to force the battalion of *cholos*, and perhaps their general, to leave the country. Although Alvarado later claimed that this action was taken prematurely and without his knowledge, apparently he was involved in planning some way to get rid of the obnoxious Mexicans. William Wood, a surgeon from the U.S. warship *Savannah*, recalled that when he stopped at Rancho El Alisal on November 13, Alvarado was "surrounded by several of his countrymen, with drinking materials on the table at which they were sitting, and from subsequent events it is certain they had assembled in furtherance of a political conspiracy, which soon developed itself."[8]

As soon as Don Juan heard of the uprising, he rode northward to secure assistance and recruit men for the rebel forces. On November 20, at his mother-in-law's Rancho San Pablo, he wrote a six-page letter to his uncle in Sonoma, Colonel Mariano G. Vallejo, telling him what had occurred, declaring the movement to be just, and asking him to support it, either in person or by sending his brother Salvador with horses and supplies. Having heard of the uprising, Vallejo had already written to Micheltorena, stating that the *cholo* battalion was the problem and suggesting that peace could be secured if he sent them back to Mexico. In reply to Alvarado's request,

Vallejo sent Salvador for a conference at San Pablo, seeking details of what the rebels had done, what they planned to do, and what the prospects for success were. In the end, Vallejo did not support the revolt—he remained neutral. And to avoid the necessity of sending reinforcements to aid his superior officer, Micheltorena—a call that surely would be made—he disbanded the Sonoma garrison on November 28 with the excuse that he could no longer support the soldiers at his own expense, as he had been doing. Doubtless, some of the Sonoma veterans joined the rebels who were gathering at Santa Clara.[9]

Meanwhile, Micheltorena took action to put down the revolt. On November 18 he issued a proclamation saying that all who took part in the movement would be brought to trial and lose their property; any foreigners who joined the rebels would be put to death; and foreigners found to have given aid to the rebels would be imprisoned or executed, depending on the degree of their guilt; but those who presented themselves within a week would be pardoned. The governor sent two officers with eighty men to pursue the rebels and reconnoiter the area where he thought they might be camped; then he took to the field himself with about 150 men and two or three pieces of artillery, determined to crush the rebellion. At the end of November the two armed forces approached each other near the Laguna Seca, twelve miles south of the pueblo of San Jose, but each side set up camp about a mile apart before any hostilities erupted.[10]

The rebel army was composed of about 220 men under Colonel José Castro, who had been on an expedition with twenty-five men in the interior valley when the revolt began. Alvarado was second in command. Besides the original band of young "hotheads" under Lieutenant Manuel Castro, a kinsman of José, the rebels were reinforced by the contingent brought by Alvarado from Rancho San Pablo, thirty men recruited in Yerba Buena by Lieutenant Francisco Rico, volunteers from the Santa Cruz area, and a company of foreigners under Charles Weber of San Jose.[11]

After a few days, during which it rained continually, General Micheltorena opened negotiations under a flag of truce. Following meetings with Alvarado, who demanded that the *cholos* be sent back to Mexico, the governor finally acceded to the wishes of the Californians, and a formal peace agreement was drawn up and signed on December 1, 1844. By terms of this treaty, Micheltorena pledged on his word of honor that within three months he would discharge and send back to Mexico all the vicious soldiers and officers of his infantry battalion. Alvarado and Castro would be permitted to keep an armed force, called the Division of the North, at San Jose as insurance that the terms were fulfilled, and when that was accomplished the rebel career soldiers would be reintegrated into the army without prejudice. Alvarado wrote, "We later learned that General Micheltorena signed the treaties of La Laguna de Alvirez [sometimes called Santa Teresa from a nearby rancho] in order to gain time and maintain himself in office until reinforcements, which he was expecting at any moment, could arrive from Mexico."[12]

Most of the civilian rebels returned home, leaving Alvarado and Castro with fewer than one hundred men at San Jose, and Micheltorena went back to the capital, where he resolved to break the treaty and made plans to continue the struggle. He sent two officers to Mazatlan, urgently requesting additional soldiers and a store of munitions; he ordered Captain Andrés Pico to organize a company of volunteers in Los Angeles; and he solicited help from foreign residents. Micheltorena found ready volunteers in Isaac Graham and his former companions in exile, who wanted to avenge what they considered wrongs at the hands of Alvarado. In several letters to Sutter, whom he had appointed a captain in the militia, Micheltorena told him to prepare his company of foreigners and Indians for action, promising him a large land grant and approval of preliminary grants that the entrepreneur had made to American settlers in the Sacramento Valley. Sutter began to drill his men and gather horses for the campaign; he also talked freely about his intention to capture Alvarado and Castro dead or alive—he even boasted that he would present their heads to Micheltorena on a silver platter.[13]

On January 1, 1845, Captain Sutter left with his men from New Helvetia to attack Castro and Alvarado. He had a company of one hundred foreign riflemen under Captain John Gantt, a company of armed Indians commanded by Ernest Rufus, eight or ten artillerymen with a brass cannon, a quartermaster, a commissary, aides-de-camp, and subordinate officers. Sutter also carried manacles with which he intended to handcuff Alvarado and Castro. Their line of march was by way of Rancho Los Médanos (belonging to John Marsh, who joined the forces) and Mission San José, where many of the men got drunk after they discovered that the rebel army had retreated to the south. Sutter's men reached the Salinas River after a week and soon were joined by Micheltorena's army— the governor's force now totaled four hundred men.[14]

Meanwhile, Alvarado and Castro, after hearing of Sutter's movements and intercepting a secret letter from Micheltorena to the Swiss captain promising to reimburse him for all his campaign expenses, determined to transfer the struggle to southern California. Alvarado was certain that the *sureños* were strongly opposed to the *cholos*, that they would react negatively to Micheltorena's duplicity, and that they would be offended by his sending an armed force of foreigners and Indians against native Californios. He also expected that it would be difficult for the governor to keep his foreign troops loyal and united during a campaign so far from home. Hastily breaking camp at San José on January 2, 1845, Alvarado, Castro, and their rebel army of ninety men made their first stop at Rancho El Alisal.[15]

From Alvarado's rancho, Don Juan and Don José Castro addressed a letter to Micheltorena. Their message rebuked the governor for violating the peace treaty he had signed; then it continued with a warning:

Our conduct has given you no cause to doubt our good faith; but notwithstanding this, you, as appears from convincing proofs in writing, were forming a combination with the foreigner Sutter to surprise us at San José with two hundred adventurers from the United States. It was hardly credible that you in the midst of peace should attempt the ruin of ourselves and our families, still less of a country entrusted by the supreme government to your care. . . . Sir, you have aroused the country. . . . The sons of California will do us justice, and we will shed our blood rather than permit our country to endure this infamous oppression.[16]

Alvarado and Castro's "Division of the North" arrived at the plaza of Los Angeles on January 21, 1845, and the governor's forces slowly pursued them, reaching Santa Barbara in February. During their stay in the *pueblo*, Alvarado and Castro brought some prominent citizens before them and, through flattery, promises of future offices, or threats of arrest, converted them into strong partisans. Another achievement was the formation of a company of about fifty foreigners under James McKinley and William Workman to counterbalance the unit under Sutter. Toward the end of January, Alvarado induced Pío Pico, who was then the president of the departmental assembly, to call an extraordinary meeting of that body so that he could explain the movement. After Don Pío opened the session and called upon the members to consider the situation and take appropriate measure to ensure tranquility, he called upon Alvarado and Castro to justify their coming at the head of an armed force. Don Juan reminded his audience of the former depredations of the *cholos* in the city and warned of outrages to be expected from Sutter's foreigners and Indians; then he excoriated the governor for breaking his solemn pledge and recommended that Micheltorena be declared a traitor and deposed. At a subsequent session it was decided to send commissioners to the governor in order to seek ways to end the conflict.[17]

On February 7, the five emissaries to Micheltorena called on him at his quarters in Mission Santa Barbara. Their instructions were as follows:

1. They were to urge Micheltorena to comply with the treaty of Santa Teresa and send his convict soldiers back to Mexico
2. They were to dismiss his foreign allies, whose presence with arms was against the law and a menace to the nation.
3. They were to send the Indians back to their villages, their arming being unwise and dangerous.
4. Should he consent to these terms, his person and position would be respected, and the assembly would aid him in restoring order.
5. Should he refuse, he would be held responsible for the war that would result.[18]

Micheltorena refused to confer officially with the representatives of the assembly, which he maintained had been convened illegally; however, he agreed to meet with them privately as he continued his march. At a brief, informal meeting, he refused any compromise but said that he would pardon the revolutionaries if they would disarm and surrender. When this news was reported to the assembly, on February 14 the members adopted a series of resolutions disavowing Micheltorena's authority as governor, declaring his office vacant, providing for formulation of a prosecution against him, and announcing that the assembly would continue to meet at Los Angeles and assume control of the government. The next day they passed a decree deposing Micheltorena and declaring Pío Pico, as first member of the assembly, temporary governor in accordance with the basic laws of the nation.[19]

Meanwhile, Micheltorena and Sutter, with confidence in their strength, resumed their march southeastward. As they approached the former mission of San Buenaventura, Colonel Castro's advance force withdrew toward Los Angeles. (In his unpublished history of California, Alvarado stated that Castro and Micheltorena had a conference at Buenaventura, but Bancroft and other writers disagree.) Finally, the two forces, each with about four hundred men and a few cannon, faced each other at Rancho Cahuenga in the southern edge of the San Fernando Valley. The opposing troops were positioned along the banks of the Los Angeles River or the *barrancas* (dry gulches) that crisscrossed it. At noon on February 20 cannonading began, and it continued all afternoon on both sides. The casualties were two horses killed; no human blood was shed. During the firing McKinley and Wilson, as representatives of Alvarado's foreign company, approached Sutter's foreigners, who were posted farther along in the same creek bed, and persuaded them that it was not in their interest to fight in this civil war between Mexicans and Californians. Before night they withdrew from the field. At about the same time, Sutter and his secretary, John Bidwell, were captured by a party of Californians and sent to Los Angeles under parole.[20]

During the night, the two armies repositioned themselves, moving to Rancho Verdugo, about twelve miles away. At dawn the following morning Micheltorena's artillery opened fire. Alvarado's account tells what happened next:

Fate decreed that I should be in charge of the troops, since [José] Castro and [José Antonio] Carrillo, who had patrolled the camp during the night, had gone to rest. We did not fire back with our cannon right away, but after we opened up, General Micheltorena sent an emissary, Captain Castañares, under a white flag to our camp. . . . The spokesman was conducted to Don Pío Pico, then he returned to Micheltorena's camp, accompanied by José Castro, José A. Carrillo, and Lieutenant Manuel Castro. Micheltorena agreed to leave the territory, provided he were granted a capitulation that should read in such a way as to leave his military reputation unsullied.[21]

Alvarado's notes include a copy of the Treaty of San Fernando, signed on February 22, 1845, by the commissioners and by Micheltorena and Castro. Don Juan thought that the overly favorable peace terms were a result of Castro's obligation to Micheltorena, stemming from the latter's legal defense of him in Mexico City four years earlier during the Graham affair. According to the eight initial treaty articles, Micheltorena and his Mexican troops were to march to San Pedro, where, except for those who wished to remain in the country, they were to embark for Monterey on a vessel to be provided by Castro. At Monterey they would take on board Micheltorena's family and the remainder of his soldiers and then sail for Mexico. The arms and munitions of war at the armory in Monterey were to be delivered to the insurgent forces. The political command of the department was to be recognized as properly vested in Pío Pico, the *primer vocal* of the departmental assembly, and the military command in José Castro as *comandante general.* Citizens who had aided Micheltorena were to be reimbursed from public funds and their lives and property guaranteed. Before signing the document, Micheltorena insisted on adding another article that permitted him to preserve his honor as a high-ranking military officer. It stated that his troops would be permitted to march out with all the honors of war, to the sound of trumpets and drums, with colors flying, the flag to be saluted by Castro's drummers, and their three cannon to be given up at San Pedro.[22]

Don Juan's adversaries had been defeated, and soon the participants returned to their homes. Micheltorena and his troops marched to San Pedro, boarded the American bark *Don Quixote,* and proceeded to Monterey; toward the end of March, the battalion set sail for San Blas. Micheltorena's departure marked the end of Mexico's direct rule of California—that is, he was the last governor sent from central Mexico.[23]

Micheltorena's ally, Captain Sutter, while under house arrest in Los Angeles, wrote a long letter to Governor Pío Pico explaining his connection with Micheltorena and justifying his conduct on the grounds that he had been acting entirely under the orders of his superior. He said that he had been unable to prevent the American immigrants from joining him and that he had only recently come to recognize his mistake and repent his action. After begging to be allowed to return to his establishment on the Sacramento, Sutter's request was granted, and he went home carrying the handcuffs he had prepared for Castro and Alvarado.[24]

In May 1845 Don Juan returned to Monterey, where he had been appointed by Governor Pío Pico to the post of administrator of the customhouse. One advantage of this position was that the holder could get his pay by simply deducting it from the customs duties and receipts collected before turning the rest over to the department treasury. After so long in military camps and in the saddle, Alvarado was pleased to be back home with his wife and family, which at that time included his three-year-old daughter, Delfina, a twenty-month-old son, Juan Cosme, and a newborn baby named Augustus. At the end of the year, Don Juan resigned from his customhouse position, turning the office over to Pablo de la Guerra.[25]

Alvarado thought he would be taking his family to Mexico City early in 1846 because he had been elected to a two-year term as deputy to the Mexican Congress. But Governor Pico did not authorize any funds for his projected trip or any advance on his congressional salary. So Don Juan remained in Monterey with no official position or any regular income. He still had extended family and friends there, and he kept in close touch with national and international developments affecting California.

# 6

# Colonel against the Yankees
# 1846–1848

THE STIRRING EVENTS OF 1846, culminating in the U.S.-Mexican War, were momentous for California and for Don Juan Alvarado. At the beginning of the year the region was ineptly governed and divided: The civil governor, Don Pío Pico, and the assembly (sometimes called *diputación*) were based in Los Angeles, whereas the military commandant, José Castro, had his headquarters in Monterey, site of the customhouse and treasury. The two men did not work in harmony—in fact, each was conspiring to overthrow the other. In addition, many Californios felt estranged from the government in Mexico City, which habitually had failed to provide money for salaries of bureaucrats and soldiers as well as arms for the defense of the region. The central government's political instability, with various generals playing musical chairs in the presidential seat, did not inspire great confidence or hope for the future. Rumors of an impending war with the United States, or some other foreign power, complicated the situation.[1]

Don Juan and other Californios were concerned about the growing number of Americans who came into the country by overland routes. During 1845 at least two hundred emigrants left the United States and made their way across the plains and mountains to settle in California—Consul Thomas Larkin estimated the number at four hundred. But most startling was the appearance at the end of that year of John Charles Frémont, a captain in the U.S. Topographical Engineers, who had come across the Sierra Nevada with sixty armed men and a mountain howitzer. After a brief stop near Sutter's Fort, where he acquired additional supplies and had his horses shod, Frémont rendezvoused his men in the San Joaquin Valley. From there he went alone to Monterey, where he arrived on January 27, 1846, and lodged at the home of the U.S. consul. Upon hearing of Frémont's activities, the California authorities asked the consul to inform them of the purpose of his visit. Larkin and Frémont met with a committee composed of the prefect, the *alcalde*, and the commanding general and with Colonel Alvarado, to whom they explained that Frémont was on a scientific exploring expedition looking for a route to the Pacific. The American captain reported that he had left his company of hired men, not soldiers, on the frontier of the department to rest themselves and their animals and that when the men were recuperated, they would leave for Oregon. This explanation seemed to be satisfactory, and notes of the meeting were transmitted to Governor Pico and to the supreme government in Mexico. Frémont then returned to his encampment.[2]

Alvarado was soon alarmed to learn that Frémont, instead of heading for Oregon, led his men westward over the Coast Range to the Salinas Valley, where they encamped on March 3 at William Hartnell's Rancho Alisal, adjacent to Don Juan's own El Alisal property. Two days later General Castro dispatched a note to the American captain notifying him that his presence in the settled area with armed men was prohibited by Mexican laws and ordering him to leave the department as soon as he received the note. After sending Castro a verbal refusal to obey his command, Frémont moved his camp to the summit of Gavilán Peak (now called Frémont Peak), near the former mission of San Juan Bautista, where he defiantly raised the Stars and Stripes and began construction of a log fort.[3]

Frémont's act in defying the California authorities obliged them to call out the militia, "in order to repel the invasion and vindicate the national honor." Dispatches to organize and

*General José Castro*. Courtesy of the Bancroft Library.

arm the able-bodied male citizens were sent to San Jose, Sonoma, Yerba Buena, and other communities. Agustín Escobar, one of Colonel Alvarado's recruits, later recalled that he and Alvarado did some drinking while they were camped in Pilarcitos Canyon during the march toward Gavilán Peak:

> Our total force was about sixty or seventy men who were divided into two encampments, one under the command of Alvarado, the other, at some distance away under the command of the Prefect Don Manuel Castro. . . . About nine o'clock that night I was on sentinel duty near the big bonfire because it was cold. On the other side was Señor Alvarado, who had his bed laid out. At this moment Tiburcio Soto, a soldier of my company, arrived. He was also a little drunk. He started toasting Colonel Alvarado, and he repeated it so often that Alvarado became angry and told him to go to bed. Soto did not obey, and there ensued a big altercation. Alvarado, furious, ordered me to take a shot at Soto. However, the official Don Estevan de la Torre made signs not to shoot. I told Soto several times to leave, but he did not obey. Finally, Señor Alvarado, very disturbed, ordered the official, la Torre, to take Soto, form a guard, and there on one side of the ring, to shoot at him four times. La Torre obeyed by taking Soto away, but it seems he conformed only in putting Soto outside.[4]

The next day Alvarado's militiamen joined forces with General Castro, who then had two hundred men and three pieces of artillery at San Juan Bautista, in full view of the Americans on Gavilán Peak. This show of force, and a warning note from Larkin indicating that the Californios were determined to fight if he did not retreat, convinced Frémont that he should abandon his fort, which he did on the night of March 9. The American intruders moved back to the interior valley, then proceeded north toward Oregon. Castro sent the citizen soldiers home and reported the affair to Governor Pico and to the minister of war in Mexico City.[5]

Because of the Frémont affair and other serious matters, in mid-March 1846 General Castro sent an agent to Mexico for aid and called a junta of military officers in the northern district to meet at Monterey. In his summons he mentioned that the ongoing revolution in Mexico would preclude aid from that quarter if California were invaded by an enemy. That revolt, which had begun the previous December when General Manuel Paredes overthrew President José Herrera, had repercussions in California, where Governor Pico and his partisans supported the ousted general, while Alvarado and the northern California leaders favored the new regime. Vallejo thought that Castro had really called the meeting in order to solidify his own plans to overthrow Governor Pico. Meanwhile, according to Alvarado, the governor was intriguing to promote a popular movement that would give both civil and military control to Pío Pico, "who knew as much about military science as I do about watchmaking."[6]

Don Juan attended several meetings of California leaders in Monterey in the first part of April 1846, but he was at Rancho El Alisal when a *junta mixta* (meaning that it included civilian residents) met on March 27 at the home of Thomas Larkin. General Vallejo's secretary, who took notes at that meeting, said that it was presided over by José Castro, whose opening words surprised the audience: "How greatly to be pitied is the condition to which Mexico has reduced us! . . . The mother country. . . refuses us arms, money and materials of war in which we are so lacking for our defense. She does not do this because she has forgotten us long since, for she very well recalls us to mind in order to send us her minions, who, dressed in the garb of soldiers and of civil officials, penetrate into our society, the morals of which they corrupt and the strongboxes of which they rifle."[7]

From some friends who attended the meeting, Alvarado learned that Castro warned his audience about the increasing number of American immigrants, predicting that within two years the newcomers would outnumber the Spanish-speaking population. And he drew laughter when he remarked, "The Americans are so clever that some day they will build ladders reaching to the sky, and once there, they will change the face of the whole universe and even the color of the stars." In a final flourish, Castro declared that he was in favor of placing California under a French protectorate—of annexing California to Catholic France![8]

Alvarado had notes of other speeches and suggestions made at this boistrous meeting, which he later incorporated into his "History of California." He noted that British-born David Spence and William Hartnell favored an arrangement with England, a powerful nation that would afford protection impartially to Catholics and Protestants and would not sanction slavery, as might happen if the United States gained control of the territory. Retired Captain Rafael González ended his speech with the following declaration: "Gentlemen, since Mexico refuses to do us justice and insults us to the extent of sending to our country her most hardened criminals, I, although born in Mexico, propose that we raise together the cry '*Viva* California, free, sovereign, and independent!'" Pablo de la Guerra, administrator of customs at Monterey, seconded the motion.[9]

Lieutenant Colonel Victor Prudon, who had formerly been Alvarado's secretary and then held the same position with General Vallejo, spoke next. He recommended that measures be taken to procure the annexation of California to the United States. Alvarado learned that Prudon's speech was not warmly received, probably because he was looked upon as a foreigner who should not influence local policy. Captain Francisco Sánchez also addressed the group, siding with Prudon. Finally, General Mariano Vallejo took the floor and declared, "We can no longer base our hopes on the promises of Mexico. . . . Would it be glorious or dignified to go far away to Europe in search of a master? To become subjects of a monarch? We are republicans. . . our future demands that we be annexed to the United States of America."[10] The meeting broke up without a vote on the proposals.

A few days later Don Juan attended a military *junta* convoked by Castro to deliberate on the condition of the country and to recommend measures that might be taken. On April 2 the six members and the military secretary signed a declaration that recognized General Paredes as president of Mexico and disavowed certain acts of the previous administration—one of those acts being confirmation of Pío Pico as governor. Subsequent deliberations of the *junta* led to the following decisions signed on April 11:

1. In view of the possibility of a foreign invasion, General Castro's presence was necessary in the northern towns, which must be fortified and defended.
2. Governor Pico should be requested to come to Monterey to take part in the salvation of the department.
3. If Pico should not comply with the invitation, the general (Castro) might act as seemed best and establish his headquarters at Santa Clara.
4. This arrangement should last until the arrival of orders and resources solicited from Mexico by the agent, Andrés Castillero.[11]

In spite of talk about the possibility of foreign invasion, Alvarado and other Mexican officers seemed not to worry when the U.S. warship *Cyane* anchored in Monterey Bay on April 17, 1846. Indeed, Don Juan sponsored a ball for Captain Samuel Dupont and the ship's officers. He later remembered, "My residence was decorated in the best possible manner, the music obtained was the best there was in the capital, and the supper prepared was as good as circumstances permitted."[12] One of the guests was Archibald Gillespie, who had arrived on the vessel from Mazatlan and was introduced as an American businessman traveling for his health. Alvarado learned from General Castro, who heard it from David Spence, that Gillespie was in the service of the U.S. government and on a secret mission. (Actually, he was a lieutenant in the U.S. Marine Corps and carried dispatches for Frémont.) Gillespie left the ball without saying goodbye and headed overland to Yerba Buena. From there he went up the river to Sutter's Fort and eventually rendezvoused with Frémont in southern Oregon.[13]

Meanwhile, when Governor Pico and members of the assembly at Los Angeles, all of them southerners, heard of the actions of the Monterey junta, they were furious and denounced Castro's "abuse of powers." Then Pico decided to raise a military force, ostensibly to resist foreign invasion, which would march northward in pretended compliance with Castro's invitation, but with the goal of forcefully removing that officer from his command. Leaving Los Angeles on June 16, the governor's army moved along the coast and arrived at Santa Barbara five days later. Meanwhile, in May and early June, Castro was at Santa Clara and other points recruiting men and supplies for the alleged purpose of resisting foreign invasion, but with the chief intention of using the force to subdue Pico. With the south in arms against him, he declared martial law. Then, unexpectedly, the general at Santa Clara, the governor at Santa Barbara, and militia Colonel Alvarado at Monterey received news that Frémont had returned to California and instigated a band of armed Yankees to capture the town of Sonoma.[14]

Alvarado learned that Frémont and his men had been camped north of Sutter's Fort, where the captain met with agitated American settlers. These frontier pioneers complained about official Mexican hostility toward them and expressed fears that their lands would be taken away. Rumors that Castro was raising troops to expel them seemed valid when they heard that his soldiers were driving a large band of about 170 horses south of Sutter's Fort. Then, after conferring with Frémont, a group of a dozen men—mostly roving immigrants and hunters—attacked the Mexican soldiers, seized the government horses, and took them to Frémont. The next day a party of some thirty men who called themselves "Bears," or "Osos," left for Sonoma, where at dawn on June 14 they surprised Don Juan's uncle Mariano Vallejo, arrested him, his secretary, and his brother Salvador, and sent the prisoners to Frémont's camp. Frémont then escorted the prisoners to Sutter's Fort. They also arrested Vallejo's brother-in-law Jacob Leese, who was acting as translator. After declaring California an independent republic, the insurgents in Sonoma replaced the Mexican flag with a newly made one featuring a red star, red bar, and a grizzly bear on a white background with the words "California Republic" painted in the center.[15]

Upon hearing of the American settlers' revolt, Colonel Juan Alvarado, accompanied by twenty citizen-soldiers he had enlisted, hurried to the Mexican military headquarters in Santa Clara. There, General Castro resolved to liberate Sonoma. After dividing his army into various sections, he sent a cavalry unit of seventy men under Lieutenant Joaquín de la Torre to Rancho San Pablo, where they obtained boats and crossed the bay to San Rafael. From there, they planned to ride toward Sonoma, but instead they had a bloody skirmish with a detachment of "Bears" and finally retreated back across the bay. Meanwhile, José Antonio Carrillo, in command of the second contingent of the Californios, took his men to Rancho San Pablo and was joined the next day by the third section of the army, whose officers included General José Castro, Colonel Juan Alvarado, and Captain Manuel Castro. The Californio forces at Rancho San Pablo could not find boats to transport them across the bay to the former mission of San Rafael, where Captain Frémont, who had joined the "Bears," was bivouacked with about 130 followers. Alvarado later wrote, "Although both leaders desired to come to grips, the lack of boats and launches prevented the realization of their wishes." Referring to Frémont and his men, Don Juan said, "I think I shall be down in my grave without forgiving them for the insults which they gave to the flag and authorities of my country on Gavilán Peak and the Sonoma frontier."[16]

While Frémont's men were at San Rafael, a tragic incident occurred—the killing of three innocent Mexican civilians. The victims were an old man named José de los Reyes Berreyessa and his twin nephews, Francisco and Ramón de Haro, who were nineteen years old. Berreyessa, who had a ranch near San Jose, was a brother of Alvarado's mother-in-law; he was on his way to see his son, the *alcalde* of Sonoma, who reportedly had been imprisoned by the "Bears." One of the twins may have been carrying a message to Californio militiamen. The three men had first gone to Rancho San Pablo, where Victor Castro, Don Juan's brother-in-law, took them in his launch across the bay to a landing near the mission; then Castro sailed back home while the three men headed on foot toward the mission. As the three strangers approached, Frémont sent Kit (Christopher) Carson with two or three men to intercept them, saying, according to an eyewitness, "I have no room for prisoners." Thus, the civilians were shot dead. Alvarado later wrote, "The sacrifice of those three lives not only did not advance the interests of the 'Bears,' but it alienated from them the sympathy of many persons who were desirous of seeing another government, rather than the Mexican government, in California."[17]

At the end of June, Alvarado and the California army of the north retreated from Rancho San Pablo to Rancho San Lorenzo and then to their prior base at Santa Clara. There, early in July a council of war determined that any further military operations should include the cooperation of Governor Pico and his forces in southern California. Selected to mediate with the governor, Captain Manuel Castro took a squad of six cavalrymen with him and rendezvoused with Pico at the former mission of Santa Inés. Meanwhile, General Castro's force, including Colonel Alvarado, moved to San Juan Bautista, where they were camped on July 8 when they learned that an American naval and marine force had landed and without opposition raised the Stars and Stripes over Monterey, announcing that war had broken out between the two neighboring republics. Two days later the Yankees raised their flag in Yerba Buena and Sonoma.[18]

For several years, Don Juan and other Californios had heard rumors of war between the United States and Mexico. They had been told that American agents had offered to purchase, or exchange for Mexican debts, parts of New Mexico, Texas, or California—proposals that were offensive to Mexican officials. And they knew that relations between the two countries had deteriorated after Texas became independent and later was annexed to the Union. The disputed boundary was another problem—Texas and the United States claimed that the Rio Grande (Río Bravo y Grande) was their southern frontier, thereby shifting the line many miles southwest of the Nueces River, the traditional boundary. Now, in July 1846, the Californios learned that hostilities had erupted on the Rio Grande frontier two months earlier, which had led to war between the two countries.

Although Colonel Alvarado was in San Juan Bautista at the time of the landing, his friends in Monterey sent him a copy of the proclamation made by Commodore John Sloat, commander of the invading force. Don Juan remembered that it included the following:

The central government of Mexico, having commenced hostilities against the United States of America by invading its territory and attacking the troops stationed on the north side of the Rio Grande . . . and General Arista's army of 7,000 men being destroyed by a force of 2,300 men under General Taylor . . . the two nations being actually at war . . . I declare that, although I come in arms with a powerful force, I do not come as an enemy to California; on the contrary, I come as their best friend, as henceforward California will be a portion of the United States, and its peaceable inhabitants will enjoy the same rights and privileges they now enjoy.[19]

The American takeover of northern California ended the Bear Flag Republic and partially mended the schism between Governor Pico and General Castro. Because of the foreign invasion, Castro, joined by Don Juan and about 150 northern California troops, quickly rode south to San Luis Obispo; near there, on July 12, they met Pico's forces, who had been heading to Monterey planning to defeat Castro. From central California the two armies then moved separately to Los Angeles, arriving there about two weeks later. Ordering all male citizens between fifteen and sixty to arms, Governor Pico called upon the people to defend the country against the "unjust aggression by the invaders," but only a few men joined the militia, and rancheros and residents reluctantly contributed horses, arms, and supplies. The situation in Los Angeles was tense: Partisans of north and south were antagonistic, as were civil and military officials; troops of the regular army and militia were incompatible; and the citizens had little confidence in their leaders. Because the California government had lost its prestige, resources, and credit, the army and militia were inadequately provided for, and their numbers were consequently diminished by desertions. During the first week in August, General Castro was in command of about one hundred armed Californios camped at La Mesa, a short distance from Los Angeles. Don Juan tells us that he, Castro, and other leaders were in an emergency "war council" when they learned that two separate American forces were headed toward Los Angeles.[20]

Alvarado and the Californio leaders in southern California learned that late in July Commodore Robert F. Stockton had replaced the ailing Commodore Sloat as commander of

American military forces in California. Don Juan was glad to hear that Stockton had ordered the release of his uncle Mariano Vallejo and others from confinement at Sutter's Fort, but he ridiculed Stockton's proclamation to the people of California, calling it "stupid." In that address, the commodore asserted that Castro had violated principles of international law and hospitality by pursuing, "with wicked intent," Captain Frémont, who had come to refresh his men after a perilous journey across the mountains. In order to redress these "outrages," Monterey had been occupied and the civil officials invited to continue in office, but they had fled, creating a state of anarchy. Stockton claimed that he would end the lawlessness and protect the people. Don Juan later wrote, "If Stockton had sent a commission to confer with Castro and myself, it is very probable that as a result of such an interview, a treaty satisfactory to both sides might have been arranged."[21]

Commodore Stockton was determined to subdue all of California, and he hoped to capture General José Castro. After appointing Frémont to the rank of major and putting him in command of the "California Battalion" of land forces (Bear Flag veterans plus additional American volunteers), on July 23 he sent him and his 165 men to San Diego aboard the sloop-of-war *Cyane*. From that place they were to gather horses and recruits and prevent Castro's escape to the south. A week later Commodore Stockton embarked on the flagship *Congress* and headed for San Pedro, where on August 6 he landed 260 marines and sailors who immediately began to practice military maneuvers. Hearing of the invasion, Castro sent two commissioners, Pablo de la Guerra and José Flores, with a letter to the commodore expressing a willingness to enter into negotiations on the condition, usual in such cases, that all hostilities be suspended. But Stockton would not halt his operations or negotiate on any principle other than that California would declare its independence under the protection of the United States and raise the American flag. Castro, of course, refused those terms. Their mission a failure, the commissioners returned to Los Angeles with news that the enemy was about to march to the *pueblo*. About the same time, Don Juan and others learned that Frémont's California Battalion was moving rapidly toward Los Angeles.[22]

General Castro and Governor Pico decided that their small and poorly armed force could not successfully oppose the invading Americans. On August 9 Castro announced his intention to go overland to central Mexico, where he would report to the government. In a speech to the California assembly (*diputación*) the next day, Governor Pico reiterated the impossibility of defense, said he saw no way to preserve the honor of the government other than to leave the country, and recommended that the assembly adjourn. Both leaders wrote patriotic farewell addresses to the people; the governor's statement included the words "between ignominy and emigration, I choose the latter." Pico went to Baja California, and Castro fled to Sonora. Before leaving, the commanding general appointed Captain Manuel Castro to command the regular army troops and ordered him to take them north, where they were to interdict the enemy's supplies.[23]

Colonel Juan Alvarado accompanied Captain Manuel Castro and a contingent of regular soldiers when they pointed their horses northward from Los Angeles on August 10, 1846. Bypassing Santa Barbara, they rode north to San Luis Obispo, where Castro disbanded his demoralized soldiers and he himself took refuge in the mountains. At this time a detachment of Frémont's California Battalion, sent in pursuit of the Californios, captured Alvarado and a few others of the group, including two of Don Juan's relatives: his half brother Joaquín Estrada and a cousin, Julián Estrada. One of the captured Californios was José de Jesús Pico, who later described what happened: "The same day that Alvarado was to leave for Monterey, an American contingent of Frémont's battalion fell upon San Luis Obispo. They called us to a room in my house, where I had a small shop, and demanded of us an oath and word of honor that we would not fight against the government of the United States during the war with Mexico, or until we were regularly exchanged prisoners of war."[24]

After the prisoners were freed under parole, they headed for Monterey, which they reached on September 2. Two weeks later Stockton arrived, and Alvarado recalled, "I was treated to champagne by Commodore Stockton and was honored with an evening party, the cost of which was borne by the Americans who tried in this way to show me that they were not indifferent to my welfare."[25]

From Stockton and others Don Juan learned that the American forces had met no opposition to hinder their triumphal entry into Los Angeles on August 13. During the following weeks the commodore arranged for the election of *alcaldes* and other civil officials, appointed Captain Frémont to the post of military commandant of California with orders to march north to the Sacramento Valley, and left Los Angeles in charge of Captain Gillespie with a garrison of fifty soldiers. But in late September Don Juan and the American military contingent in Monterey were stunned to learn that the Californios, led by Captain José Flores (who broke his parole), had revolted and recaptured Los Angeles, forcing Gillespie to retreat to San Pedro. Flores assumed the titles of commanding general and governor of California.[26]

On receipt of news about the revolt in Los Angeles, Commodore Stockton organized reinforcements to move south—some would go by sea and others would march overland. Frémont, newly promoted to lieutenant-colonel, ordered his men to obtain horses and supplies from rancheros, giving receipts payable by the U.S. government at the end of the war. Alvarado later claimed $11,605 for horses and cattle requisitioned from Rancho El Alisal by men of the California Battalion, but his claim was never paid. Neither was that of José María Amador, who stated, "Upon one occasion they took sixty animals from me at my Rancho San Ramón, but they took no arms or anything else. I sent to where Frémont was and demanded my horses or their value and he sent me word by messenger that he would pay me for them with an ounce of lead from every rifle in his troop."[27]

In the latter part of 1846 the Mexican minister of war, who was not too current on the military affairs in Alta California, appointed Don Juan Alvarado to the post of adjutant and inspector of the Presidial Companies of California. The position had a salary of three thousand *pesos*, beginning with the date of the commission. News of this appointment was communicated from Mexico City to Don Juan on January 15, 1847, by his friend Captain Andrés Castillero, to whom he had earlier granted Santa Cruz Island, off the Santa Barbara coast.[28] But by the time Don Juan received the news, he had already agreed to take no further military role in the Mexican army.

During the remaining months of the U.S.-Mexican War, Don Juan honored his parole and remained in Monterey, occasionally visiting his Rancho El Alisal. At this time the Anglo American population of the town increased, and the newcomers rapidly acquired urban landholdings. Although social life in Monterey was dominated by the occupying American forces, whose officers sponsored various parties and dances, there were also Spanish-language events. In January 1847 a local theatrical troupe put on a play entitled "Adam and Eve," which was attended by local citizens as well as Americans. In his published memoirs Lieutenant William T. Sherman wrote, "Eve was personified by a pretty young girl known as Dolores Gomez, who, however, was dressed very unlike Eve, for she was covered with a petticoat and spangles. Adam was personated by her brother [Vicente]. . . . God Almighty was personated, and heaven's occupants seemed very human. Yet the play was pretty, interesting, and elicited universal applause."[29]

As a civilian in Monterey, without a government position and its income, Don Juan found it difficult to support his family. Besieged by several creditors, especially the merchants Henry Mellus and William Howard, he decided to sell his Rancho Las Mariposas, which had been granted to him in 1844 by Governor Micheltorena. This property of ten square leagues (44,386 acres) was located in the foothills of the Sierra Nevada, not far from Yosemite Valley. Because Alvarado had neither visited the property, nor made any improvements or put livestock on the land, as required by Mexican law, his title was questionable. Nevertheless, on February 14, 1847, through the agency of Thomas Larkin, who received a commission of seven and a half percent, Don Juan sold the rancho to Colonel John Frémont for three thousand dollars. (Gold discovered on the property the following year made a fortune for Frémont.)[30]

As the war continued, Don Juan was kept abreast of the military news through communication with friends and by reading the newly established Monterey weekly newspaper, the *Californian*, part of which was printed in Spanish. This first paper ever published in the territory was a joint venture of two Americans, Robert Semple, who knew something of typesetting, and Walter Colton, a navy chaplain who had been an editor in Philadelphia and was now *alcalde* (justice of the peace) of Monterey. Alvarado followed the progress of the American reconquest of Los Angeles, spearheaded by armies under Stockton and Frémont, plus those of General Stephen W. Kearny, who had marched overland from New Mexico. The California campaigns ended in mid-January 1847, but fighting continued in mainland Mexico for another eight months.[31]

When the California battles ended, the new American military governor, General Kearny, and naval Commodores James Biddle and William Shubrick attempted to gain the good will of the inhabitants. In March 1847 they issued several public circulars, which were printed in the *Californian*. The joint circulars included the following points: The Americans wanted the residents to share the good government enjoyed by citizens of the United States, the religious institutions of the country would be protected, losses suffered because of the war would be investigated and restitution made, and office-holders would continue at their posts. The American commanders also decided to court the favor of former governor Juan Bautista Alvarado. On March 12 they invited him on board the flagship *Columbia*, where he was saluted with thirteen guns and treated as if he were governor. Two days later Alcalde Colton called on Don Juan, in the name of the military governor and commodores, to offer him the office of secretary of state, with an annual salary of four thousand dollars and a promise that on General Kearny's departure, he would exercise the duties of governor.[32] Alvarado refused the offer, undoubtedly because he knew that his Californio friends would consider him a puppet of the Yankees.

The U.S.-Mexican War ended with the Treaty of Guadalupe Hidalgo, tentatively signed in February 1848 and ratified on May 30. News of the definitive end of the war reached California on August 6 of that year. Besides establishing peace between the belligerent powers, the treaty made California officially a part of the United States of America. Article VIII of the treaty specified that Mexican citizens who lived in the ceded area could continue to live there and retain any property they possessed, or they could dispose of their property and move to Mexico at any time. Those who remained could keep their Mexican citizenship by declaring their intention within one year; otherwise, they would automatically become American citizens.[33] Don Juan made no declaration. He had spent his first years under the Spanish flag and his middle years as a Mexican, and he would live the last half of his life under the Stars and Stripes.

In later years Don Juan reflected about the changeover from Mexican to American rule. "Although certain of my fellow citizens and relatives, and I, myself, have suffered by the change of flag, the majority have benefited. . . . In my opinion, the improvements in public education introduced by the North Americans are of themselves alone great enough for Californians to celebrate enthusiastically the anniversary of the day on which Mexican domination was done away with forever in this state."[34]

# 7

# *Ranchero* at Rancho San Pablo
# 1848–1882

IN MID-1848 DON JUAN decided to move his family from Monterey to Rancho San Pablo on the east side of San Francisco Bay. Thus, he changed his status from town dweller to *ranchero*. Two years earlier, when the Americans took control of California, he had lost his government pension and political prestige in the old capital and thus his livelihood there. Don Juan, who was not yet forty years old, had never been a businessman or a career military officer, and although he had owned ranches, he had not been an active *ranchero*. He had already sold his two large ranchos, El Sur and Las Mariposas, but his wife, Martina, had an inheritance interest in the sprawling Rancho San Pablo. Furthermore, it was close to the new center of activity—the growing city of San Francisco, which had been renamed by the Americans from its original designation as the *pueblo* of Yerba Buena.

Doña Martina's mother, Gabriela Castro, begged her daughter and her family to join her on Rancho San Pablo, to which the Alvarados finally agreed. In May 1848 three of Martina's brothers and a niece went to Monterey to help with the move. The return journey by horseback, with oxcarts carrying some furniture, clothing, and household goods, took almost a fortnight, including stops at several ranchos along the way. Having no home on the ranch, the Alvarados asked permission to move in with Gabriela, who lived with her son Jesús María and his wife, Josefa, in their recently built adobe home. Martina's brother reluctantly agreed, with the under-

130

standing that it would be a temporary arrangement while the newcomers had another house built. At this time the Alvarados had three young children: Delfina, six-and-a-half years old; Juan Cosme, almost five; and Augustus, who was three.[1]

Rancho San Pablo embraced almost eighteen thousand acres on the eastern shores of San Francisco Bay and San Pablo Bay. Early in the nineteenth century, when it had been established as a ranch and farm for Mission San Francisco (Dolores), some rude buildings had been erected—a dwelling for the caretaker, huts for Indian laborers, and animal shelters and corrals. In 1817 Martina's father, Francisco Castro, who was then a forty-five-year-old corporal in the Spanish army and overseer of the mission ranch, supervised the Indians in building an adobe house for his family and petitioned for a grant of the land. His request was denied because the mission continued to claim the property. But five years later he reapplied and received a tentative grant to the land, which was called Los Cuchiyunes (named for the local Indian tribelet) or, more commonly, Rancho San Pablo, for the prominent Point San Pablo, which defined the southeastern portion of San Pablo Bay. After he died in 1831, his widow and children continued to live on the ranch. By 1848, when Don Juan Alvarado's family moved to the ranch, there were six adobe houses on the rancho property, occupied by Martina's brothers and their families. Some of the land was planted to wheat, potatoes, vegetables, orchards, and grape-vines, but most of it was covered with native grasses, which supported large herds of livestock.[2]

The ranch house where the Alvarados were accommodated had three-foot-thick adobe walls, a gable roof covered with shingles, roofed *portales*, or porticos, running along the front and back, and an outdoor stairway to the half-story attic, which served as an extra dormitory bedroom. The main building was 79 feet long by 26½ feet wide (2,094 square feet)

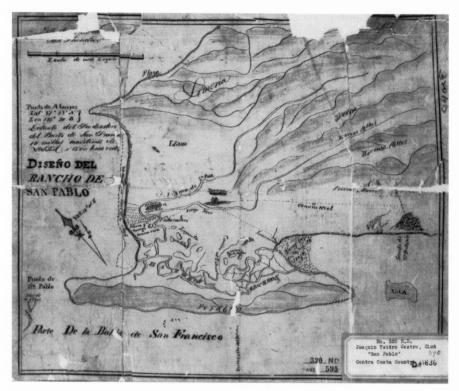

*Diseño of Rancho San Pablo, 1830.* Courtesy of the Bancroft Library

divided into four rooms; attached to it were two wooden structures, each twelve by fifteen feet, one of which was used as a kitchen. Separate outbuildings included a large stable with its adjacent tack room; a barn; tool sheds; a *ramada* (shelter) eleven by thirty feet made of adobe bricks, with a shingled roof that covered a large outdoor oven; a well house; and, of course, the *retrete* (toilet). A few ranch hands and household servants—the personnel and numbers changed from time to time—lived nearby in their own dwellings. North of the main house was a six-acre orchard, planted earlier in pear and other fruit trees by Martina's father, and close at hand was the Arroyo Seco, later called Wildcat Creek, which flowed year-round. Martina's brother Gabriel and his wife and family lived just across El Camino Real, the dirt road that ran southeast to Mission San Jose, and another married brother, Joaquín Isidro, had his home not far away, in the midst of a vineyard.[3]

The arrival of the former governor's family put a strain on the ranch household. Besides the three Alvarado children, there were now five adults in the house: Grandma Gabriela; Jesús María and his wife, Josefa; and Don Juan and his wife, Martina. The two younger women were both pregnant. As the head of the family and owner of most of the ranch land, Gabriela exercised matriarchal rights, but Josefa considered the house to be hers because she and her husband had built and paid for it. Nevertheless, strong-willed Martina, who was the favorite of Gabriela and seven years older than her brother, attempted to control household affairs. After a short time, Josefa and her husband fled and went to live with her parents at Rancho Milpitas, near Mission San Jose, leaving the Alvarados to live in the adobe house for the rest of their lives. (A few years later, Jesús María and Josefa Alviso de Castro moved back to Rancho San Pablo and built another home.)

During his years at Rancho San Pablo, Don Juan remodeled the ranch house so that it more closely resembled a Victorian house than the Mexican adobe that he and his family had moved into. Clapboard siding was put over all the exterior walls, and green louvered shutters were added to the window frames. He hired an itinerant French carpenter to construct an ornamental wooden arbor that extended the length of the house and to the street, giving shade to the house and support to his flourishing grapevines. His granddaughter, Lucille Alvarado Skinner, later recalled the bower: "It was a latticed roof with many ornamental arches underneath that surrounded many odd-shaped flower beds. The arbor was covered with mission grapes and California red and yellow

*Castro-Alvarado home on Rancho San Pablo.* Courtesy of the San Pablo Historical Society.

roses and was unlike anything in beauty in this country at that time. That unique decoration made it quite a showplace in the very early days. Many people from all over the country would come to see the old hacienda."[4]

Don Juan had two fireplaces built in the house, one of them a large, elaborate one built in the *sala* (parlor), which provided better heat than the charcoal braziers previously used.[5] Gradually, the Alvarados acquired handsome furniture: a rosewood square grand piano, an upholstered settee and a John Henry Belter chair, Oriental carpets, lacquered tables, gilt picture frames, brass bed frames and a wooden four-poster, fancy dishes, pressed-glass goblets, and other items that made for refined living. Don Juan had one of the four largest private libraries in California, rivaling that of his uncle, General Mariano Guadalupe Vallejo, who lived about fifty miles northwest in the town of Sonoma. The other two extensive book collections belonged to William P. Hartnell and José Castro.

Don Juan was a *ranchero* in name only—although he was an accomplished horseman, he did virtually no tending of cattle at Rancho San Pablo. Of course, the ranch land and livestock belonged to his wife, Martina, and her mother and brothers. Besides Indian laborers, there were *vaqueros* (cowboys), such as Juan Vargas and Juan Pérez, who had charge of Señora Alvarado's cattle. About five thousand head of cattle and one thousand horses grazed on the rancho and adjacent lands. Because the livestock ran free over broad, unfenced ranges, resulting in the intermingling of animals belonging to different owners, an old Spanish-Moorish method was used to identify and segregate the herds. Each *ranchero* was obliged by law to brand his livestock, and every spring neighboring ranchers held a rodeo, or roundup, during which *vaqueros* segregated the livestock by their brands. At that time the unbranded young calves and colts that followed their mothers were lasooed and held while a red-hot branding iron was applied to their flanks. The annual *matanza* (butchering), when a number of cattle were slaughtered and their hides and fat prepared, took place in August or September.

Don Juan and the Californio ranchers were greatly affected by the discovery of gold in 1848 and the subsequent events. After mid-May, when there was a public announcement of the startling news, a human tide headed for the Sierra Nevada— hundreds departed from the cities, sailors quit their ships, soldiers deserted from barracks, and ranch hands left their employers. At the beginning of the year there had been about 12,500 non-Indian residents of California, but by the end of the year that number had greatly increased as about six thousand gold seekers arrived. The next year more than 100,000 newcomers—eighty thousand Yankees among them—swelled the population. In 1848 the miners unearthed gold worth about $10 million; the following year's production was two or three times as large; and in 1850 they obtained $80 million. Most of the newly arrived miners were Americans, but there were sizeable contingents from Mexico, Great Britain, Germany, France, Chile, Peru, Australia, and the Sandwich Islands. The influx of so many Americans submerged the Californios and their lifestyle; henceforth the preodominant culture would be Anglo-Saxon.[6]

Neither Don Juan nor any of his *ranchero* neighbors— members of the Martínez, Moraga, and Peralta families—went to the mountains to search for gold. Instead, they subscribed to the advice given by the patriarch of the Peralta clan to his sons: "God has given this gold to the Americans. Had he desired us to have it, he would have given it to us ere now. Therefore, go not after it, but let others go. Plant your lands, and reap; these be your best gold fields, for all must eat while they live."[7] Records indicate that California ranchers provided great quantities of beef, wheat, vegetables, and other foodstuffs, as well as horses and mules, for the miners.

Although Don Juan did not rush for gold, he was involved in a speculative silver mining venture near Monterey. In the spring of 1849, he and his family returned to the capital city, where they stayed for three months in their two-story home. One room of the house was rented to an American officer, Major Edward Canby, and his wife. In Monterey, Alvarado talked with his friend and neighbor, William Hartnell—for many years the two men had owned and occupied adjacent parts of Rancho Alisal—who introduced him to Dr. Alexander Smith Taylor, a recently arrived American. On June 24 the three men filed a statement of intent to form the "Alisal Silver Mining Company for the purpose of working and extracting the ores of silver and other metals on the Ranchos of Alisal and Patrocinio." To finance the project, which involved construction of buildings and smelters, they would issue two thousand shares, half of which were to be sold to the public and the others to be reserved for the promoters. Some building plans were drawn up, but there is no record that any construction took place or that any shares were ever sold. A biographer of Hartnell noted, "Alvarado was drinking heavily by this time, and Hartnell had become known through three decades as a business failure."[8]

In July 1849, a Chilean named Vicente Pérez Rosales knocked at the door of the Alvarado house in Monterey, hoping to get permission to spread his *sarape* (blanket worn as a cloak) on the floor of the *portal.* Impressed by the eloquence and demeanor of the man, Don Juan insisted that he come in and stay in his own bedroom, and he provided him with a change of clothes. A week later, the Alvarados gave a party for the departing visitor, who long remembered the affair:

The guests were numerous. . . . Delightful was the appearance of the halls and corridors adjoining the reception room; they were draped with green branches and flowers forming arches and borders, and illuminated with wax lights, an almost unheard-of luxury. In each corner of the exterior rooms there were fragrant baskets filled with boxes of cigars of various sizes, among which, artistically arranged, was a little spirit flame. . . . And the fair guests, after a quadrille played on the piano by the sexton of the adjoining chapel, walked through the corridors two by two, helped themselves to cigars as they passed the baskets, and returned to the ballroom only after throwing away the stubs.[9]

Although Don Juan was in Monterey in the summer of 1849, he did not stay on and participate in the constitutional convention that met there in September. He was interested in how California was to be governed and whether Mexican laws were still valid, but he would not accept a seat in the convention or any office under the Americans. Because the Treaty of Guadalupe Hidalgo had not specified a transition to civilian rule, nor had Congress acted on the matter, the military governor, Colonel Richard Mason, proposed a temporary scheme of civilian government, calling for the election of local officials and for delegates to a constitutional convention. The convention met in Monterey on September 1, 1849, with a contingent of seven Californio delegates, including Don Juan's uncle Mariano Guadalupe Vallejo. Later that year, the constitution was ratified and state officials elected; then on September 9, 1850, California was admitted as the thirty-first state of the Union. The first legislature passed an act repealing virtually every Spanish and Mexican law, but not the community property law. One article of the constitution required that all major laws be published in Spanish as well as English (this bilingualism lasted for thirty years).[10]

Don Juan returned to Rancho San Pablo in the late summer of 1849, but having spent most of his life as a townsman, he disdained the dull, rural life and preferred to spend as much time as possible in San Francisco. Although many of his friends had moved there and he had purchased property in the rapidly growing center, it appears that he could not afford to live permanently in the city or keep his family there. Sometimes he stayed at the home of his friend Juan Cooper, but often he was registered at the City Hotel (later renamed Brown's Hotel), on the southeast corner of the plaza, or the California Hotel at the southeast corner of Dupont and Commercial Streets. In their letters and memoirs, various residents and visitors mentioned seeing the former governor at one of the bars, billiard saloons, theaters, or gambling dens that surrounded Portsmouth Square, formerly the Mexican plaza. Occasionally, the entire Alvarado family was in residence in San Francisco for a few months at a time.[11]

The discovery of gold made San Francisco important as a port of debarkation and soon propelled it to become the commercial, banking, and social center of California. From January 1848 to December 1854, the city's population swelled from eight hundred residents to fifty thousand. Meanwhile, streets were paved; hundreds of substantial buildings of brick and granite erected, following a series of fires that destroyed the wooden structures; factories and mills established; wharves and warehouses built; and gaslights installed along the principal streets. From the first, San Francisco was a cosmopolitan city whose inhabitants spoke a variety of languages, including Chinese, English, French, German, Hawaiian, Italian, and Spanish. Social amenities improved rapidly with the establishment of eighteen schools, more than thirty churches, four hospitals, thirteen daily newspapers printed in several languages, and a number of benevolent and fraternal organizations. After joining the Society of California Pioneers in 1850, Don Juan frequented the clubroom and participated in the society's social events. He also enjoyed the city's theatrical performances featuring melodramas, operatic numbers, Shakespeare, minstrel shows, and dancers such as Lola Montez, who perfomed her dazzling "Spider Dance."[12]

Toward the end of 1850, the Alvarados employed a Chilean, Juan N. Espejo, to build them a new house on the rancho. The contractor was paid two thousand dollars for the two-story wooden structure, which was erected near the Alvarado corral, about a mile from the adobe house where they lived. Don Juan later testified, "We first intended to live in the house, then changed our minds."[13] Espejo lived in the wooden house for two years; it was later sold to David Goodale, who acquired additional parcels of the rancho. Undoubtedly, the Alvarados decided to stay in the adobe home because of the frail condition and wishes of Martina's mother. The matriarch died in December 1851, but a few months before dying she deeded all of her property to Martina, an act that caused resentment on the part of Martina's brothers. This rift in the Castro family brought on a series of lawsuits that lasted for many years and will be taken up in the next chapter.

While living at Rancho San Pablo, the Alvarado family was increased with the birth of five additional children, one arriving about every three years until the last child was born in 1860. At the end of that year there were four sons and two daughters living at home. The boys were Juan Cosme, age 17; Augustus, 15; Valentín, 6; and Enrique (Henry), 3 years old. The oldest girl, 19-year-old Delfina, was a boarding student at St. Catherine's Convent School in Benicia; her sisters at home were Celinda, age 9; and a baby named Adelina. (Another daughter, Clorina, had died as a toddler in 1850.) The federal census of 1860 listed six other members of the household, who undoubtedly lived in adjacent outbuildings. Besides a retired handyman who had come from Mexico and had been with them a long time, there was a cook and a gardener, both of whom had been born in France; a Portuguese clerk; a German painter; and a thirteen-year-old Indian servant girl named Semona.[14] Other Indian servants and *vaqueros* lived nearby.

Don Juan also kept in touch with his "natural" daughters who lived in or near Monterey. In 1851, when one of them, fifteen-year-old Francisca, wanted to marry Victorino Chávez, she asked her father's permission, leaving the decision completely up to him. After meeting the young man when he came to Rancho San Pablo, Don Juan told him, "This matter rests with her—that is to say, that I cannot make her consent to the marriage, choosing the person I like for her husband— because this choice depends entirely on her and on her own wishes. If it is understood that Francisca wants my permission to marry the person most agreeable to her, she certainly can count on it."[15]

Edward Bosqui, a clerk at Palmer and Cook's bank in San Francisco, where he became acquainted with Don Juan, visited the Alvarados at their ranch home in May 1852. When he arrived in midmorning, the former governor was not there, but he soon rode up on a handsome horse, saying that he had just returned from a remote part of the ranch, searching for a band of cattle rustlers who had been regularly killing his cattle and shipping the meat to San Francisco. Bosqui's *Memoirs* gives an account of a meal served during his visit:

> The table was embellished by wild flowers and also by some old pieces of solid silver plate; but the food consisted of "carne con chili colorado," jerked beef, tortillas and coffee. Within view of the veranda of the house were thousands of cattle roaming over the hills belonging to the rancho; notwithstanding this, there was no milk, no fresh butter, and no fresh meat on the table. The Governor's household consisted of his wife, a woman past middle age, with a sad, careworn face, and a number of children, none of whom seemed to possess their father's high breeding and distinguished appearance.[16]

After moving to Rancho San Pablo, Don Juan was much occupied with real estate and money matters, subjects about which he seemed to be inept. In September 1848 he signed an agreement with James McKinley, mortgaging his Monterey townhouse in exchange for $3,500 in cash. Two years later Don Juan received an extension of time to repay the loan, but when it still was not repaid in 1855, McKinley foreclosed the mortgage and sold the house to Durrel S. Gregory. About that time, it was valued on the Monterey Assessor's List at five thousand dollars. Meanwhile, in 1851 Alvarado borrowed five thousand dollars from Clemente Pinard, giving as collateral a mortgage on his Rancho El Alisal, which was assessed for $7,696. The next year, Don Juan's ranch, which he had purchased a decade earlier, was sold by the sheriff to meet Pinard's debt judgment.[17]

What were the reasons for Don Juan's need for money? After 1846 he had no job, pension, or regular income. His wife's share of Rancho San Pablo was in constant and costly litigation, and the property was in Martina's name, not Don Juan's. Family expenses included groceries, clothing, tuition for the children's education, and transportation, as well as taxes on their real estate, improvements, and personal property. Receipts in the family papers show that they purchased relatively expensive farm equipment, including a reaper and threshing machine for $1,450 on credit, a wagon, and a carriage. Another factor involved gambling debts—like many Californios, Don Juan was fond of card games such as monte. A record from the Third Judicial Court shows that he was sued by Henry Vanderstice for a gambling debt in the amount of eighty ounces of gold. Other card players in this particular instance were Andrés Pico and Captain Acklen, who gave testimony in the case. Alvarado, who claimed that he owed nothing and that he had won that amount at cards, was found not liable.[18]

The influx of population in California generated a rising demand for land to be used for farming, residential and commercial purposes, or speculation. However, the newcomers found that most owners of Mexican ranchos did not want to sell their land, at least not in small parcels, and those who agreed to sell their land could not provide a clear title. Many of the recently arrived Americans, believing that all of California belonged to the United States by right of conquest, simply became squatters, building homes, appropriating livestock, and cultivating land without regard to who had a prior claim of ownership. In addition, under the American preemption system these settlers were accustomed to occupy tracts on unclaimed land or public property before they were surveyed and then be permitted to purchase them at the minimum price when the lands were opened to settlement.[19] To address the matter of titles, Congress passed the Land Act of 1851, which provided for a board of land commissioners to decide the validity of all claims to land under Mexican titles.

Between 1852 and 1856, Don Juan spent much time in San Francisco as a witness testifying before the U.S. Board of Land

Commissioners. This board of three men required all California claimants to appear before them to have their titles confirmed. Many of the grantees did not have documents proving their ownership, and most of the grants had ill-defined borders using trees, rocks, and other natural objects as reckoning points. Some of the grants had not been recorded in government archives; others overlapped each other; and several of the grants were thought to be fraudulent. The grantees or their heirs were obliged to employ attorneys to prepare and present their case and to have all of the documents translated into English, as required by the board. With the exception of a brief term in Los Angeles, all sessions were conducted in San Francisco, which meant that most of the Californios had to stay in hotels while their cases were being heard. Not having ready cash, they borrowed money or often agreed to pay their attorneys in land. Interest rates of three to ten percent compounded monthly were common, while small amounts often were billed at twelve and one-half percent, compounded daily. Historian Hubert H. Bancroft remarked that "the commissioners . . . were able and honest men, though knowing nothing of the Spanish language, and very little of Mexican law and customs."[20] The result was a bonanza for translators and especially for lawyers.

In 1859 Antonio María Pico and forty-nine other Mexican land grantees submitted a letter to the U.S. Congress detailing their troubles in trying to get their titles confirmed. To submit their claims they had to engage lawyers, which involved mortgaging their ranches. Even after the land commission approved their titles, there were delays because of appeals to higher courts. Meanwhile, the flood of immigrants, perceiving that the titles were in question, squatted on the land, took possession of improvements, butchered cattle, and destroyed crops. The new state government had levied taxes on the property, and if these were not paid, the land was put up for sale. Eventually, many of the titles were confirmed, but by then most of the Californios had lost their property to banks, lawyers, or money lenders.[21]

One of the land claimants was María Amparo Ruiz de Burton, putative owner of Rancho Jamul, east of San Diego. Litigation to defend her title, which lasted more than twenty years, finally resulted in confirmation of 987 acres, rather than the 8,926 acres originally held. In addition, she had a serious problem with squatters, and the legal costs financially ruined her. Based on her experience, she wrote a novel, *The Squatter and the Don*, published in 1885, which mixed romance and history and excoriated the United States land commissioners for their mistreatment of Californio landholders. In the introduction to a recent edition of the novel, the editors point out that the author "presents a heroic, cultured people who were unjustly deterritorialized, economically strangled, linguistically oppressed and politically marginalized after 1848."[22]

Don Juan Alvarado testified 137 times in cases before the land commission—his total was more than that of any other witness. Besides giving information about Spanish and Mexican laws and customs regarding land titles, he also bore witness in many cases, verifying that the claimant had received a grant and had fulfilled the necessary requirements for a title. Having given out more grants than had any other governor, he was an appropriate choice to offer evidence under oath. Of course, he was paid for his expertise, and he enjoyed seeing many of his Californio friends, living in a hotel, and eating in restaurants during the sessions. Because all cases were appealed by one side or the other to the district court, and some went all the way to the U. S. Supreme Court, it took an average of seventeen years to validate the claims. Meanwhile, the grantees were in limbo, as were later purchasers of land and the squatters. Of the 813 claims presented, 605 were finally confirmed, 190 rejected, and nineteen withdrawn.[23]

Besides testifying about other cases, Don Juan filed three claims in his own name with the Board of Land Com-

missioners. The first was an attempt to gain clear title to
26,500 acres of former Mission San Jose lands, which he
declared that Governor Pío Pico had granted to him and
Andrés Pico on May 5, 1846. During the proceedings, it was
revealed that the grant was the result of a sale of surplus
mission lands for twelve thousand *pesos* plus an agreement
that the purchasers would pay the mission debts. The board
rejected the claim, citing a lack of evidence in the Monterey
archives and declaring that Governor Pico had no authority to
sell the land. A second case involved the orchard and vineyard
of Mission San Jose, a tract known as the Garden of San
Cayetano, granted by the same governor to the same two
individuals on May 12, 1845. Again, the board rejected the
claim for similar reasons.[24]

Don Juan's third claim was for part of Nicasio Valley, which
formerly had belonged to Mission San Rafael. The complicated story began in 1835, when that mission was secularized and Governor Figueroa had ordered Mariano Vallejo
to give the resident Indians twenty leagues of land as well as
cattle, sheep, horses, and implements from the mission stores.
Five years later Vallejo gave them a written conveyance to one
league of land at the southern end of Nicasio Valley, where
most of them lived. In 1844, Alvarado conspired with his
uncle to acquire the remaining part of Nicasio by inviting the
Nicasio Indian chiefs to Sonoma, where they signed away their
ownership to Alvarado, receiving in return an "order" on
Vallejo for one thousand *pesos*, an amount they apparently
never collected. Later that year, Don Juan wrote to Governor
Micheltorena requesting that he be considered the rightful
owner of Nicasio since he had just purchased it from the
Indians. But the governor rejected Alvarado's request on two
grounds: the Indians did not have the right to transfer the
grant, and he had already granted the land to Don Pablo de la
Guerra and Don Juan Cooper. Nevertheless, Alvarado considered Nicasio his property, and he and his brother-in-law

Victor Castro ran cattle there, expecting ultimate victory. Don Juan filed his claim on March 1, 1853, but after much testimony, it was rejected.[25]

About this time, two old friends of Don Juan, who were also distant relatives of his wife, invited him to join their business venture to exploit some salt deposits in northern Baja California. Title to this property at Cabo San Quintín on the Pacific coast had been awarded in 1841 to General José Castro, a boyhood friend and political supporter of Alvarado, but he had never developed the salt mines thereon. So, on March 4, 1853, a contract was drawn up in San Francisco and signed by the four principal partners: José Castro; his cousin and fellow military officer, Manuel de Jesús Castro; Juan B. Alvarado; and Jacques Antoine Moerenhaut, the French consul in California between 1846 and 1848. Moerenhaut, who was given fewer shares than the others, was delegated to keep the books and make a written report every two months. In mid-1853 José Castro went to Baja California, where he was appointed to political and military offices. Subsequent correspondence between Alvarado and the partners indicates that the salt business was unsuccessful in producing income, at least for Don Juan.[26]

During the 1850s, Don Juan learned about several expeditions that were organized in San Francisco to exploit the legendary wealth of Mexico. Finally, he, too, succumbed and became part of one of these ventures. Apparently, officials of the state of Sonora had invited and encouraged foreigners to settle in the interior region, partly as a way to control hostile Indian uprisings. As a result, some of the undertakings were labeled as colonizing projects; a few had "mining" in their name; and one or two were outright filibustering movements. All were failures. At the end of 1851, Charles de Pindray, an impoverished French nobleman, left California with 150 men for Sonora, where the group was disbanded after their leader died. The following year another Frenchman, Count Gaston de Raousset-Boulbon, enticed by an offer from the Mexican government to open a mining field in northern Sonora, took 260 men from San Francisco to Guaymas, where they were denounced as outsiders and, after an armed conflict, had to surrender. In 1853–1854, William Walker and his men from California suffered a similar experience after they took possession of Baja California and moved into Sonora.[27]

Thus, it is surprising that Alvarado became involved in a scheme to send colonists to the Mexican state of Sonora. Perhaps he thought that the previous expeditions had failed because their leaders and followers were Yankees or foreigners. In any event, on February 12, 1855, a group of Spanish-speaking natives of California and Sonora convened in San Francisco, where they formed a company called "Empresa de Colonización en el Estado de Sonora" (Enterprise for Colonization in the State of Sonora). Don Juan was elected president of the company. In a move to explain the project and secure official approval of it, Alvarado wrote to the chief executive of Mexico, Antonio López de Santa Anna, who styled himself, "His Most Serene Highness, President of Mexico." In addition to pointing out the problem of Indian depredations in Sonora, his letter stated:

> The history of the sad and lamentable happenings, which the press daily describes, will suffice to make known the causes of this movement, which has generated a great deal of confusion among Mexican journalists.
>
> A deputation which will soon depart for Sonora to confer with the government of that state, and the petitions which will arrive thereafter at the federal government will serve to illustrate the great and important Mexican interest for which these two peoples find themselves so closely united in sentiment.
>
> I hasten to apprise your Most Serene Highness of this project, with the hope that when the petitions reach the federal govern-

ment, they will be welcomed, imploring your powerful influence in support for these, our unfortunate compatriots.[28]

There is no record that Alvarado received a reply to his letter or that his company subsequently sent colonists or other assistance to Sonora, Mexico.

Some of Don Juan's activities during these years involved family matters. A son, Valentín Alvarado, was born in 1854, but he was a sickly child and died at the age of seven. The two oldest children were away at school—Delfina boarded at a school operated by the Dominican Sisters in Benicia, and her brother, Juan Cosme, attended a private school for boys in San Francisco. Eventually, Celinda would go to San Jose to study under the Sisters of Notre Dame de Namur.[29]

In April 1857, Don Juan moved his family and some of his furniture about twelve miles south to the growing town Oakland, where they stayed for a few months. Their reason for moving may have been that Martina was having a difficult pregnancy and wanted to be near a doctor and maternity facility—Oakland at that time had seven physicians who were medical school graduates. The Alvarado's eighth child, Enrique (Henry) Victor Alvarado, was born in Oakland in mid-July 1857 and baptized at St. Mary's Catholic Church in that town. Compared with rural San Pablo, Oakland was a cosmopolitan place of about one thousand inhabitants and had three hotels, three newspapers, a fire department, and regular steamboat ferry service to San Francisco.[30]

In the late summer of 1857, the Alvarados moved their furniture permanently back to their home on Rancho San Pablo, but they also spent some time in San Francisco, probably in rented rooms. City directories show them living there in 1858 and 1859. In September of the latter year, Don Juan suffered from a freak accident, as reported in a newspaper: "Juan B. Alvarado, a former Governor of California, was severely injured at San Francisco on the 5th inst. He was riding in a cab, in company with two friends, when the horse commenced kicking, and with such violence as to break through the front of the vehicle and force those on the box to jump for their lives. The horse finally kicked high enough to project his hoof through the front window of the cab and strike Governor Alvarado on the head, inflicting an ugly gash about two inches long."[31]

By 1860 Don Juan was back at San Pablo, where, across the road from his home, he opened the area's first public hostelry, the Union Hotel, with an adjacent livery stable. In addition to rooms, the two-story wooden hotel featured a restaurant, bowling alley, and a bar. Two years later, when the bartender, J. Rosa, sued Alvarado for the back payment of wages in the amount of $450, the defendant counterclaimed five hundred dollars, the value of unauthorized credit extended to customers. During the trial, a waiter named Juan Coeyo testified as follows:

On the first day the restaurant was opened, a good many of the guests came without money, and I said to defendant [Alvarado] I must give some credit, and defendant said, "Yes, certainly, for all the people of San Pablo have not got money but will pay when they have money." The defendant said I might give credit to those I knew. I gave credit to different persons, according to defendant's orders. At night I gave account of the credits I had given during the day to plaintiff [J. Rosa] and he entered them in the books. . . .

Defendant Alvarado was in and about the hotel often during all the time I was at work there, usually took his coffee in the restaurant three or four times a day. I have seen the plaintiff and defendant together looking over the books of the hotel . . . to ascertain the amount of cash taken in and credits given. . . . I never heard defendant find fault [with] plaintiff for giving credits.[32]

The court records are incomplete, but it appears that the case was settled in favor of the plaintiff.

# Grand Patriotic Ball.

To be given at the UNION HOTEL, in San Pablo, on Thursday, November 20, 1862, for the Benefit of the suffering defenders of our Country. Please come and join us.

## COMMITTEE OF INVITATION.

### OAKLAND,

| | | |
|---|---|---|
| J. B. Harris, | Judge Blake, | N. Knowlton. |

### MARTINEZ.

| | | |
|---|---|---|
| J. J. McEwen. | L. C. Wittenmeyer, | Mark Shepard. |

### SAN PABLO.

| | | |
|---|---|---|
| J. M. Tewksbury, | George H. Barrett, | David S. Goodale, |
| J. B. Alvarado, | Henry A. Benson, | Captain James Gill, |
| D. S. Hubbell, | James Duncan, | L. E Morgan, |
| C. E Wetherbee, | M. S. Grover, | H. Rockefellow, |
| L. D. Reynolds, | C Maybourn, | G. W Christian, |
| Job Whipple, | N. Barovich, | John Galvin, |
| John Welch, | T. Falvy, | Frank Castro, |
| J. Y. Castro, | E Hubbell, | T. J Wright. |

## RECEPTION COMMITTEE.

| | | |
|---|---|---|
| A. F. Dyer, | Adam Hagy, | Daniel Boone, |
| Justin Goodale, | Augusto Alvarado, | L Benson. |

**Floor Managers**—D. B. AUSTIN, E. TUCKER
**Director**—W. P. BALDWIN.

*DANCING TO COMMENCE AT SEVEN O'CLOCK.*

**TICKETS, (INCLUDING SUPPER,) FIVE DOLLARS.**

*Invitation to a patriotic ball in San Pablo, 1862.* Courtesy of the San Pablo Historical Society.

The very name of Alvarado's Union Hotel expressed his political opinion about the growing division of the United States. During the American Civil War (1861–1865), the hotel was the setting for rallies and meetings of supporters of the Northern or Union cause. For example, on November 20, 1862, there was a "Grand Patriotic Ball for the Benefit of the Suffering Defenders of our Country." Although the major battles of the Civil War were fought east of the Mississippi River, and there was no draft of men from the western states, volunteers from California did participate in the war—some went to the South to aid the Confederacy, and nearly seventeen thousand joined the Union armies. Don Juan's cousin Platón Vallejo, who was a medical student at Columbia College of Physicians and Surgeons, served with federal forces at the second Battle of Bull Run.[33]

In the midst of the Civil War period Juan Bautista and Martina Alvarado deeded all of their property, with the exception of a homestead around their home, to their oldest child, twenty-year-old Delfina. This transfer was doubtless a strategy to avoid problems arising from claims to parts of Rancho San Pablo by relatives and individuals, as well as a way to preclude foreclosures and lawsuits. At this date the Alvarados were living in "a stately home" at 418 Greenwich Street in San Francisco. This was a difficult time for California ranchers because of  squatters, floods in 1861–1862, and a severe drought the next year. One account says that "During the squatter problems of the 1850s and '60s, he [Alvarado] lost thousands of acres and a large portion of his wealth through costly litigations. Eighteen sixty-two was the beginning of a serious, three-year drought during which he . . . and many others lost a fortune in cattle, sheep and horses."[34]

While the Alvarados were residing in San Francisco, they witnessed some of the events associated with triumphs of the Union army. William Brewer, principal assistant with the Whitney Geological Survey of California, recorded in his journal the hubub of March 16, 1862, following receipt of news that Manassas, Virginia (site of Bull Run battles), had been occupied by federal troops: "The city was wilder with excitement that I have seen it before over war news. The legislature adjourned. The streets were filled. From the top of our building a hundred flags could be counted floating in the stiff breeze. Hurrahs were heard in the streets, and as night came on a hundred guns were fired on the plaza, the bands in the theaters played patriotic tunes, the streets were crowded with people . . . boys and Chinese exploded firecrackers, and columns in the papers teemed with telegraphic news."[35]

Don Juan and others kept abreast of the war news because of the progress in communications and transportation. In the 1850s it had taken months for steamship mail from the East Coast via Panama; the time was shortened when overland stage service between St. Louis and Los Angeles began in 1858; and the following year the Pony Express, which charged five dollars per half-ounce of mail, took only ten days from St. Joseph, Missouri, to Sacramento. Then in 1861 the transcontinental telegraph line was completed, carrying news and information almost instantaneously for one dollar per word. There are several telegrams among Don Juan's papers, most of them dealing with real estate matters. The railroad soon replaced the stagecoach for mail and passengers—on May 10, 1869, the Golden Spike was driven, opening a convenient transportation link between the Atlantic and Pacific. Eventually, railroad tracks crossed Rancho San Pablo, and later the town of San Pablo was the headquarters of the California & Nevada Railroad Company.[36]

During the American Civil War, Don Juan and other Californios were surprised and dismayed when they learned that a French army had invaded Mexico and installed Maximilian von Hapsburg as emperor. Meanwhile, Mexico's fugitive president, Benito Juárez, retreated to the Texas border, from where he dispatched agents to various American cities.

In 1864 Don Juan became acquainted with one of the emissaries, General Plácido Vega, a former governor of the state of
Sinaloa, who set up an office in San Francisco. During his two-
and-a-half years in California, Vega floated bond issues and
purchased thousands of muskets and other war material,
which he forwarded to his home country. He also distributed
several thousand dollars to friendly newspaper editors, organized *juntas* or patriotic clubs throughout California, and
raised money and volunteer soldiers for the countermarch.
On one occasion Agustín Alviso, Salvio Pacheco, and Victor
Castro, Don Juan's brother-in-law, lent the agent twenty-four
thousand dollars; Alvarado also lent money to the enterprise.
(The loans were never repaid to Alvarado or the other
lenders.) Finally, in July 1866 General Vega sailed from San
Francisco to western Mexico with a group of four hundred
armed Californians. Among the volunteers were sons of the
Alviso, Castro, Pacheco, and Vallejo families. From Sonora,
General Vega's California contingent marched eastward to
Chihuahua, where they joined the main republican army, and
then moved south to participate in the final battles that
defeated Maximilian's army.[37]

Don Juan's benevolence also extended to the Catholic
Church. In 1864 he donated almost four acres of land, across
Wildcat Creek from his home on Rancho San Pablo, as a site
for a new church. The men of the parish raised money for the
materials, and with their own labor they constructed the
building. Archbishop Joseph Alemany dedicated St. Paul's
Catholic Church in July 1864. Six years later, Virgilio Tojetti,
an Italian artist in San Francisco, painted a portrait of Saint
Paul that was purchased for the reredos, or altar wall, of the
new church. The priest's nephew and Don Juan's son Henry,
who was only thirteen years old, sailed to San Francisco in a
small skiff to pick up the large, framed painting; on the way
back, "the gusty winds made it an arduous sailing," Henry
remembered.[38]

The 1870 federal census for San Pablo Township listed the Alvarado family as "Household 159." Don Juan's first name was given as "John"; his family real estate was valued at twenty-five thousand dollars, and personal property at four hundred. Besides his wife, Martina, five children were named as living at home: Delfina, Augustus, Celinda, Henry, and Adelina; their ages ranged from twenty-eight to ten years old. The Contra Costa County Assessor's file for 1870 shows a tax liability of $170 for the following categories: land, improvements, personal property, furniture, a buggie, a horse, poultry, and a dog tax of five dollars.[39]

Don Juan's oldest son, Juan Cosme Alvarado, was living in San Francisco, studying law. In 1870 the California Supreme Court admitted him to the bar; city directories of subsequent years show him listed as an attorney with an office on California Street and a specialty in mining law. After it opened in 1875, Juan Cosme lived at the Palace Hotel, which one writer said was "at least four times too large for its period and place." The hotel covered two and one-half acres, had a lavish, marble-paved, glass-roofed grand court, and had eight hundred rooms equipped with "noiseless water closets" and gadgets designed to make life at the hotel effortless and luxurious. Don Juan often visited his son at the Palace Hotel.[40]

From his correspondence and remarks made by his contemporaries, it appears that Juan Alvarado was greatly depressed in the 1870s. He was in ill health and quite poor, though his pride kept him from admitting it publicly. He had been much less Americanized than his uncle Mariano Vallejo, and he could scarcely speak the language of the people who had taken over California. His acquaintance Bancroft, wrote, "In common with all his countrymen he fancied that he had been badly abused, had been tricked and robbed of millions of dollars which he had never possessed, and of hundreds of leagues of land which he had neglected to secure to himself. To the accursed Yankees were to be attributed all his follies and failures, all his defects of character, all the mistakes of his life."[41]

In 1875 the deaths of two beloved family members further affected the former governor. In April, Don Juan's twenty-three-year-old daughter, Celinda, died suddenly while she was living in San Rafael, across San Pablo Bay. Lacking the necessary funds to have her body transported home and for funeral expenses, he appealed to Bancroft, for whom he was then compiling notes for a projected history, and received one hundred dollars. The next month his wife of thirty-five years, Doña Martina, died. After her funeral at St. Paul's Catholic Church in San Pablo, the mourners, including their five living children, traveled to St. Mary's Cemetery in Oakland for the interment. An obituary in a San Francisco newspaper included the following words: "The death of Señora Martina Castro de Alvarado has brought sorrow to many of our prominent native California families. In her honor, on the day of the funeral, business was suspended in San Pablo, the inhabitants uniting in paying the last sad honors."[42]

Alvarado's association with the historian Hubert Howe Bancroft began in the autumn of 1874. Proprietor of a book-store and publishing firm in San Francisco, Bancroft had acquired an astounding collection of books and manuscripts focused on the Pacific coast, with California as a central subject. With this resource, he began to write a series of history books and hired a number of staff members to help with the research and writing. Some of his agents were sent to interview "old-timers" who dictated their recollections and gave or sold their documents to the historian. Persuaded by his uncle Mariano Vallejo, and by one of Bancroft's bilingual agents, Henry Cerruti, a former general in the Bolivian army, Don Juan agreed to write an account of California history. On December 4, 1874, he notified Vallejo that he had completed 241 pages of notes, arranged in twenty-one chapters that

*Celinda Alvarado, c. 1867.* Courtesy of the San Pablo Historical Society.

formed three of the five projected parts of his history.[43] Three days later Vallejo visited his nephew and borrowed the notes. During the following year, Don Juan added to these pre-liminary notes and wrote narratives on some specific topics, such as a brief account of his administration and a history of the *pueblo* of Yerba Buena–San Francisco.

Bancroft, the California historian and publisher, later wrote about his negotiations with Don Juan:

> Next among the Hispano-Californians in historical importance to Mariano G. Vallejo stood his nephew Juan B. Alvarado. . . . His recollections were regarded by every one as very important, but exceedingly difficult to obtain.
>
> At length promises were extracted from the governor that he would write a history. . . . So he went to work; for in truth, old and ill as he was, he had more working power and pluck than any of them. . . . In writing his history he displayed no little enthusiasm, and seemed specially desirous of producing as valuable a record as that of any one. . . .
>
> I had told Alvarado plainly that I would not pay him for his information; indeed, he never asked me to do so. He would accept nothing in direct payment, but he was determined to make the most of it indirectly.[44]

In January 1876, Bancroft provided rented rooms in San Francisco, "plentifully supplied with liquor and cigars," where for six months Don Juan dictated his recollections of California history to Henry Cerruti. Both men had copious notes and outlines to follow, and Cerruti was familiar with the subject, having recently worked with General Vallejo in recording his reminiscences ("Recuerdos historícos"). When they were partway through, Alvarado made a trip to Rancho San Pablo to prune his fruit trees. Finally, on July 4, 1876 (the American centennial), the project was completed. The result was a manuscript of 1,250 numbered leaves written in five large ledger books and entitled "Historia de California" (History of California).[45]

In his "Historia de California," Don Juan blended autobiographical data with the major political events of his times. He also included descriptions of leading personalities, giving his frank opinion of their virtues or worthlessness. Social history was touched on in his mention of fiestas, recreational activities, legal proceedings, and relations between Californios and the Indians of California. In a sense, this dictated "history" was not written by Alvarado—it is in the handwriting of Cerruti; thus, the narrative is a product of the interviewer as well as the informant. Yet Don Juan attempted to give his version of events, as did his uncle Mariano Vallejo, who told Cerruti, "It is my history, and not yours, I propose to tell."[46]

Don Juan also provided historical material to his Yale-educated attorney, Theodore H. Hittell, who planned to write a history of California. The two men first met in 1868; five years later Hittell interviewed the former governor for three days at Rancho San Pablo. Finally, Don Juan gave the attorney eighty handwritten pages of notes on California history as well as depositions in September 1878. Undoubtedly, he was paid for providing this information. Volume two of Hittell's *History of California*, published in San Francisco in 1885, has seventy-eight pages of text about Alvarado's governorship.[47] The third and fourth volumes of Bancroft's *History of California*, covering that period, were published the following year, but by that time, Don Juan was dead.

On July 13, 1882, after a bronchial illness of several months, Juan Bautista Valentín Alvarado died at his home in San Pablo. A few days later, a front-page article in the San Francisco *Bulletin* described the funeral observances:

The body of the venerable soldier and beloved statesman lay in state most of the morning in one of the rooms of the old homestead. Here it was viewed by the visitors present, who had assembled

*Juan Bautista Alvarado, 1881.* Courtesy of the San Pablo Historical Society.

to pay the last sad rites to the dead. Many old Spanish and Mexican residents of the neighborhood who had known the Governor for many years were there. About the door and gateway groups of villagers were standing in knots and talking in low tones. In the front hallway of the house the friends and relatives of the family were gathered about the coffin. About eleven o'clock the pallbearers carried the body, followed by the assemblage, down the garden walk, under the vine-covered arbors, to the hearse at the gate. From there the procession moved slowly down the road to the little Catholic Church nearby. Here the mourners gathered and listened to the short service.[48]

After the religious service, Alvarado's body was taken to St. Mary's Catholic Cemetery in Oakland for burial alongside his wife and other family members.

In honor of their deceased member, the Society of California Pioneers prepared a long eulogy and sent a copy of it to his three sons and two daughters. After summarizing highlights of the former governor's life, the encomium concluded with the following words: "Alvarado was a man of fine feelings, of enlarged views, and of fine conversational powers. His knowledge of English did not enable him to speak it with fluency; yet he had among those speaking that language many strong friends. . . . In his death the Society of loses one of its oldest and most esteemed members, whose life was upright and honorable, and whose departure . . . will be deeply regretted by all classes of our people."[49]

# 8

# The Great Land Case and Legacy
# 1867–1894

LEGAL DISPUTE OVER OWNERSHIP of Rancho San Pablo was a central concern during the last thirty years of Don Juan Alvarado's life, and it continued for more than a decade after his death. It became known as "the Great Land Case" as dozens of lawsuits concerning various aspects of the extensive property were filed, some of which were appealed to higher courts. Meanwhile, title to all seventeen thousand acres of the rancho was clouded, precluding development of the property, the village, and its waterfront. Furthermore, the litigation caused rancor and difficulty between descendants of Martina Castro de Alvarado and her brothers.

The quarrel had its origin in Francisco Castro's last will and testament, which he had signed before he died in November 1831. By this document he gave half of his ranch property to his wife, Gabriela, the remainder to be divided equally among his eleven children. Thus, the land was divided into twenty-two shares. An old record was more explicit: "eleven equal undivided twenty-second parts thereof to his widow, and one equal undivided twenty-second part thereof to each of his ten living children, and a like undivided twenty-second part thereof to his grandchildren, heirs of his deceased daughter Francisca." In 1835, his son Joaquín, who had been appointed executor of the will and administrator of the estate, received from Governor Figueroa confirmation of the grant as well as an addition to the property of one square league, making in all about four square leagues of land (17,712 acres). During the next fifteen years, although some of Castro's sons built homes at various locations on the ranch, no actual physical division of the land was made, and all the siblings used the ranch land in common. Meanwhile, three other unmarried children had died, whereupon their individual shares became the property of their mother, increasing Gabriela's total to fourteen of the twenty-two shares.

In 1850, with the influx of people to the area, some of them interested in buying or leasing part of the property, there was an effort to partition the ranch. Gabriela asked her son-in-law Don Juan to draw up a plan for splitting the ranch, which he did. He then employed Cándido Gutiérrez, a settler who lived on the ranch and had married into the Castro family, to go to each of principals and explain his proposition for a partition. Unfortunately, Don Juan's plan included the adjacent Rancho El Sobrante of twenty thousand acres, which had been granted separately to two of Martina's brothers, Victor and Juan José, so naturally they objected to that inclusion, and the proposed partition failed.[1]

In August 1851 lawyers, notaries, witnesses, and an interpreter gathered at the Alvarado home for the signing of some legal papers. Gabriela was told that it would facilitate confirmation of the Rancho San Pablo title in the U.S. courts if she would sign (put her mark on) a deed, transferring her interest in the ranch to her favorite daughter, Martina. She was led to believe that this action would benefit all of her children, although none of Martina's brothers was at the meeting. Key phrases of the deed, dated August 4 and acknowledged before a justice of the peace on August 12, stated that Gabriela Castro, widow of Francisco M. Castro, "gives, grants, aliens, conveys and confirms the entire undivided interest in all the tract of land and premises known as Los Cuchigunes, or San Pablo . . . also gives and grants all her interest in the cattle on said Rancho, and all the privileges and appurtenances" to Martina Castro, wife of Juan B. Alvarado and daughter of said Gabriela.[2]

That meant that Don Juan's wife was now owner of more than half of the rancho—fifteen of the twenty-two parts.

The next four months were difficult ones for the Alvarados. At the end of August, Martina gave birth to a new baby, named Celinda, and caring for her and for the failing Gabriela was a strain on Martina. Then her brother, Jesús María, who had built the house in which the Alvarados lived and who now was in deep financial trouble, begged Martina and Don Juan to pay him at least one thousand dollars for the adobe house; but the Alvarados did not pay, probably because they did not have any ready money. In late November all of the extended family gathered at the nearby home of Martina's brother, Joaquín, for his birthday party. While the fiesta was under way, Gabriela went into the yard and fell to the ground uncon-scious—she had suffered a stroke. For the next three weeks the seventy-one-year-old matriarch was quite ill; finally she died at home four days before Christmas and was buried in San Francisco at Mission Dolores. Martina Castro was executrix of her mother's estate. The cost of Gabriela's medical expenses and funeral came to $881, a substantial amount of money in those days; it doubtless meant that she had an elaborate funeral with memorial masses.[3]

After Gabriela's death, Martina's brothers became aware that the large inheritance they had expected from their father's estate was almost all in the hands of their sister. They tried to overturn Gabriela's donation of her property to Martina, claiming that their mother had not been mentally capable, that the deed had been signed under duress, that it was not properly signed and sealed, and that the estate had not been probated properly. In addition, the brothers accused Martina and Don Juan of coercion and fraud. But these charges were never proven.[4]

At the same time, the Castro brothers initiated legal action to contest their father's 1831 will. Their suit cited a Mexican law that, they claimed, permitted a widow only a lifetime interest in real estate, after which the property would be divided equally among her children. But when the case went to court, it was determined that Spanish and Mexican laws recognized the rights of married women to independently inherit, own, mortgage, and convey property they acquired before or during marriage. Furthermore, it was shown that a number of California land grants had been made to women, or were conveyed by gift or bequest to women.[5] The case went to a probate court, a district court, and finally the California Supreme Court, which upheld Francisco Castro's will. The final decision stated that the plaintiffs, "after twenty years acquiescence, ought not to be allowed to come in and dispute their own acts or impeach the validity of their ancestor's will upon abstract points of law, which are shown never to have been in force in California."[6]

In order to validate the Castros's claim to Rancho San Pablo, it was necessary to file a claim with the U.S. Board of Land Commissioners, which was established in San Francisco in 1852. Martina's brother Joaquín, as administrator of Francisco Castro's will, employed an attorney named Eugene Musson (who had drawn up Gabriela's deed to Martina of August 1851) to take the family's case before the board. Musson presented papers relating to the original grant and the will of Francisco Castro. The attorney's contract stated that he would receive one-tenth part of the value of the rancho as payment for his services. The next year Musson added two associates, John Saunders and H. Hepburn, to help him with the claim; these three lawyers would share equally in the one-tenth fee.[7]

Meanwhile, Victor Castro employed another lawyer, John Wilson, to defend the rights and position of Martina's brothers, who wanted to split the ownership of the property equally among the children of the original grantee. On February 18, 1854, attorney Wilson wrote to the Castro brothers, urging them to sue the Alvarados or settle with them: "In my opinion, the time has come when you can not and ought not to wait any longer without having that matter settled, either by an amicable arrangement (as I hope it will be) or a suit. And I now say I will not consider myself in any way responsible for any loss that may come by delay, for I have for a year been urging you to have it settled, or order me to bring the suit. . . . You will consider this my last effort to make you see your interests in this matter."[8]

On April 17, 1855, the Board of Land Commissioners confirmed the title to Rancho San Pablo according to the will of the original grantee, and an appeal was dismissed March 10, 1858. With the title confirmed, Musson and his partners' legal fee became due and payable, but when it was not paid, the three attorneys filed suit on March 10, 1856, in the District Court of Contra Costa County against the Francisco Castro heirs. In the ensuing case, four of Martina's brothers, through their attorney, D. W. Perley, claimed that they had no knowledge about the contract between Joaquín Castro and Musson; that Joaquín, as administrator of the estate, had no power of authority to enter into such a contract; that the will of Francisco Castro was illegal; that all of his property should have gone to his children and none to his widow; that the 1851 deed of Gabriela to Martina was fraudulent; and that Gabriela Castro was incompetent in her last years. When they won their case, Musson and his partners received their tenth part of the land, which they soon sold.[9]

In 1856 the brothers of Martina determined to partition the ranch on a plan of eighths instead of twenty-seconds; that is, the property would be divided into eight portions, one for each of the surviving children of Francisco Castro. To make the partition, they appointed three commissioners: James Alexander Forbes, a bilingual settler and friend of Francisco Castro who had drawn the original *diseño* of the rancho in 1830 and had written out Francisco's will in 1831; John R. B. Cooper, an American sea captain and *ranchero* married to

General Vallejo's sister, Encarnación; and Nicholas Gray, deputy surveyor of the United States. The commissioners produced a plat of Rancho San Pablo and gave the property a total valuation of $148,251. On the basis of this partition, numerous land transactions were made—some were outright sales, others were mortgages or leases. But this informal partition failed in subsequent legal proceedings; the map was set aside as erroneous, and many of those who purchased from the Castros, except the Alvarado interest, finally found themselves without title.[10]

On October 10, 1859, Joaquín Castro, as administrator, published a legal notice entitled "Caution to Purchasers of Land." The names of thirty-five Castro descendants were printed at the end of the sheet, but Martina and Juan Bautista Alvarado's names were not included. The notice stated "The undersigned heirs and divisees of Francisco Castro, original grantee of the Rancho de los Cochiyunes (San Pablo in the counties of Contra Costa and Alameda) hereby caution all who may wish to purchase land in said Rancho, not to buy from any one who claims under the so-called Partition Deed of the Rancho de San Pablo, recorded at Martinez, Book of Records, Vol. 6, pages 1 to 10, as the said deed is Fraudulent, Null and Void, and will not convey any legal title to the purchaser."[11]

In the proposed informal partition of 1856, Martina Castro de Alvarado received only two thousand acres, not the twelve thousand acres she would have received under a fifteen-twenty-seconds split, so she and Don Juan determined to claim what they considered their rightful interest. Allying with Joseph Emeric, who had purchased a large tract of the rancho, and with others who objected to the 1856 division, they determined on further court action. On November 19, 1867, Emeric filed an amicable suit against the Alvarados and others (the et alia numbered nearly two hundred) in order to have the ownership legally determined. Those who had agreed to the 1856 decision fought this new suit, and although they did not win, they succeeded in protracting the proceedings for seventeen years.[12]

The *Emeric v. Alvarado* lawsuit finally ended in 1884, when the California Supreme Court confirmed the Alvarado claim and title. A pertinent paragraph of the legal decision follows:

A portion of said rancho, equivalent to fifteen-twenty-second parts thereof, quality and quantity relatively considered, and as far as practicable, without prejudice to any other interests, including the so-called "Alvarado homestead," and the improvements and possessions of persons claiming under said Martina Castro de Alvarado, to be allotted and set aside by the referees, to be known as the "Martina Castro de Alvarado share and interest," which will thereafter . . . be separately partioned between those persons claiming under said Martina Castro de Alvarado according to their respective rights.[13]

When the California Supreme Court confirmed the Alvarado title in 1884, both Don Juan and his wife were dead, and only one of Martina's brothers, Victor, was still alive. In the intervening years, the heirs had made a number of sales, mortgages, liens, and transfers of parcels of the rancho, further complicating the lawsuits and clouding the titles. The county recorder's office lists twenty-five land transactions for this period by Juan B. and Martina Alvarado, some of the individual transfers involving as many as thirty-eight deeds. An even larger number of land transactions are listed under the Castro brothers' names. A newspaper account noted that "during the long litigation, nearly all the lawyers in San Francisco have been from time to time more or less connected with one or more branches of it."[14]

After confirmation of the title in 1884, a new set of commissioners worked for ten additional years on a final partition of Rancho San Pablo. When in 1894 a judge handed down the

*Delfina Alvarado, c. 1865.* Courtesy of the San Pablo Historical Society.

final decree of partition, it recognized 148 owners of parcels of the old rancho. By that time Joseph Emeric was deceased, but his son Henry acquired nearly two thousand acres, a princely inheritance valued at $246,000. The widow of Dr. Jacob Tewksbury, an early settler on the rancho, was awarded 2,215 acres, and Alvarado's attorney, Theodore Hittell, received 460 acres. In contrast, the original Castro heirs had disposed of most of their interest; Martina's brother Victor and all of the other Castro heirs together received title to less than one hundred acres. The Alvarado descendants were allocated the least: Anna Chevesich Alvarado, Don Juan's daughter-in-law (she was married to his youngest son, Henry) was awarded 2.26 acres, including the old adobe home, and the estate of Don Juan's oldest daugher, Delfina Alvarado Carrick, received 9.66 acres.[15]

At the time of the California Supreme Court decision of 1884 confirming the Alvarado title, only five of Don Juan and Martina's nine children were living. The oldest was Delfina, then forty-three years old, who had married George W. Carrick in 1870. They had three children: George William, Alice Delfina, and John Alvarado Carrick. Delfina (who had no grandchildren) lived nearby in Oakland, where she died in 1888, and her husband followed her a year later. One of her legacies was a Mexican silver chalice, which she donated to St. Paul's Catholic Church in San Pablo.[16]

All three of the Alvardo boys studied law—perhaps they were attracted to that profession by the drawn-out legal squabbles over Rancho San Pablo land and the influence of lawyers who were involved in the case. The mysteries and vagaries of the American legal system must have been a principal topic of conversation when they got together with other family members.

The oldest of Don Juan's sons was Juan Cosme Alvarado, who was born in 1843. By 1870, as an attorney specializing in mining law, he had an office in San Francisco, where he

*Juan B. Cosme Alvarado, c. 1895.* Courtesy of the San Pablo Historical Society.

resided in the Palace Hotel. In 1882 he married Mary Ann Bolton, and they had a son, John Bolton Alvarado, before the marriage was dissolved two years later. Juan Cosme practiced law for two years in New York. Then, after 1884, he lived in London, England, where he was manager of the Anglo-Mexican Mining Company. He died in London in 1910. His death certificate, dated January 14, 1910, gave his occupation as a mining share broker, his residence as De Kaysers Royal Hotel on Victoria Embankment, and his cause of death as kidney disease before admission to the City of London Lunatic Asylum.[17]

Although Augustus Alvarado, who was two years younger than Juan Cosme, also studied law in San Francisco, he did not pass the bar. Augustus, who never married, worked as a legal clerk and court interpreter and later taught school in San Antonio, Texas. In 1887 he moved to Socorro, New Mexico, where he secured a position as translator and interpreter with a law firm. In June of that year he committed suicide. A newspaper account of his death said that "he had been despondent and complained of being defrauded out of a large estate in California, inherited from his father. His despondency terminated in a heavy debauch."[18]

Don Juan's youngest son, Henry, had a happy marriage and a long and productive career. In 1886, when he was twenty-nine years old, following an engagement of six years, he married a San Pablo neighbor and childhood sweetheart, Anna Virginia Chevesich. Four years later they had twin daughters named Lucille and Grace, both born in the old Alvarado adobe in San Pablo. In 1896 Henry moved his family to the county seat of Martinez, where he established a law office. From 1902 to 1910 he was district attorney, and later he served as a superior court judge in Contra Costa County, continuing in that office for another twenty years. When the new St. Paul's Catholic Church in San Pablo was dedicated in 1931, Henry donated a crucifix that had been in the family

*Henry Alvarado, c. 1920.* Courtesy of the San Pablo Historical Society.

for generations. Henry died in 1932, but the fact that he had a Masonic funeral and his remains were cremated and deposited in a public crematorium suggest that he was no longer a staunch Roman Catholic.[19]

The youngest child of Don Juan and Martina Alvarado was named Adelina. In 1879, at the age of nineteen, she eloped with a neighbor, Lucian M. Tewksbury, but after they were discovered at the Palace Hotel in San Francisco, the marriage was annulled. She then moved to Washington, D.C., where she met and married in 1882 Major Frank I. Tedford, a career army officer, from whom she later separated, saying that "he had tricked her into signing away her share in her ancestral estate at San Pablo." During her last years Adelina conducted a boardinghouse in Chicago; then a newspaper account in 1930 stated that she was living in poverty and waiting for a vacancy in a Chicago home for the aged operated by the Little Sisters of the Poor. She died in that city two years later.[20]

It is worthy of note that the Alvarado children were well educated, and all spoke and wrote English correctly, even though their mother did not know the language and their father never mastered it. Furthermore, Don Juan's offspring who married all chose American-born spouses who did not speak Spanish; their surnames were Bolton, Carrick, Chevesich, Tedford, and Tewksbury. Even Don Juan's favorite dog had a non-Hispanic name—he was called Beauregard.

The history of the adobe dwelling on Rancho San Pablo, where Don Juan and his family lived for so many years, is interesting. Built about 1842, it was first occupied by Gabriela Castro and her son Jesús María and his wife, Josefa. In 1848 Don Juan and his wife, Martina, moved in, and they lived there most of the time until their deaths in 1875 and 1882, respectively. Their son Henry and his wife, Anna, occupied the house until 1896, when they moved to Martinez. In 1907 they sold the old adobe building to Henry Belding, who used it for storage behind a new store that he built on San Pablo

*Adelina Alvarado Tedford, c. 1887.* Courtesy of the San Pablo Historical Society.

Avenue. The structure lasted until 1954, when it was razed to make way for new construction nearby. Then in the 1970s, a replica of the historic home of Governor Alvarado was rebuilt on the site to form part of a new Spanish-architectural-style civic center, known as Alvarado Square, in the town of San Pablo. The reconstructed building now serves as a museum, open to the public, where visitors can see where and how the Alvarados lived in the mid-nineteenth century. Some of their original furnishings, photographs, and personal possessions are on display, and the library of the San Pablo Historical Society contains documents and data about the Castro and Alvarado families.

Don Juan Alvarado's most important legacy for California was not the houses he lived in or his personal estate—it was the accomplishments he achieved during his governorship. He tirelessly insisted that California's governors should be native-born sons, not strangers sent from central Mexico, and he stressed the preference of civilian over military leaders. In the legal realm, he stressed that laws should be enacted by the territorial legislature rather than by executive decrees, and he created a supreme court for California. Don Juan expanded public education and used government funds to improve public buildings, bridges, and roads. It was his idea, success-fully carried out, that the territory should acquire a seagoing vessel to facilitate transport of officials, mail, and trade goods between ports in California and the west coast of Mexico. But his most important accomplishment was the vast distribution of millions of acres of public (former mission) lands. These more than two hundred land grants—to Californios, Indians, and foreigners—resulted in a change in the economy and a redistribution of the population of California.

Some writers have accused Alvarado of being irreligious and of having destroyed the missions. In truth, the Mexican government had ordered the missions to be secularized and their lands and livestock distributed, but because much of the phasing out occurred during his governorship, Don Juan was blamed, especially by pro-Church supporters. In his manu-script "Historia de California," Alvarado acknowledged that "religion and ministers of the altar were necessary to train the ignorant masses in the path of morality . . . but the poor natives were reduced by the friars to such a state of servility that they dared not entertain even a thought without the consent of the priest. . . . I want the Church and the world to know that, prompted by motives of humanity, I resolved to free the Indians from that bondage." He added that he was a Roman Catholic "who tried to regard very highly the ministers of the religion in which I was reared and in whose bosom I hope to die."[21]

Several of his contemporaries mentioned Don Juan in their memoirs or narratives of their experiences in California. Juan Espejo, an educated Chilean who lived for a time on Rancho San Pablo, recalled that Alvarado was an educated and talented man who lacked an ambition for wealth. Another acquaintance, San Francisco bank clerk Edward Bosqui, commented that the former governor was a man of more than ordinary intelligence and that he was one of the most courteous gentlemen he had ever met. William Heath Davis, an American trader and rancher, remembered Alvarado as a fine-looking man who was a powerful speaker and who possessed great geniality and tact. The American consul in Monterey, Thomas O. Larkin, wrote that his friend Don Juan was "a man of the best general knowledge, information, and talents, mild in demeanor but violently disposed when under the effect of inebriation."[22]

Thomas Jefferson Farnham, a fiery journalist who was prejudiced against Alvarado because of the governor's deportation of Isaac Graham and other Americans, left a colorful description of Don Juan. In 1841 he and Consul Larkin visited Alvarado, but first they had to pass by what Farnham described as a poorly armed guard "of five half-breed Indians, and what passed for a white corporal, lounging about the door." Farnham wrote, "We passed this valorous body, ascended a flight of stairs, and entered the presence of governor Juan Baptiste Alvarado; a well-formed, full-blooded, Californian Spaniard, five feet eleven inches in height, with coal-black curly hair, deep black eyes, fiercely black eye-brows, high cheek bones, an aquiline nose, fine white teeth, brown complexion, and the clearly marked mien of a pompous coward, clad in the broadcloth and whiskers of a gentleman."[23]

Except for a brief period when they quarreled about public policy, Don Juan and his uncle Mariano Guadalupe Vallejo were very close. The general's correspondence is filled with letters to and from Alvarado, and more than once he visited the former governor at Rancho San Pablo. In his manuscript history of California, Vallejo commented that Alvarado was no great grammarian or profound thinker but that he had good ideas and was an eloquent speaker who was able to convince his listeners. Writing about Don Juan's last years, he noted, "Good fortune never filled Alvarado with pride, neither could the misfortunes which, one after another, fell upon him from 1847 to 1854, abate his courage. He saw, without even complaining, his cattle and horses disappear, which hundred by hundred the 'honest immigrants' stole; saw himself involved in expensive law suits to save even a mile of land; saw all his fortune pass into strange hands; and I do not remember ever to have heard him murmur. . . . It almost seems a dream, but is yet the truth that he, who gave away as gifts so much land, has seen himself stripped of the last inch of land he possessed."[24]

The historian Hubert Howe Bancroft, who came to know Don Juan very well, said that he had a genial temperament, courteous manners, and rare powers of winning friends. Admitting that there were some negative aspects to his conduct, he judged these were attributable to his environment, his position as a politician that required him to engage in intrigues, and his unfortunate indulgence in intoxicating drink. He concluded his appraisal of Alvarado as follows: "In his favor it may be said that he had more brains, energy, and executive ability than any three of his contemporaries combined; that in most of his many controversies he was right as well as successful; that he was patriotic . . . ; that the politicians who forced him to expend his energies and the country's substance in sectional quarrels are largely responsible for his failure; that none of his countrymen could have done so well in his place; that he was honorable in his private dealings, true to his political friends, and never used his position to enrich himself."[25]

Later historians, too, have written favorably about Don Juan. Calling Alvarado "one of the finest and most distinguished sons of the state," Rockwell Hunt added the following tribute: "Conspicuous for his industry in an age of easy-going indolence, deeply interested in education when California was practically without schools, he will always be remembered for his generous and liberal disposition, his sincerity of purpose, and his high sense of justice."[26]

It is clear that Don Juan Bautista Alvarado was brilliant, energetic, honest, and popular—all qualifications for success. But unfortunately, the petty quarrels of political rivals and his increasing dependence on alcohol destroyed his ambition and prevented him from making a greater name for himself. Although there are no statues or marble plaques dedicated to Alvarado, a town named for him was founded in 1852, and a dozen years earlier the town of San Jose was briefly called Pueblo de Alvarado. Furthermore, there are a number of streets, several parks, a shopping center, and even a motel that honor his name. Now, with this full-length biography, readers can discover many facets of Don Juan Bautista Alvarado's life and evaluate his shortcomings and accomplishments.

# Typical Land Grant Awarded by Governor Alvarado

(From William Halley, *The Centennial Year Book of Alameda County, California*, 40–41)

WHEREAS, The citizen Joaquín Estudillo has petitioned for his personal benefit and that of his family for a part of the land known under the name of San Leandro, the boundary of which being on the north the Arroyo San Leandro, on the east the drainage of the springs in the lands occupied by the Indians now settled there; from this point in a straight line south to the Arroyo de San Lorenzo, without including the lands cultivated by the Indians already mentioned, and on the west by the bay, having previously taken all the necessary steps and regulations on this subject: In virtue of the powers conferred on me, in the name of the Mexican nation, I hereby grant him the land mentioned, giving to him the right of possession thereof by these presents, and by the approbation which he has obtained from the Departmental Junta, being subject to the following conditions:

1st. He has the power to fence it without interfering with the passages, roads, and other rights. He shall enjoy it freely and exclusively, applying it to any use or culture most agreeable to him, but within a year he shall build a house, and said house must be inhabited.

2d. He shall solicit to be placed in lawful possession in virtue of this document, from the competent judge by whom the boundaries shall be marked out, and on their borders he

179

shall, besides placing land marks, plant some fruit trees or some forest trees of some utility.

3d. The land granted is one square league, a little more or less, as it is shown by the sketch annexed to the folder on this matter. The judge who shall place him in possession must have the land measured according to law, leaving the remainder for the uses the nation may decree proper.

4th. Should he contravene these conditions he shall lose his right to the land, and it shall be denounced by any other person.

In virtue whereof I order this title, being good and valid, that a copy of it be recorded in the Book of Record, and that it be delivered to the party interested for his security and other ends.

Given in Monterey, October 16, 1842.

[signed] Juan Bautista Alvarado

Constitutional Governor of the Department of the Californias.

# Children of Juan B. and Martina Castro de Alvarado

1. María Alvino Alvarado. Born July 6, 1840. Died August 29, 1840.

2. María Victoria Delfina Alvarado. Born December 25, 1841, baptized February 27, 1842. Married George W. Carrick; had three children: George, Alice, and John Alvarado. Died February 11, 1888.

3. Juan B. Cosme Alvarado. Born September 22, 1843, baptized December 26, 1843. Married Mary Ann Bolton; had one son: John Bolton Alvarado. Died in London, England, January 14, 1910.

4. José Francisco Augusto (Augustus) Alvarado. Born May 1845, baptized April 3, 1846. Died June 21, 1887.

5. María Clorina Viviana Alvarado. Born mid-December 1848, baptized May 12, 1849. Died May 10, 1850.

6. María Celinda Alvarado. Born August 28, 1851, baptized November 30, 1851. Died April 5, 1875.

7. Valentín Alvarado. Born 1854. Died June 7, 1861.

8. Enrique (Henry) Victor Alvarado. Born July 15, 1857, baptized July 15, 1857. Married Anna Chevesich; had twin daughters: Lucille Valentina and Grace Alvarado. Died May 30, 1932.

9. Adelina Natalia Alvarado. Born 1860. Married (1) Lucian M. Tewksbury, (2) Frank I. Tedford. Died in Chicago in 1932.

# Children of Juan B. Alvarado and Juliana ("Raymunda") Castillo

1. Nicolasa Ana Josefa Alvarado. Born December 6, 1831. Married John Escobar; had 14 children, including María Elena and Virginia Escobar. Died October 18, 1915.

2. Estéfana del Rosario Alvarado. Born April 4, 1834. Married Ygnacio Esquer on May 10, 1850. Died September 8, 1916.

3. María Francisca de la Ascención Alvarado. Born May 31, 1836. Married Victorino Chavez.

4. María Gerarda Alvarado. Born October 10, 1838. Probably died young.

5. María Antonia de la Trinidad Alvarado. Born February 22, 1841. Married a man with the surname Ríos.

# Notes

## 1. BOYHOOD IN MONTEREY, 1809–1827

1. Number of *neophytes* in Engelhardt, *Missions and Missionaries of California*, 2: opp. 72; estimate of *gentiles* in Sturtevant, ed., *Handbook of North American Indians*, 8:92; population of *pueblos* in Bancroft, *History of California*, 2:111, 133, 156, and presidios, 2:189.

2. Langum, *Law and Community*, 13; Jones, *Los Paisanos*, 218–19.

3. Description of the presidio in Alvarado, "Notes on California History"; Howard, *California's Lost Fortress*, 6, 15–16; Conley, "We All Lived Together," 21–23, 26–27, 29–30.

4. Bancroft, *California*, 2:141 n. 40; Alvarado, *Vignettes*, 1.

5. Vallejo, "Recuerdos históricos, " 1:225–26; Bancroft, *California Pioneer Register and Index*, "Vallejo, Ignacio."

6. Juan Buatista Alvarado's baptismal record, no. 2732, Mission San Carlos, Real Presidio; José Francisco's burial record, May 29, 1809, Mission San Luis Obispo; Alvarado, *Vignettes*, 1–3.

7. Chidren of Ignacio Vallejo listed in Northrop, *Spanish-Mexican Families of Early California*, 1:350–52; Alvarado, *Vignettes*, 2.

8. Alvarado, "Historia," 2:45–46.

9. Bancroft, *California Pastoral*, 404; Amador, "Memorias sobre la historia de California," 123–24.

10. Alvarado, "Historia," 1:72–74, 124; José de Jesús Pico, "Acontecimientos en California," 2–3.

11. Alvarado, "Historia," 1:72–74; Bancroft, *History of California*, 2:428–29, 3:451.

12. Vallejo, "Recuerdos históricos," 1:273–77.

13. Alvarado, "Historia," 1:125–31.

14. Alvarado, "Historia," 1:146–48, 151–53, 155; Alvarado, *Vignettes*, 5; Bancroft, *History of California*, 2:222, 225, 231.

15. Alvarado, "Historia," 1:152–53; Bancroft, *History of California*, 2:228–29; Burgess, "Pirate or Patriot?," 40–47; Cerecedo, "Hipolito Bouchard," 5–8.

16. Alvarado, "Historia," 1:155–57; Bancroft, *History of California*, 2:231–34, 253–54. For an account by Peter Corney, captain of the *Santa Rosa*, see his *Early Voyages in the North Pacific*, 215–19.

17. Alvarado, *Vignettes*, 5–8, 11. Clara Ortega later married John Gilroy, a Scottish sailor turned rancher, whose name lives on in the town of Gilroy. Pierce, *East of the Gabilans*, 153.

18. Alvarado, *Vignettes*, 12–13, 17–21.

19. Alvarado, *Vignettes*, 12–13, 17–21, 26–27, 30.

20. Schuetz-Miller, *Building and Builders in Hispanic California*, 165–66; Osio, *History of Alta California*, 52–53; Alvarado, "Historia," 1:149; Bancroft, *History of California*, 2:253–54.

21. Alvarado, *Vignettes*, 30–33; Dakin, *Lives of William Hartnell*, 97, 159. Hartnell College in Salinas commemorates his name.

22. Alvarado, "Historia," 1:197, 202–3; Bancroft, *History of California*, 2:450–59.

23. List of goods shipped to California in Dana, *Two Years Before the Mast*, 401–405; description of the trade and profits in Phelps, *Alta California*, 20.

24. Alvarado, "Historia," 1:203, 217; Bancroft, *History of California*, 2:461–62, 466–67, 473.

25. Alvarado, "Historia," 2:110–11; also see 2:14–15.

26. Alvarado, "Historia," 2:93–94; Bancroft, *History of California*, 3:24–26.

27. Bancroft, *History of California*, 3:16–19; Alvarado, "Historia," 2:20–25, 159–60.

28. Alvarado, "Historia," 2:33–34; Alvarado, "Notes on California History," 31–33; ban of the waltz also mentioned by Vallejo, "Recuerdos históricos," 2:95, and Sánchez, *Spanish Arcadia*, 317.

29. Hittell, *History of California*, 2:313, citing California State Archives, Provincial State Papers, Benicia, 25:564.

30. Torre, "Pre-American Monterey," 30; Sánchez, *Spanish Arcadia*, 316, 320; Vallejo-Cooper wedding noted in Woolfenden and Elkinton, *Cooper: Juan Bautista Rogers Cooper*, 33–34.

31. Briones, "A Glimpse of Domestic Life in 1827," 470.

32. Briones, "A Carnival Ball at Montery in 1829," 468–69.

33. Alvarado, "Historia," 2:102, 105–6, 139; Bancroft, *History of California*, 3:8–10, 13–14.

## 2. CIVIL SERVANT AND LEGISLATOR, 1827–1836

1. Miller, *Mexico: A History*, 203; Mexican chief executives are listed in the *Enciclopedia de México*, s.v. "Gabinetes."

2. Alvarado, "Historia," 2:121; Bancroft, *History of California*, 3:36 n. 9.

3. Bancroft, *History of California*, 3:36–38; Alvarado, "Historia," 2:139.

4. Alvarado, "Historia," 2:139.

5. Alvarado, "Historia," 2:118; Bancroft, *History of California*, 3:51–52, 93.

6. Alvarado, "Historia," 2:126–27; 3:16–18.

7. Fitch, "Narración de la Viuda Fitch," 5; Alvarado, "Historia," 2:127–31.

8. Alvarado, "Historia," 2:148–49, 155–56; Bancroft, *History of California*, 3:69–80, 82–85. Summary of the revolt by a participant, Pico, "Acontecimientos," 10–14.

9. Híjar, "California in 1834," in *Three Memoirs of Mexican California*, 14.

10. Bancroft, *History of California*, 3:34–35, 43 n. 24; English translations of the pertinent Mexican colonization and naturalization laws can be found in Wright, *A Yankee in Mexican California*, apps. A, B, and C.

11. Tays, "Revolutionary California," 339–40, 342; Antonio Ríos-Bustamante, ed., Regions of La Raza, 238, 240; Osio, *History of Alta California*, 185.

12. Bancroft, *History of California*, 3:47–49; Wright, *A Yankee in Mexican California*, 16 n. 22.

13. Alvarado, "Historia," 3:10–11.

14. Bancroft, *History of California*, 3:43, n. 24, 301–3.

15. Bancroft, *California Pioneer Register and Index*, s.v. "Padrés, José María; Alvarado, "Historia," 2:172–73; Bancroft, *History of California*, 3:102–3, 301–2.

16. Bancroft, *History of California*, 3:54, 303–5 (summary of decree, 305 n. 6); Alvarado, "Historia," 3:6.

17. Alvarado, "Historia," 3:6.

18. Alvarado, "Historia," 2:167, 3:7; Osio, *History of Alta California*, 102–3.

19. Quoted in Sánchez, *Spanish Arcadia*, 95; Alvarado, "Historia," 2:6; Ogden, *California Sea Otter Trade*, 106–7, 146–47.

20. Vallejo, "Recuerdos históricos," 3:109–12; Bancroft, *California Pastoral*, 524; listed books belonging to Alvarado were given by his grandson, John Bolton Alvarado, to the Monterey History and Art Association, Monterey *Peninsula Diary*, Nov. 16, 1950.

21. Alvarado, "Historia," 2:34–37; Vallejo, "Recuerdos históricos," 3:113–16; Bancroft, *California Pastoral*, 524–25.

22. Baer and Fink, *Adobes in the Sun*, 20–21; Bancroft, *California Pioneer Register*, s.v. "Alvarado, Juan Bautista."

23. Alvarado, "Historia," 2:122–23.

24. Testimony of Espejo in Emeric, *Emeric vs. J. B. Alvarado, et als.*, 2:1242.

25. Davis, *Seventy-five Years in California*, 64.

26. Alvarado, "Historia," 2:169–73; Bancroft, *History of California*, 3:186–209.

27. Pico, *Historical Narrative*, 54.

28. Alvarado, "Historia," 2:196–97; Bancroft, *History of California,* 3:240–41, 246–47, 296.

29. Pico, "Acontecimientos," 27; Amador, "Memorias," 79.

30. Bancroft, *History of California,* 3:318, 321; Alvarado, "Historia," 2:194–95.

31. Hutchinson, *Frontier Settlement in Mexican California,* 210–12, 215, 348; Alvarado, "Historia," 2:225–26; Bancroft, *History of California,* 3:324–26, 336–37.

32. Alvarado, "Historia," 2:232–34; Bancroft, *History of California,* 3:342–44.

33. Alvarado, "Historia," 2:238, 244, 3:27–29; Bancroft, *History of California,* 3:279–80.

34. Bancroft, *California Pioneer Register,* s.v. "Alvarado, Juan Bautista"; grant of El Sur in Cowan, *Ranchos of California,* 100; lot deed from Manuel Jimeno Casarín to Juan Buatista Alvarado, Mar. 21, 1835, Monterey County Recorder's Office, Salinas.

35. Estrada, "Padrón general que manifiesta el."

36. David Langum, "Sin, Sex, and Separation in Mexican California," 48–49; Bancroft, *California Pioneer Register,* s.v. "Madariaga, Bonifacio."

37. Alvarado, "Historia," 3:39–40; Bancroft, *History of California,* 3:295–96.

38. Figueroa, *Manifiesto a la república mexicana,* 178–81.

39. Bancroft, *History of California,* 3:292, 298–300; Alvarado, "Historia," 3:43–45; Weber, *The Mexican Frontier,* 258.

40. Weber, *The Mexican Frontier,* 243–44; Miller, *Mexico: A History,* 210.

41. Pico, "Acontecimientos," 16; Alvarado, "Historia," 3:51–52.

42. Alvarado, "Historia," 3:52.

43. Alvarado, "Historia," 3:53–55, 79–80; Bancroft, *History of California,* 3:422–24, 428–29; Osio, *History of Alta California,* 136.

44. Alvarado, "Historia," 3:87, 101–5; Bancroft, *History of California,* 3:439–41.

45. Alvarado, "Historia," 3:115.

## 3. REVOLUTIONARY GOVERNOR, 1836–1839

1. Bancroft, *History of California,* 3:449.

2. Bancroft, *History of California,* 3:447–48, 450.

3. Alvarado, "Historia," 3:125, 128–31; Bancroft, *History of California,* 3:453–55.

4. Alvarado, "Historia," 3:32–33.

5. Alvarado, "Historia," 3:137–39.

6. Alvarado, "Historia," 3:14–42; Bancroft, *History of California,* 3:456–58; Osio, *History of Alta California,* 153–54; Pico, "Acontecimientos," 33.

7. Alvarado, "Historia," 3:144–53.

8. Alvarado, "Historia," 3:157–58, 165; for an eyewitness view of the revolt, see Atherton, *California Diary*, 28–33.

9. Alvarado, "Historia," 3:159, 170–72, 175. The original one-star flag is in the Southwest Museum, Allen W. Welts, "The Lone Star Flag of California," 40–43.

10. Bancroft, *History of California*, 3:470–71, n. 28.

11. Alvarado, "Historia," 3:175; Bancroft, *History of California*, 3:467–71, 474–75 & n. 36.

12. Bancroft, *History of California*, 3:474–76.

13. Osio, *History of Alta California*, 158.

14. Alvarado, "Historia," 3:190–91, 194, 205–6.

15. Alvarado, "Historia," 3:213, 215–16, 222, 224–25; José de Jesús Pico, "Acontecimientos," 21.

16. Alvarado, "Historia," 3:230, 232–35; liaison in Bancroft, *California Pastoral*, 592.

17. Alvarado, "Historia," 3:235–38; in 1846 Prudon changed his name, see Prudhomme, "Leon Victor Prudon [Prudhomme]," 2.

18. Bancroft, *History of California*, 3:506–7, 510.

19. Bancroft, *History of California*, 3:517–20, 522.

20. Bancroft, *History of California*, 3:521, 526–28; "Las Siete Leyes" in Arrillaga, compiler, *Recopilación de leyes, decretos, bandos, reglamentos*, 2:317–380.

21. Bancroft, *History of California*, 3:529, note 24.

22. Woolfenden and Elkinton, *Cooper*, 1–2; Alvarado, "Historia," 4: 13.

23. Dupetit-Thouars, *Voyage of the Venus*, 33.

24. Pico, *Historical Narrative*, 79; Janssens, *Life and Adventures in California*, 83.

25. Osio, "Historia de la California," 190; Alvarado, "Historia," 4: 34, 36, 39–40.

26. Alvarado, "Historia," 3:243–45; Bancroft, *History of California*, 3:558–64.

27. Alvarado, "Historia," 4:65–71; Bancroft, *History of California*, 3:565–68.

28. Alvarado, "Historia," 4:74; Bancroft, *History of California*, 3:569, 573.

29. Alvarado, "Historia," 4:76–79; Bancroft, *History of California*, 3:570–71, 573.

30. Pico, *Historical Narrative*, 85–86.

31. Bancroft, *History of California*, 3:574–75; Vallejo, "Documentos para la historia de California," 1:12; 5:225, 269.

32. "Juan B. Alvarado, gefe político de la Alta California; á sus habitantes . . . ," Santa Barbara, Nov. 21, 1838; Bancroft, *History of California*, 3:595.

33. Alvarado, "Historia," 4:113–15, 123; Bancroft, *History of California*, 3:577–81.

## 4. CONSTITUTIONAL GOVERNOR, 1839–1842

1. Osio, *History of Alta California*, 193–94; Bancroft, *California Pioneer Register*, s.v. "Abrego, José," and "Jimeno Casarín, Manuel."

2. Bancroft, *History of California*, 3:584.

3. Alvarado, "Historia," 4:131; Bancroft, *History of California*, 3:585–86, 590.

4. Osio, *History of Alta California*, 196, 306 n. 33.

5. Alvarado, "Historia," 4:128–30; Cerruti, *Ramblings in California*, 127.

6. Miller, *Captain Richardson*, 68; Alvarado, "Historia," 4:128–30.

7. Hittell, *History of California*, 2:294; Duflot de Mofras, *Travels on the Pacific Coast*, 1:214; Shinn, "Spanish-California Schools," 30–41.

8. Alvarado, "Historia," 4:206–10.

9. Pinedo, "Early Days in Santa Clara," 1.

10. Mission Santa Clara, Book of Marriages, no. 2735.

11. Alvarado, "Historia," 4:170–71; Bancroft, *History of California*, 3:593. Mention of California gold nuggets found in 1824, Vallejo, "Recuerdos," 1:370; in 1829–1830, Pico, "Acontecimientos," 14–15; Altrocchi, *Spectacular San Franciscans*, 29.

12. Alvarado, "Historia," 4:169–70; Laplace, *Campagne de circumnavigation*, 6:293. Don Juan's illness in Bancroft, *History of California*, 3:593.

13. Alvarado, "Historia," 3:200, 4:172–73.

14. Laplace, *Campagne de circumnavigation*, 6:24.

15. Blue, "Report of Captain La Place," 321.

16. Until he died four years later, Raoul cooked in Los Angeles for Louis Vignes (Alvarado, "Historia," 4:18–20).

17. Sale of the house in Augusta Fink, *Monterey: The Presence of the Past*, 101. María Alvino Alvarado was born July 6 and died August 29, 1840. Raymunda was married at age thirty–five in 1844; her husband, whose first wife was María Isidora Vallejo, was forty–eight years old.

18. Bancroft, *History of California*, 3:593–95.

19. Bancroft, *History of California*, 3:604 n. 49.

20. Bancroft, *History of California*, 3:605–6.

21. Bancroft, *History of California*, 4:50, 54; Gleeson, *History of the Catholic Church in California*, 2:148–49.

22. Manuscript copy of Alvarado's mission regulations in Pico, "Documentos para la Historia, de California," doc. 89, Bancroft Library; summarized in Bancroft, *History of California*, 4:54–55.

23. Dakin, *Lives of Hartnell*, 213–14; Alvarado, "Historia," 4:144–45.

24. Dakin, *Lives of Hartnell*, 232; Alvarado, "Historia," 4:144–45; Bancroft, *History of California*, 4:57–58.

25. Alvarado, "Historia," 4:59, 127; Bancroft, *History of California,* 4:57 & n. 26.

26. Guerra de Hartnell, "Narrativa," 3; Bancroft, *History of California,* 3:601, 4:58–61; Alvarado, "Historia," 4:144–45; Dakin, *Lives of Hartnell,* 213–40.

27. Alvarado, "Historia," 4:200–202; Bancroft, *History of California,* 3:595–604; Tays, "Mariano Guadalupe Vallejo and Sonoma," 16:50–61.

28. Robinson, *Life in California before the Conquest,* 225; Alvarado, "Historia," 5:3–4; Bancroft, *History of California,* 4:5; Garner, *Letters from California,* 24–25.

29. Alvarado, "Historia," 5:4–6; Bancroft, *History of California,* 4:11, 16–17; Garner, *Letters from California,* 25–26.

30. Alvarado, "Historia," 5:7–9; Bancroft, *History of California,* 4:13–15, 28; Garner, *Letters from California,* 26–27; see also Nunis, *Trials of Isaac Graham.*

31. Alvarado, *Gobernador Constitucional del Departamento de Los Californias; á sus Habitantes* [Monterey, c. April 26, 1840]; translation in Robinson, *Life in California,* 222–23.

32. Robinson, *Life in California,* 228; Alvarado, "Historia," 5:10–11; Bancroft, *History of California,* 4:29–31; Garner, *Letters from California,* 27.

33. Bancroft, *History of California,* 4:31, 34.

34. Bancroft, *History of California,* 4:35–36, 38–39.

35. Alvarado, "Historia," 4:192–93.

36. Alvarado's 226 land grants from 1837 to 1842 are listed in Cowan, *Ranchos of California;* also see Jimeno Casarín, *Index of Land Concessions from 1830–1845;* and Perez, *Land Grants in Alta California.*

37. Original grant in the U. S. General Land Office; photostatic copy in the Bancroft Library.

38. Woolfenden and Elkinton, *Cooper,* 61, 85–86; Fink, *Monterey: Presence of the Past,* 77.

39. Hittell, *History of California,* 2:282, 287.

40. Rosenus, *General M. G. Vallejo,* 23–26; Hittell, *History of California,* 2:285–88.

41. Alvarado, "Primitivo descubrimiento de placeres de oro en California," the Bancroft Library; Hoover, et al., *Historic Spots in California,* 4th ed. rev., 159.

42. Alphabetical lists of ships in Bancroft, *History of California,* 4:100–106 n. 54; 562–70, n. 42.

43. Phelps, *Alta California,* 307.

44. Douglas, *James Douglas in California,* 7–9.

45. Douglas, *James Douglas in California,* 11–15; see also copy of Douglas's "Journals, 1840–41," Bancroft Library.

46. Simpson, *Narrative of a Voyage to California Ports*, 89–90, 92–93.

47. Alvarado, "Historia," 4:174–75; Duflot de Mofras, *Travels*, xxviii–xxix; Foucrier, "Spy or Explorer?," 21, 24.

48. Wilkes, *Narrative*, 5:160–272; Bancroft, *History of California*, 4:243–46; Kinnaird, *Greater San Francisco Bay Region*, 1:325–29.

49. Population figures in Francis, *Economic and Social History*, 153–54; Hittell, *History of California*, 2:284–85.

50. Osio, *History of Alta California*, 207; Wright, *A Yankee in Mexican California*, 111–12; Bancroft, *History of California*, 4:281–90.

51. Bancroft, *History of California*, 4:290–91, 293–94; Hittell, *History of California*, 2:314. A copy of the proclamation is in the Bancroft Library.

52. Harlow, *California Conquered*, 4–5; Maxwell, *Visit to Monterey in 1842*, 17–18; Bancroft, *History of California*, 4:307–09.

53. Osio, *History of Alta California*, 208–9; Ord, *Occurrences in Hispanic California*, 52–53; Harlow, *California Conquered*, 7.

54. Hague and Langum, *Thomas O. Larkin*, 99–100; Harlow, *California Conquered*, 7.

55. Larkin to Faxon Dean Atherton, Monterey, Oct. 20–21, 1842, in Larkin, "Six New Letters," 67–71; Hague and Langum, *Thomas O. Larkin*, 100.

56. Larkin, "Six New Letters," 68–69; Davis, *Seventy-five Years in California*, 88; Harlow, *California Conquered*, 7.

57. Maxwell, *Visit to Monterey*, 32–33.

58. Bancroft, *History of California*, 4:313–14.

59. Osio, *History of Alta California*, 210.

## 5. REVOLT AGAINST MICHELTORENA, 1843–1845

1. Alvarado, "Historia," 5:33; Carreño, *Jefes del ejército mexicano en 1847*, 205–6; Bancroft, *History of California*, 4:402–3, 418–19, 513–14.

2. Osio, *History of Alta California*, 212–13.

3. Alvarado, "Historia," 5:20; Osio, *History of Alta California*, 207; Bancroft, *History of California*, 4:350–54.

4. Alvarado, "Historia," 5:21; Bancroft, *History of California*, 4:355, 364 n. 32, 377 n. 16.

5. Bancroft, *History of California*, 4:357–58, 358 n. 16.

6. Serrano, "Apuntes para la Historia, de Alta California," 90–91; Bancroft, *History of California*, 4:403–4; Alvarado sold Las Mariposas to John C. Frémont in Feb. 1847 for $3,000.

7. Bancroft, *History of California*, 4:406–8; Thomas O. Larkin, *The Larkin Papers*, 2:205.

8. Wood, *Wandering Sketches of People and Things*, 254; Bancroft, *History of California*, 4:458–60; Alvarado, "Historia," 5:22.

9. Alvarado's letter in Vallejo, "Documentos," 12:108; Vallejo to Alvarado, n.d., seeking data, in Vallejo, "Documentos," 14:21–22; Bancroft, *History of California*, 4:465.

10. Bancroft, *History of California*, 4:461, 466; Alvarado, "Historia," 5:23–24.

11. Alvarado, "Historia," 5:23–24; Bancroft, *History of California*, 4:462–63.

12. Alvarado, "Historia," 5:24; Bancroft, *History of California*, 4:468–69.

13. Bancroft, *History of California*, 4:471, 474 n, 478, 482; Osio, *History of Alta California*, 219.

14. Bancroft, *History of California*, 4:485–86, 488.

15. Bancroft, *History of California*, 4:489.

16. Letter to Micheltorena quoted in Bancroft, *History of California*, 4:489–90.

17. Hittell, *History of California*, 2:350–51; Bancroft, *History of California*, 4:490–91, 493–97.

18. Bancroft, *History of California*, 4:497–98.

19. Hittell, *History of California*, 2:352.

20. Alvarado, "Historia," 5:29, 66, 70; Bancroft, *History of California*, 4:500–506, 508.

21. Alvarado, "Historia," 5:71–74; Pico, *Historical Narrative*, 108–9.

22. Alvarado, "Historia," 5:75–78; Bancroft, *History of California*, 4:509–10.

23. Bancroft, *History of California*, 4:511–12; Alvarado, "Historia," 5:89.

24. Hittell, *History of California*, 2:355–56; Alvarado, "Historia," 5:89; Bancroft, *History of California*, 4:511–12.

25. Vallejo, "Documentos," 34:122, 182; baptismal records, Mission San Carlos Borromeo, Presidio Chapel.

## 6. COLONEL AGAINST THE YANKEES, 1846–1848

1. Alvarado, "Historia," 5:128–29, 131.

2. Bancroft, *History of California*, 4:586–87, 5:2–5; Larkin to U.S. Minister in Mexico, Monterey, April 3, 1846, *Larkin Papers*, 4:278; Egan, *Frémont*, 317.

3. Bancroft, *History of California*, 5:6–7, 9–11; Egan, *Frémont*, 318–20.

4. Híjar, Pérez, and Escobar, *Three Memoirs of Mexican California*, 109.

5. Bancroft, *History of California*, 5:15, 17–18, 19 n.

6. Alvarado, "Historia," 5:128, 130–31; Vallejo, "Recuerdos históricos," 5:71.

7. Vallejo, "Recuerdos históricos," 5:71–76.

8. Alvarado, "Historia," 5:134–36.

9. Alvarado, "Historia," 5:137–38.

10. Vallejo, "Recuerdos históricos," 5:80–84; Alvarado, "Historia," 5: 133–144; Bancroft, *History of California*, 5:59–62.

11. Bancroft, *History of California*, 5:41–43; "Documentary," *California Historical Society Quarterly* 5 (June 1926):193–95.

12. Alvarado, "Historia," 5:171.

13. Alvarado, "Historia," 5:171–78; Egan, *Frémont*, 327–29.

14. Bancroft, *History of California*, 5:45–46, 48, 51–53, 105; Alvarado, "Historia," 5:150–55.

15. Alvarado, "Historia," 5:185–86, 195, 197; Bancroft, *History of California*, 5:104–5, 107–8, 109–10, 112, 145, 151.

16. Alvarado, "Historia," 4:136, 5:199–200, 207; Bancroft, *History of California*, 5:134–36, 165–67, 171.

17. Alvarado, "Historia," 5:207, 214; Bancroft, *History of California*, 5:171–72.

18. Alvarado, "Historia," 5:212, 230–31; Bancroft, *History of California*, 5:136

19. Alvarado, "Historia," 5:215–20; Sloat's proclamation is printed in Manning, *Diplomatic Correspondence of the United States*, 8:877–78.

20. Alvarado, "Historia," 5:231, 239; Bancroft, *History of California*, 5:261–67.

21. Alvarado, "Historia," 5:234–36, 242; Harlow, *California Conquered*, 137, 141–42.

22. Alvarado, "Historia," 5:245–46; Harlow, *California Conquered*, 139–40, 146–48.

23. Alvarado, "Historia," 5:246–47; Bancroft, *History of California*, 5: 275–79.

24. Pico, "Acontecimientos," 67–68; Alvarado, "Historia," 5:249–50.

25. Alvarado, "Historia," 5:250; Monterey *Californian*, Sept. 5 and 12, 1846.

26. Alvarado, "Historia," 5:253–54; Bancroft, *History of California*, 5:284, 286–87, 303, 314–15.

27. Amador, "Memorias," 95; United States, 33 Cong., 2d sess., *House Exec. Doc. 13* (Frémont's Calif. Claims), Alvarado's claim 169, suspended; Bancroft, *History of California*, 5:358.

28. Original letter from Castillero to Alvarado, Jan. 15, 1847, in Thomas Savage, "Documentos para la historia de California," 2:69.

29. Sherman, *Memoirs*, 1:20; Tucey and Hornbeck, "Anglo Immigration," 5–6.

30. Alvarado, "Historia," 5:250–51; Rolle, *John Charles Frémont*, 112, 178.

31. Alvarado, "Historia," 5:267–68, 274; Bancroft, *History of California,* 5:291, 388–96, 399.

32. Jacques Antoine Moerenhout [French consul] to French Foreign Minister Guizot, Monterey, March 15, 1847, in France, Archives du Ministère des Affaires Etrangères; Tays, "Revolutionary California," 808; Harlow, *California Conquered,* 252.

33. Treaty in Miller, ed., *Treaties and other International Acts,* 5:207–36.

34. Alvarado, "Historia,," preface, ii–iii.

## 7. *RANCHERO* AT RANCHO SAN PABLO, 1848–1882

1. Conley, *Long Road to Rancho San Pablo,* 28.

2. Hendry and Bowman, " Spanish and Mexican Adobe," pts 5–6: 487, 490, 497, 499, 501, 503; McGinty, "Spanish and Mexican Ranchos," 48–49, 53.

3. Hendry and Bowman, "The Spanish and Mexican Adobe," pts 5–6: 498–501; Emeric, *Emeric vs. Alvarado,* et als., 2:795.

4. Letter, Lucille Alvarado Skinner to Agnes Hoey, 1947, Contra Costa County History Center.

5. Hendry and Bowman, " Spanish and Mexican Adobe," ps 5–6: 498.

6. Pitt, *Decline of the Californios,* 52–53; Wright, "Making of Cosmopolitan California" 19:323.

7. Quoted in Bancroft, *History of California,* 6:65–66.

8. Dakin, *Lives of William Hartnell,* 286; Sherman, *Memoirs,* 1:70.

9. Pérez Rosales, *California Adventure,* 87–88; also see Pérez Rosales, *We Were '49ers!,* 79–83.

10. Richman, *California under Spain and Mexico,* 356–57.

11. *Langley's San Francisco Business Directory;* Estudillo, *Sketches of California in the 1860s,* 38–39, 126–27.

12. Society of California Pioneers, *Centennial Roster; Commemorative Edition;* Bancroft, *History of California,* 4:6, 778, 781–86; Writers' Program, *San Francisco,* 135–36.

13. Emeric, *Emeric vs. J. B. Alvarado,* et als., 2:1355.

14. U.S. Federal Census, Contra Costa County, San Pablo Township no. 1, June 1860.

15. Alvarado to Ignacio Ezquer, San Pablo, Nov. 1851, in Ezquer, "Memorias de cosas pasadas," C-D 77, pt. 2, Bancroft Library.

16. Bosqui, *Memoirs,* 72–73.

17. Vallejo, "Documentos," 35:257, 281; Monterey County Recorder's Office, assessment list for 1852; details of the house sale in a letter from Amelie Elkinton to Frances Conley, Carmel, Jan. 20, 1983, Frances and Earl Conley Collection.

18. *Vanderstice vs. Alvarado*, 3rd Judicial Dist. Court, May 27, 1851; copy of case summary and other receipts at the San Pablo Historical Society.

19. For a discussion of conflicting land policies see Bakken, "Mexican and American Land Policy," 237–62.

20. Bancroft, *History of California*, 4:542; Morefield, *Mexican Adaptation in American California*, 25, Robinson, *Land in California*, 31, 100–105, 253–58.

21. Weber, *Foreigners in Their Native Land*, 195–99. A manuscript copy of the petition is in the Huntington Library, San Marino, Calif.

22. Ruiz de Burton, *Squatter and the Don* (the original edition was published with the author's pseudonym of C. Loyal).

23. Morrow, *Spanish and Mexican Private Land Grants*, 14; Bowman, "Index of Witnesses," 5; Pitt, *Decline of the Californios*, 86–95.

24. U. S. District Court, Northern District, Land Cases 407 and 414, Bancroft Library.

25. U. S. District Court, Northern District, Land Case 404; Mason, *Early Marin*, 70–76.

26. Copy of the contract in Castro, "Documentos," C-B 52:226–28; copy of San Quintín land grant in Manuel de Jesús Castro documents, C–B 232, Bancroft Library.

27. Bancroft, *History of California*, 6:585–94, 598–600.

28. Alvarado to Santa Anna, Feb. 15, 1855, copy in Vallejo, "Documentos," 36:377–78, Bancroft Library.

29. Valentín Alvarado was buried June 7, 1861, in St. Mary's Cemetery, Oakland; Delfina's schooling is mentioned in a letter from her niece, Lucille Alvarado Skinner, to Agnes Hoey, Nov. 18, 1947, Contra Costa History Center; Celinda's education, in a letter from Sr. Anne C. Stark, Dominican Sisters, Calif. Province Archivist, to Ann Roberts, Mar. 23, 1990, San Pablo Historical Society library.

30. Bagwell, *Oakland*, 38, 40–41, 132–33; U.S. Census of 1860 gave the population as 1,543; testimony of Juan B. Alvarado in U.S. District Court, Northern District, Land Case 299:277, Bancroft Library. Henry's baptismal record in Northrop, *Spanish-Mexican Families*, 1:11.

31. Nevada City *Democrat*, Sept. 14, 1859.

32. *J. Rosa vs. J. B. Alvarado*, July 3, 1862, copy of Contra Costa County Court record at San Pablo Historical Society library.

33. Emparan, *Vallejos of California*, 317, 320; Orton, *Records of California Men*, 12.

34. Estudillo, *Sketches of California*, 39, 127.

35. Brewer, *Up and Down California*, 250.

36. Fickeworth, *California Railroads*, 23; telegrams in Alvarado papers in the San Pablo Historical Society Library.

37. Miller, "Californians against the Emperor," 193–214; Alvarado, "Historia," 1:181–82, 5:179.

38. Soito, *The Saint Paul Story*, 16, 18; Emeric, *Emeric vs. J. B. Alvarado, et als.*, 2:998.

39. United States Federal Census, Contra Costa County, San Pablo Township no. 1, June 1870; Contra Costa County, California, Assessment Records, 1870, Bancroft Library.

40. San Francisco *Daily Alta California*, Sept. 22, 1877, Sept. 22, 1878; *Langley's San Francisco Directory*, 1870, 1875; *Elite Directory for San Francisco and Oakland*, 1879; Writers' Program, *San Francisco*, 191–92.

41. Bancroft, *Literary Industries*, 407–08.

42. San Francisco *Alta California*, May 12, 1875; Bancroft, *Literary Industries*, 418–20.

43. Alvarado to Vallejo, Dec. 4, 1874, quoted in Bancroft, *Literary Industries*, 410. See also Alvarado to Cerruti, Dec. 9, 1874, Vallejo, "Documentos," 36:298–99.

44. Bancroft, *Literary Industries*, 407, 410.

45. Bancroft, *Literary Industries*, 412. The five original manuscript volumes are in the Bancroft Library, University of Calif., Berkeley; they have never been published. In his preface, Alvarado used an alternate title, "California antes del '48" (California before 1848).

46. Vallejo's statement is in Bancroft, *Literary Industries*, 393, and is quoted in Padilla, *My History, Not Yours*, 90. Also see Sánchez, Pita, and Reyes, "Nineteenth Century Californio Testimonials," vii.

47. Hittell also published an article, "Juan Bautista Alvarado," *Overland* 6 (1885):337–52, 459–84. Also see Alvarado, *Vignettes*, xiii; Alvarado, "Notes on California History," Sutro Library.

48. San Francisco *Bulletin*, July 17, 1882, p. 1.

49. Eulogy dated Sept. 4, 1882, copy in the San Pablo Historical Society Library.

## 8. THE GREAT LAND CASE AND LEGACY, 1867–1894

1. Testimony in Emeric, *Emeric vs. J. B. Alvarado, et als.*, 2:870–71, 1352; Land Case 320 N.D. (Rancho San Pablo), Bancroft Library.

2. Wittenmyer, compiler, *Complete Search and Abstract*, 39–40; Emeric, *Emeric vs. J. B. Alvarado, et als.*, 2:1235–38, 1357, 1380.

3. Francisco Castro Estate Papers, Frances and Earl Conley Collection; Emeric, *Emeric vs. J. B. Alvarado, et als.*, 2:860, 867, 1356–57.

4. Emeric, *Emeric vs. J. B. Alvarado, et als.*, 2:1247.

5. Wittenmyer, *Complete Search and Abstract*, 39–40; on women's rights see Lothrop, "Rancheras and the Land," 59–62.

6. *Castro vs. Castro* (Calif. Supreme Court, 1856) 6 C 158–61; Wittenmyer, *Complete Search and Abstract,* 39–40.

7. Petition to U.S. Land Commission in Wittenmyer, *Complete Search and Abstract,* 1–3; *Musson, et al, vs. Antonio Castro, et al.,* March 10, 1856, Seventh District Court, Contra Costa County, San Pablo Historical Society Library.

8. Wilson to Juan José Castro, et al., Feb. 18, 1854, John Wilson Papers, box 3, Bancroft Library.

9. Hoffman, *Reports of Land Cases,* app. 54, Rancho San Pablo; *Musson, et al, vs. Antonio Castro, et al.,* March 10, 1856, Seventh District Court; Emeric, *Emeric vs. J. B. Alvarado, et als.,* 1:270–71.

10. Sheehan, " Story of the San Pablo Rancho," 521–22; Emeric, *Emeric vs. J. B. Alvarado, et als.,* 2:1345.

11. Copy of the notice in John Wilson papers, box 3, Bancroft Library.

12. Emeric, *Emeric, vs. J. B. Alvardo, et als.;* the transcript of the case covers 1,702 pages in 3 vols.

13. Emeric, *Emeric vs. J. B. Alvarado,* et als., 64, 613; *Reports of Cases Determined in the Supreme Court of Calif.,* vol. 64 (1884).

14. *Contra Costa Gazette,* Feb. 16, 1884; land transactions in Grantor's Index, Contra Costa County Recorder's Office, Martinez.

15. List of owners and acreage allocated in Whitnah, *History of Richmond, California,* 19–25; Sheehan, " Story of the San Pablo Rancho," 517, 521–22.

16. Data on Alvarado children in San Pablo Historical Society Library; chalice donation mentioned in unidentified newspaper clipping, Aug. 17, 1914, in Irene Soberanes Scrapbook, Contra Costa County History Center.

17. Certified copy of death certificate, Frances and Earl Conley Collection; data on his marriage and career in San Pablo Historical Society Library.

18. San Francisco *Call,* June 23, 1887:8; data on Alvarado children in San Pablo Historical Society Library.

19. Copy of published obituary of Henry Alvarado in Irene Soberanes Scrapbook, Contra Costa County History Center.

20. Newspaper clipping about Mrs. Tedford in Irene Soberanes Scrapbook, Contra Costa County History Center; Northrop, *Spanish-Mexican Families,* 1:10–11.

21. Alvarado, "Historia," 4:71–72.

22. Larkin, *Larkin Papers* 4:328; Espejo's comments in Emeric, *Emeric vs. Alvarado, et als.,* 2:1242; Bosqui, *Memoirs,* 73; Davis, *Seventy-five Years in California,* 96, 113.

23. Farnham, *Life, Adventures, and Travels in California,* 54.

24. Vallejo, "Recuerdos históricos," 3:217–20.

25. Bancroft, *California Pioneer Register,* "Alvarado, Juan Bautista."

26. Hunt, "Juan Bautista Alvarado: California Cavalier," 109, 112.

# Bibliography

## MANUSCRIPTS

*The Bancroft Library, University of California, Berkeley*

Alvarado, Juan Bautista. Correspondence and Papers.

Alvarado, Juan Bautista. "Historia de California," 5 vols. 1876.

Alvarado, Juan Bautista. "Primitivo descubrimiento de placeres de oro en California."

Alvarado, Juan Bautista, and José Castro. "Exposición contra Micheltorena, Jan. 20, 1845.

Amador, José María. "Memorias sobre la historia de California." 1877.

Archives of California, 1767–1848. 63 vols.

Bowman, Jacob N. "Index of the Spanish-Mexican Private Land Grant Records and Cases of California." 2 vols., typescript. 1958.

Bowman, Jacob N., compiler. "Index of Witnesses in the California Private Land Grant Cases, 1833 to 1937."

California Biography. Binders, "Alf to Alvires."

Carrillo, Julio M. "Narrative." 1875.

Castro, Kenneth, and Doris Castro. "Castro of California; Genealogy of a Colonial Spanish California Family."

Castro, Manuel de Jesús. "Documentos para la historia de California, 1828–1875." 2 vols.

Contra Costa County, California, Assessment Records, 1870.

Douglas, James. Extracts of "Journals, 1840–1841."

Downing, Mary Margaret. "Juan Bautista Alvarado, Politician." M.A. thesis, University of California, Berkeley, 1938.

Escobar, Agustín. "La campaña de '46 contra los Americanos en California." 1877.

Estrada, José Ramón. "Padrón general que manifiesta el número de havitantes que exsisten en la municipalidad de Monterey [1836]."

Ezquer, Ignacio. "Memorias de cosas pasadas en California." 1878.

Fitch, Josefa María A. N. "Narración de la Viuda Fitch." 1875.

France. Archives du Ministère des Affaires Etrangères. Correspondance des Consuls. Monterey, Calif., Vol. 1 (microfilm).

Guerra de Hartnell, María Teresa de la. "Narrativa de la distinguida matrona californiana." 1875.

Hendry, George W., and Jacob N. Bowman. "The Spanish and Mexican Adobe and Other Buildings in the Nine San Francisco Bay Counties, 1776 to about 1850." 11 parts in 7 vols. 1940–1945.

Hertzog, Dorothy A. "Isaac Graham, California Pioneer." M.A. thesis, University of California, Berkeley, 1941.

McGinty, Ruth Mary. "Spanish and Mexican Ranchos in the San Francisco Bay Region; San Antonio, San Pablo, and San Lorenzo." M.A. thesis, University of California, Berkeley, 1921.

Mission San Carlos Borromeo (Carmel). Baptismal Records (microfilm).

Mission San Francisco de Asís (Dolores). Baptismal and Death Records (microfilm).

Mission San Luis Obispo de Tolosa. Death Records (microfilm).

Mission San Rafael Arcángel. Marriage and Death Records (microfilm).

Mission Santa Clara. Book of Marriages (microfilm).

Osio, Antonio María. "Historia de la California, 1815–1848," 1878 copy of original 1851 manuscript at Santa Clara University.

Pico, José de Jesús. "Acontecimientos en California de que hace memoria." 1878.

Pico, Pío. "Documentos para la historia de California, 1825–1852; Archivo de la familia Pico." 1877.

Savage, Thomas. "Documentos para la historia de California." 3 vols.

Serrano, Florencio. "Apuntes para la historia de Alta California." 1877.

Spence, David. "Historical Notes." 1872.

U.S. District Court. Land Cases, Northern District, 1 (Las Mariposas); 320 (San Pablo); 403 (El Sobrante); 407 (former Mission San Jose); 404 (Nicasio); 414 (Garden of San Cayetano).

U.S. General Land Office. Land Grant of Mare Island to Victor Castro in 1841. Photostat of original.

Vallejo, Mariano Guadalupe. "Documentos para la historia de California, 1769–1850." 36 vols.

Vallejo, Mariano Guadalupe. "Recuerdos históricos y personales tocante á la California, 1769–1848." 5 vols. 1875.

Wilson, John. Wilson Papers (Castro Land Suit).

*Contra Costa County History Center, Pleasant Hill, California*

Castro, Francisco María. Will, November 3, 1831.

Rancho San Pablo, Agreement of Partition, 1856.

Skinner, Lucille Alvarado. Letter to Agnes Hoey, 1947.

Irene Soberanes Scrapbook; clippings about Alvarado and Castro families.

*Contra Costa County Recorder's Office, Martinez, California*
Grantor's Index; deeds signed by Juan B. and Martina Castro.

*Frances and Earl Conley Collection, El Cerrito, California*
Census data for Monterey, California, 1830s.
Francisco Castro Estate Papers (extract).
Amelie Elkinton correspondence about Juan Bautista Alvarado.
Genealogy of Francisco María Castro's family.
Genealogy of Juan Bautista Alvarado's family.
Research Notes for Alvarado–Castro families.
Research Notes about Rancho San Pablo.
U.S. Federal Census data, extracts for 1860, 1870.

*Monterey County Recorder's Office, Salinas, California*
Deed from Manuel Jimeno Casarín to Juan B. Alvarado, Mar. 21, 1835.
Property Assessment Lists, 1851, 1852.

*San Pablo Historical Society Library, San Pablo, California*
Alvarado Family. Papers and Photographs.
Collier, George. "Mexican Land Grants in Contra Costa County," typescript.
Collier, George. "San Pablo: A History of a Rancho," typescript.
Court Records, *Musson, et al., vs. Antonio Castro, et al.* (1856); *J. Rosa vs. J. B. Alvarado* (1862).
Dominican Sisters, San Rafael, California. Correspondence.
Mutnick, Dorothy. "The Alvarado Interest in Rancho San Pablo," typescript.
Rancho San Pablo. Maps and Papers.
Society of California Pioneers. Eulogy for Juan B. Alvarado, 1882.

*Sutro Library, California State Library, San Francisco, California*
Alvarado, Juan Bautista. "Notes on California History."

## NEWSPAPERS

Martinez, *Contra Costa Gazette.* Feb. 16, 1884; Sept. 23, 1893; Jan. 31, 1897.
Monterey, *Californian.* Sept. 5, 12, 1846.
Monterey, *Peninsula Diary.* Nov. 16, 1950.
Nevada City, *Democrat.* Sept. 14, 1859.
San Francisco, *Alta California.* May 12, 1875; Sept. 22, 1877; Sept. 22, 1878; Aug. 2, 1882.
San Francisco, *Bulletin.* July 14, 17, 1882; June 9, 1901.
San Francisco, *Call.* June 23, 1887.
San Francisco, *Chronicle.* July 15, 1882; Jan. 31, 1897.

## BOOKS, MONOGRAPHS, AND PRINTED ARTICLES

Altrocchi, Julia C. *The Spectacular San Franciscans.* New York: E. P. Dutton, 1949.

Alvarado, Juan Bautista. *Vignettes of Early California.* Translated by John H. R. Polt; introduction and notes by W. Michael Mathes. San Francisco: Book Club of California, 1982. (Original MS at the Huntington Library.)

Arrillaga, Basilio José, ed. *Recopilación de leyes, decretos, bandos, reglamentos, circulares y providencias de los supremos poderers y otras autoridades de la República mexicana.* 20 vols. Mexico City: J. M. Fernández de Lara, 1828–1866.

Atherton, Faxon D. *The California Diary of Faxon Dean Atherton, 1836–1839.* Edited by Doyce B. Nunis, Jr. San Francisco: California Historical Society, 1964.

Avina, Rose H. *Spanish and Mexican Land Grants in California.* New York: Arno Press, 1976.

Baer, Morley, and Augusta Fink. *Adobes in the Sun: Portraits of a Tranquil Era.* San Francisco: Chronicle Books, 1972.

Bagwell, Beth. *Oakland: The Story of a City.* Novato, Calif.: Presidio Press, 1982.

Bakken, Gordon M. "Mexican and American Land Policy: A Conflict of Cultures." *Southern California Quarterly* 75 (1993): 237–62.

Bancroft, Hubert H. *California Pastoral, 1769–1848.* San Francisco: History Co., 1888.

———. *California Pioneer Register and Index, 1542–1848.* Baltimore: Regional Publishing Co., 1964. (Reprinted from "Pioneer Register and Index," vols. 2–5 of Bancroft's *History of California,* 1885–1886.)

———. *History of California.* Vols. 2–6. San Francisco: History Co., 1885–1888.

———. *Literary Industries.* San Francisco: History Co., 1890.

Beck, Warren A., and Ynez D. Haase. *Historical Atlas of California.* Norman: University of Oklahoma Press, 1974.

Blue, George Verne. "The Report of Captain La Place on His Voyage to the Northwest Coast and California in 1839." *California Historical Society Quarterly* 18 (Dec. 1939): 315–28.

Bosqui, Edward. *Memoirs.* San Francisco: Author, 1904.

Brewer, William H. *Up and Down California in 1860–1864: The Journal of William H. Brewer.* Edited by Francis P. Farquhar. Berkeley: University of California Press, 1949.

Briones, Brígida. "A Carnival Ball at Monterey in 1829." *Century* 41 (Jan. 1891): 468–69.

———. "A Glimpse of Domestic Life in 1827." *Century* 41 (Jan. 1891): 470.

Burgess, Sherwood. "Pirate or Patriot? Hypolite Bouchard and the Invasion of California." *American West* 11 (1974): 40–47.

California Supreme Court. *Reports of Cases Determined in the Supreme Court of California.* Vol. 64. San Francisco: Bancroft-Whitney Co., 1906.

Carreño, Alberto M. *Jefes del ejército mexicano en 1847. Biografías de generales de division y de brigada y de coroneles del ejército mexicano por fines del año 1847.* Mexico City: Secretaría de Fomento, 1914.

*Castro v. Castro* (Calif. Supreme Court, 1856) 6 C, 158–61.

Cerecedo, Carlos. "Hipolito Bouchard: Pirate or Patriot?" *La Campana* (Santa Barbara Trust for Historic Preservation), Winter 1995–96, 5–10.

Cerruti, Henry. *Ramblings in California; The Adventures of Henry Cerruti.* Edited by Margaret Mollins and Virginia E. Thickens. Berkeley: Friends of the Bancroft Library, 1954.

Conley, Frances. *Long Road to Rancho San Pablo: The Story of Francisco Castro.* El Cerrito, Calif.: Author, 1989.

———. "We All Lived Together in the Presidio." *The Californians* 5 (Jan.–Feb. 1987): 21–23, 26–27, 29–30.

Corney, Peter. *Early Voyages in the North Pacific, 1813–1818.* Fairfield, Wash.: Ye Galleon Press, 1965.

Cowan, Robert G. *Ranchos of California: A List of Spanish Concessions, 1775–1822, and Mexican Grants, 1822–1846.* Fresno: Academy Literary Guild, 1956.

Dakin, Susanna Bryant. *The Lives of William Hartnell.* Stanford: Stanford University Press, 1949.

Dana, Richard Henry. *Two Years before the Mast: A Personal Narrative of Life at Sea.* Los Angeles: Ward Ritchie Press, 1964.

Davis, William Heath. *Seventy-five Years in California.* Edited by Harold A. Small. San Francisco: John Howell Books, 1967.

"Documentary." *California Historical Society Quarterly* 5 (June 1926): 184–195.

Douglas, Sir James. *James Douglas in California, 1841; Being the Journal of a Voyage from the Columbia to California.* Vancouver, B.C.: [Vancouver Public] Library's Press, 1965.

Duflot de Mofras, Eugène. *Duflot de Mofras' Travels on the Pacific Coast.* Translated and edited by Marguerite Eyer Wilbur. 2 vols. Santa Ana, Calif.: Fine Arts Press, 1937.

Dupetit-Thouars, Abel. *Voyage of the Venus; Sojourn in California.* Translated by Charles Rudkin. Los Angeles: G. Dawson, 1956.

Egan, Ferol. *Frémont: Explorer for a Restless Nation.* Garden City, N.Y.: Doubleday & Co., 1977.

*Elite Directory for San Francisco and Oakland.* San Francisco: Argonaut Pub. Co., 1879.

Emeric, Joseph. *Joseph Emeric, Plaintiff and Respondent, vs. J. B. Alvarado et als., Defendants and Respondents, E. S. Tewksbury et als., Defendants and Appellants.* 3 vols. San Francisco: Bonnard & Daly, 1878–1879.

Emparan, Madie Brown. *The Vallejos of California.* San Francisco: Gleason Associates, University of San Francisco, 1968.

*Enciclopedia de México.* 12 vols. Mexico City: Enciclopedia de México, S.A., 1978.

Engelhardt, Zephyrin. *The Missions and Missionaries of California.* 4 vols. San Francisco: James Barry Co., 1908–1915.

Estudillo, Jesús M. *Sketches of California in the 1860s: The Journals of Jesus María Estudillo.* Edited by Margaret Schlichtmann. Fredericksburg, Tex.: Awani Press, 1988.

Farnham, Thomas J. *Life, Adventures, and Travels in California.* New York: Sheldon, Blakeman & Co., 1857.

Fickewirth, Alvin A. *California Railroads; An Encyclopedia of Cable Car, Common Carrier, Horsecar, Industrial, Interurban, Logging, Monorail.* San Marino, Calif.: Golden West Books, 1992.

Figueroa, José. *Manifiesto a la república mejicana que hace el general de brigada José Figueroa, comandante general y gefe político de la Alta California, sobre su conducta y la de los Señores D. José María de Híjar y D. José María Padrés, como directores de colonización en 1834 y 1835.* Monterey: Agustín V. Zamorano, 1835.

Fink, Augusta. *Monterey: The Presence of the Past.* San Francisco: Chronicle Books, 1972.

Foucrier, Annick. "Spy or Explorer? The True Mission of Eugène Duflot de Mofras." *The Californians* 9 (Jan.–Feb. 1992): 17–26.

Francis, Jessie Davis. *An Economic and Social History of Mexican California, 1821–1846.* New York: Arno Press, 1976.

Garner, William R. *Letters from California, 1846–1847.* Edited by Donald Craig. Berkeley: University of California Press, 1970.

Geary, Gerald J. *The Secularization of the California Missions, 1810–1846.* Washington, D.C.: Catholic University of America Press, 1934.

Gleeson, William. *History of the Catholic Church in California.* 2 vols. San Francisco: A. L. Bancroft & Co., 1871–1872.

Hague, Harlan, and David J. Langum. *Thomas O. Larkin: A Life of Patriotism and Profit in Old California.* Norman: University of Oklahoma Press, 1990.

Halley, William. *The Centennial Year Book of Alameda County, California; Containing a Summary of the Discovery and Settlement of California; a Description of the Contra Costa under Spanish, Mexican and American Rule.* Oakland: W. Halley, 1876.

Harlow, Neal. *California Conquered: War and Peace on the Pacific, 1846–1850.* Berkeley: University of California Press, 1982.

Herbert, Victor. *Natoma, An Opera in Three Acts.* New York: G. Schirmer, 1911.

Híjar, Carlos N., Eulalia Pérez, and Agustín Escobar. *Three Memoirs of Mexican California.* Translated by Vivian C. Fisher and others. Berkeley: Friends of the Bancroft Library, 1988.

Hittell, Theodore H. *History of California.* 4 vols. San Francisco: Pacific Press & Occidental Pub. Co. and N. J. Stone & Co., 1885–1897.

——. "Juan Bautista Alvarado, Governor of California." *Overland,* n. s., 6 (1885): 337–52, 459–84.

Hoffman, Ogden. *Reports of Land Cases Determined in the United States District Court for the Northern District of California, June 1853–June 1858 Inclusive.* San Francisco: Numa Hubert, 1862.

Hoover, Mildred Brooke, et al. *Historic Spots in California.* Revised by Douglas E. Kyle. Stanford: Stanford University Press, 1990.

Howard, Donald M. *California's Lost Fortress: The Royal Presidio of Monterey.* Monterey: Angel Press, 1976.

Hunt, Rockwell D. "Juan Bautista Alvarado: California Cavalier." *California's Stately Hall of Fame,* 108–12. Stockton, Calif.: College of the Pacific, 1950.

Hutchinson, C. Alan. *Frontier Settlement in Mexican California; The Híjar-Padrés Colony and its Origins, 1769–1835.* New Haven: Yale University Press, 1969.

Janssens, Victor E. August. *The Life and Adventures in California of Don Agustin Janssens, 1834–1856.* Edited by William H. Ellison and Francis Price. San Marino: Huntington Library, 1953.

Jimeno Casarín, Manuel. *Index of Land Concessions from 1830–1846.* San Francisco: Kenny and Alexander, 1861.

Johnson, Allen, ed. *Dictionary of American Biography.* 22 vols. New York: Charles Scribner's Sons, 1928–1944. Vol. 1:233–34 "Alvarado, Juan B."

Jones, Oakah L., Jr. *Los Paisanos: Spanish Settlers on the Northern Frontier of New Spain.* Norman: University of Oklahoma Press, 1979.

Kinnaird, Lawrence. *History of the Greater San Francisco Bay Region.* 3 vols. New York and West Palm Beach: Lewis Historical Pub. Co., 1966.

L'Amour, Louis. *The Californios.* New York: E. P. Dutton, 1987.

*Langley's San Francisco Directory.* San Francisco: R. L. Polk & Co., 1858, 1862–1863.

Langum, David J. *Law and Community on the Mexican California Frontier; Anglo-American Expatriates and the Clash of Legal Traditions, 1821–1846.* Norman: University of Oklahoma Press, 1987.

_____. "Sin, Sex, and Separation in Mexican California: Her Domestic Relations Law." *The Californians* 5 (May–June 1987): 44–50.

Laplace, Cyrille Pierre Théodore. *Campagne de circumnavigation de la frégate l'Artémise, pendant les années 1837, 1838, 1839 et 1840*. 6 vols. Paris: A. Bertrand, 1841–1854.

Larkin, Thomas O. *The Larkin Papers: Personal, Business, and Official Correspondence of Thomas Oliver Larkin, Merchant, and United States Consul in California*. Edited by George P. Hammond. 10 vols. Berkeley: University of California Press, 1951–1964.

_____. "Six New Larkin Letters." Edited by Doyce B. Nunis, Jr. *Southern California Quarterly* 49 (March 1967): 65–71.

Lothrop, Gloria Ricci. "Rancheras and the Land: Women and Property Rights in Hispanic California." *Southern California Quarterly* 76 (1994): 59–84.

Manning, William R., ed. *Diplomatic Correspondence of the United States; Inter-American Affairs, 1831–60*. 12 vols. Washington, D.C.: Carnegie Endowment for International Peace, 1932–1939.

Mason, Jack. *Early Marin*. San Rafael, Calif.: Marin County Historical Society, 1976.

Maxwell, Richard T. *Visit to Monterey in 1842*. Los Angeles: Glen Dawson, 1955.

Miller, Hunter, ed. *Treaties and Other International Acts of the United States of America, 1776–1863*. 8 vols. Washington, D.C.: Government Printing Office, 1931–1948. Vol. 5, *Treaty of Guadalupe Hidalgo*.

Miller, Robert Ryal. "Californians against the Emperor." *California Historical Society Quarterly* 37 (Sept. 1958): 193–214.

_____. *Captain Richardson: Mariner, Ranchero, and Founder of San Francisco*. Berkeley, Calif.: La Loma Press, 1995.

_____. *Mexico: A History*. Norman: University of Oklahoma Press, 1985.

Morefield, Richard. *The Mexican Adaptation in American California, 1846–1875*. San Francisco: R & E Research, 1971.

Morrow, William W. *Spanish and Mexican Private Land Grants*. San Francisco: Bancroft-Whitney Co., 1923.

[Munro-Fraser, J. P.] *History of Contra Costa County, California, including its Geography, Geology, Topography, Climatology . . . and Biographical Sketches*. San Francisco: W. A. Slocum & Co., 1882.

Northrop, Marie E. *Spanish-Mexican Families of Early California, 1769–1850*. 2 vols. Burbank: Southern California Genealogical Society, 1987.

Nunis, Doyce B., Jr. *The Trials of Isaac Graham*. Los Angeles: Dawson's Book Shop, 1967.

Ogden, Adele. *The California Sea Otter Trade, 1784–1848.* Berkeley: University of California Press, 1941.

Ord, Angustias de la Guerra. *Occurrences in Hispanic California.* Edited by William Ellison. Translated by Francis Price. Washington, D.C.: Academy of American Franciscan History, 1956.

Orton, Richard H., comp. *Records of California Men in the War of the Rebellion, 1861–1867.* Sacramento: State Printing Office, 1890.

Osio, Antonio María. *The History of Alta California: A Memoir of Mexican California.* Translated, edited, and annotated by Rose Marie Beebe and Robert M. Senkewicz. Madison: University of Wisconsin Press, 1996.

Padilla, Genaro. *My History, Not Yours: The Formation of Mexican American Biography.* Madison: University of Wisconsin Press, 1993.

Perez, Crisotomo N. *Land Grants in Alta California.* Rancho Cordova, Calif.: Landmark Enterprises, 1996.

Pérez Rosales, Vicente. *California Adventure.* Translated by Edwin S. Morby and Arturo Torres-Rioseco. San Francisco: Book Club of California, 1947.

_____. *We were '49ers! Chilean Accounts of the California Gold Rush.* Translated and edited by Edwin A. Beilharz and Carlos U. Lopez. Pasadena, Calif.: Ward Ritchie Press, 1976.

Phelps, William D. *Alta California, 1840–1842: The Journal and Observations of William Dane Phelps, Master of the Ship "Alert."* Edited by Briton C. Busch. Glendale, Calif.: Arthur H. Clark Co., 1983.

Pico, Pío. *Don Pío Pico's Historical Narrative.* Translated by Arthur P. Botello. Edited by Martin Cole and Henry Welcome. Glendale, Calif.: Arthur H. Clark Co., 1970.

Pierce, Marjorie. *East of the Gabilans.* Santa Cruz, Calif.: Western Tanager Press, 1976.

Pinedo, Encarnación. "Early Days in Santa Clara." San Francisco *Bulletin,* June 9, 1901.

Pitt, Leonard. *The Decline of the Californios; A Social History of the Spanish-Speaking Californians, 1846–1890.* Berkeley: University of California Press, 1970.

Prudhomme, Charley. "Leon Victor Prudon [Prudhomme]: Being the Record of One of California's Earliest Pioneers." *Grizzly Bear* 26 (Nov. 1919): 2.

*Reports of Cases Determined in the Supreme Court of the State of California,* vol. 64. San Francisco: Bancroft-Whitney Co., 1906.

Richman, Irving B. *California under Spain and Mexico, 1535–1847.* New York: Cooper Square Publishers, 1965.

Ríos-Bustamante, Antonio, ed. *Regions of La Raza: Changing Interpretations of Mexican American Regional History and Culture.* Encino, Calif.: Floricanto Press, 1993.

Robinson, Alfred. *Life in California Before the Conquest; Hispano-Californians, Leperos, & Indians, Franciscan Missionaries & Missions.* San Francisco: T. C. Russell, 1925.

Robinson, William W. *Land in California.* Berkeley: University of California Press, 1948.

Rolle, Andrew. *John Charles Frémont: Character as Destiny.* Norman: University of Oklahoma Press, 1991.

Rosenus, Alan. *General M. G. Vallejo and the Advent of the Americans: A Biography.* Albuquerque: University of New Mexico Press, 1995.

Ruiz de Burton, María Amparo. *The Squatter and the Don.* Edited by Rosaura Sánchez and Beatrice Pita. Houston: Arte Público Press, 1992.

Sánchez, Nellie Van de Grift. *Spanish Arcadia.* Los Angeles: Powell Pub. Co., 1929.

Sánchez, Rosaura, Beatrice Pita, and Barbara Reyes, eds. "Nineteenth Century Californio Testimonials." In *Crítica: A Journal of Critical Essays* 68. San Diego: University of San Diego, 1994.

Schuetz-Miller, Mardith K. *Building and Builders in Hispanic California, 1769–1850.* Tucson, Ariz.: Southwestern Mission Research Center, 1995.

Sheehan, John Francis, Jr. "The Story of the San Pablo Rancho." *Overland Monthly* 24 (1894): 517–23.

Sherman, William T. *Memoirs of General W. T. Sherman, Written by Himself.* 2 vols. New York: Appleton & Co., 1875.

Shinn, Charles H. "Spanish-Californian Schools." *Educational Review* 26 (June 1893): 30–41.

Simpson, Sir George. *Narrative of a Voyage to California Ports in 1841–42 . . . From the Narrative of a Voyage Round the World During the Years 1841 and 1842.* San Francisco: Thomas C. Russell, 1930.

Society of California Pioneers. *Centennial Roster; Commemorative Edition.* Edited by Walter C. Allen. San Francisco: n. p., 1948.

Soito, Henry C. *The Saint Paul Story: A Parish Biography.* San Pablo, Calif.: Parish of St. Paul, 1965.

Sturtevant, William C., ed. *Handbook of North American Indians.* Vol. 8, *California,* edited by Robert F. Heizer. Washington: Smithsonian Institution, 1978.

Tays, George. "Mariano Guadalupe Vallejo and Sonoma." *California Historical Society Quarterly* 16 (1937): 99–121, 216–54, 348–72; and 17 (1938): 50–73, 141–67, 219–42.

_____. "Revolutionary California: The Political History of California from 1820 to 1848." Ph.D. diss., University of California, Berkeley, 1934.

Torre, Esteban de la. "Pre-American Monterey." Translated by Nellie Van de Grift Sánchez. *Touring Topics* 22 (Oct. 1930): 28–31.

Tucey, Mary, and David Hornbeck. "Anglo Immigration and the Hispanic Town: A Study of Urban Change in Monterey, California, 1835–1850." *Social Science Journal* 13 (April 1976): 1–7.

United States Congress. 33 Cong., 2d sess. *House Executive Document 13.* Report of Board of Commissioners, Dec. 5, 1854. [Frémont's California Claims.]

Weber, David J. *Foreigners in Their Native Land; Historical Roots of the Mexican Americans.* Albuquerque: University of New Mexico Press, 1973.

_____. *The Mexican Frontier, 1821–1846: The American Southwest under Mexico.* Albuquerque: University of New Mexico Press, 1982.

Welts, Allen W. "The Lone Star Flag of California." *Masterkey* (Southwest Museum), 30 (March 1956): 40–43.

White, Stuart Edward. *The Saga of Andy Burnett.* Garden City, N.Y.: Doubleday & Co., 1951.

Whitnah, Joseph C. *A History of Richmond, California.* Richmond: Richmond Chamber of Commerce, 1944.

Wilkes, Charles. *Narrative of the United States Exploring Expedition During the Years 1838, 1839, 1840, 1841, 1842.* 5 vols. Philadelphia: C. Sherman, 1844.

Wittenmyer, L. C., comp. *Complete Search and Abstract of the Title to the Rancho de San Pablo, in Contra Costa County, California.* San Francisco: M. D. Carr, 1867.

Wood, William Maxwell. *Wandering Sketches of People and Things in South America, Polynesia, California, and Other Places Visited during a Cruise on Board of the U.S. Ships Levant, Portsmouth, and Savannah.* Philadelphia: Carey and Hart, 1849.

Woolfenden, John, and Amelie Elkinton. *Cooper: Juan Bautista Rogers Cooper, Sea Captain, Adventurer, Ranchero, and Early California Pioneer, 1791–1872.* Pacific Grove, Calif.: Boxwood Press, 1983.

Wright, Doris Marion. "The Making of Cosmopolitan California: An Analysis of Immigration, 1848–1870." *California Historical Society Quarterly* 19 (Dec. 1940): 323–43; 20 (Mar. 1941): 65–79.

_____. *A Yankee in Mexican California: Abel Stearns, 1798–1848.* Santa Barbara: Wallace Hebbard, 1977.

Writers' Program. *San Francisco: The Bay and Its Cities.* New York: Hastings House, 1940.

# Index

Abella, Ramón (fray), 43
Abrego, José, 63
Alemany, Joseph, 153
*Alert* (ship), 88
Aleuts, 30
Alta California, 3, 4, 5, 9, 28, 29, 35, 53, 55. *See also* California
Altimira, José (fray), 23
Alvarado, Adelina, 140, 154, 173, 181
Alvarado, Anna Chevesich, 169, 173. *See also* Chevesich, Anna Virginia
Alvarado, Augustus, 110, 131, 140, 154, 171, 181
Alvarado, Celinda, 140, 148, 154, 155, 163, 181
Alvarado, Clorina, 140, 181
Alvarado, Delfina, 110, 131, 140, 148, 151, 154, 169, 181
Alvarado, Enrique (Henry), 140, 148, 153, 154, 171–73, 181
Alvarado, Estéfana del Rosario, 182
Alvarado, Francisca, 140
Alvarado, Grace, 171, 181
Alvarado, Henry. *See* Alvarado, Enrique
Alvarado, John Bolton, 171, 181
Alvarado, Josefa, 32, 182
Alvarado, José Francisco (father), 5, 6, 13
Alvarado, Juan Bautista (grandfather), 5

Alvarado, Juan Bautista Valentín: accident of, 148–49; accomplishments of, 175; administrative decrees of, 64, 65, 77; alcoholism of, 32–34, 51, 57, 71, 73, 75, 85, 88, 94–95, 96, 137, 176, 177, 178; angina attack, 72; arrest of, 100, 124; arrests foreigners, 80; birth of, 3–6; blamed for spoilation of missions, 76–77; books of, 31, 134; childhood of, 6–9, 12–13; children of, 32, 74, 110, 131, 139–40, 154, 181–82; claim for requisitioned livestock, 125; colonel in militia, 51, 101, 112, 114, 118, 119, 121, 124; commander of army, 58; and Constitution of 1836, 55; as a customs administrator, 38, 45, 110; death of, 158–60; declaration of Calif. independence, 49–50, 54; deputy to Mexican Congress, 110; description of, 18, 63, 72, 90, 176–78; donation of land for church, 153; education of, 8–9, 12, 14, 16, 31, 34; eulogy of Gov. Figueroa, 40; excommunication of, 31–32; governor, 50–51, 61, 75, 63, 93, 95; grantor of land, 54, 67, 74, 84, 86, 87, 144, 175, 179–80, 189n.36; "Historia," 116, 155, 157–58, 175–76; hunter of sea otters, 30;

illegitimate children of, 32, 53, 60, 74, 182; liberalism of, 16, 17, 28, 31; in Los Angeles, 53, 59, 106; marriage of, 67, 69; mistress of, 32, 74, 182; Monterey town house, 39, 67, 73, 90, 117, 137, 141; move to Rancho San Pablo, 130–31; in Oakland, 148; owner of Union Hotel, 149–51; president of *diputación*, 41, 43, 46; ranchos of, 38, 85, 100, 127, 130, 141, 145–46; religious views of, 24, 28, 175–76; and revolt against Gutierrez, 44, 45–47; revolt against Micheltorena, 102, 103, 108; salt mine in Baja, 146; in San Francisco, 138–39, 142, 144, 147, 148, 152, 154, 157; in San Luis Obispo, 122; at San Miguel, 29; in Santa Barbara, 52, 53–54, 58, 59, 60, 62; in Santa Inés, 57; secretary of *diputación*, 21, 23, 34, 35, 38; siblings of, 6, 11, 39; silver-mining venture, 136; testimony in land cases, 144; and Vallejo, M.G., 59–60; wedding of, 69–71
Alvarado, Juan Cosme, 110, 131, 140, 148, 154, 169–71, 181
Alvarado, Lucille, 171, 181
Alvarado, María Alvino, 74, 181
Alvarado, María Antonia de la Trinidad, 182
Alvarado, María Francisca de la Ascención, 182
Alvarado, María Gerarda, 182
Alvarado, Martina: *See* Castro de Alvarado, Martina
Alvarado, Valentín, 140, 148, 181
Alviso, Agustín, 153
Amador, José María, 36, 125–26
American immigrants, 111, 115–16, 136, 142, 143. *See also* Foreign residents
Anza, Juan Bautista de, 69

Archuleta, Miguel, 7, 8, 9
*Argentina* (ship), 11–12
Argüello, Concepción, 59
Argüello, Luis Antonio, 16, 18, 20
Armstrong, James, 93
Arrillaga, José Joaquín, 5
*Asia* (Spanish ship), 16
Aspiroz, Salvador, 8
Attilan, Pierre, 99
Aulick, J. H., 83
*Ayuntamiento* of Los Angeles, 51, 53, 56, 57, 59, 96

Baja California, 24, 35, 49, 55, 64, 124, 146
Bancroft, Hubert H., 29, 37, 77, 143, 154, 155, 157, 158, 177
Bandini, Juan, 35, 37, 51, 54, 62, 75
Barron, Eustace, 82
Bear Flag revolt, 118–20, 122
Belding, Henry, 173
Berreyessa, José de los Reyes, 120
Berreyessa de Castro, Gabriela (mother-in-law), 69, 73, 130, 133, 139, 161–63, 165, 173
Biddle, James, 127
Bidwell, John, 108
Bodega Bay, 10, 85, 87
Bolton, Mary Ann, 171, 181
Boronda, Manuel, 8
Boronda, Tía, 46
Bosqui, Edward, 140, 176
Bouchard, Hipolito, 11
Brewer, William, 151–52
Bullfights, 20, 25–26

Cabot, Juan (fray), 29
Cabot, Pedro (fray), 29
Cahuenga Pass, 35
California: admission to Union, 138; constitutional convention, 137–38; government expenses and income, 100; independence of, 49–50, 54, 55, 116, 119, 123;

population of (1810) 3, (1836)
    51–52, (1840) 92, (1848–49) 135;
    supreme court established, 75;
    U.S. takeover of, 121–22. *See also*
    Alta California
*California* (ship), 55, 60, 61, 62, 74
California Battalion, 123–24, 125
*Californian* (newspaper), 127
California Pioneers, Society of, 139,
    160
Californios, 16, 26, 27, 36, 38, 84, 92,
    101, 102, 114, 119, 175; prejudice
    against Mexicans, 26–27, 45
Cambuston, Henri, 66
Campina, José, 66
Canby, Edward, 136
Cañes de Briones, Brígida, 19
Carrick, George W., 169, 181
Carrillo, Carlos Antonio, 56–62, 84
Carrillo, José Antonio, 35, 42,
    56–59, 61, 62, 84, 108, 119
Carrillo, Josefa, 24
Carson, Christopher (Kit), 120
Castañares, Andrés, 108
Castillero, Andrés, 54, 55, 60, 61,
    64, 84, 117, 126
Castillo, José, 32
Castillo, Juliana Francisca
    ("Raymunda") (mistress), 32, 74,
    182
Castro, Francisco, 69, 131, 161, 164,
    165, 166
Castro, Gabriel, 133
Castro, Gabriela. *See* Berreyessa de
    Castro, Gabriela
Castro, Jesús María, 130–31, 133,
    163, 173
Castro, Joaquín Isidro, 133, 161,
    163, 164, 165, 166
Castro, José, 25, 29, 30, 31, 40, 42,
    47, 48, 50, 52, 54, 57, 58, 62, 64,
    80–83, 91, 105, 108, 109, 135,
    146; commandant, 111, 112, 117,
    119, 120, 122, 124; court-martial
    of, 82–83; exile of, 124; and

French protectorate, 116; in Los
    Angeles, 106; and revolt vs.
    Gutiérrez, 46; and revolt vs.
    Micheltorena, 82–83, 103
Castro, Josefa, 130, 133, 173
Castro, Juan José, 162
Castro, Manuel de Jesús, 102, 103,
    108, 114, 119, 124, 146
Castro, María Gregoria, 69
Castro, María Luisa, 73
Castro, Mariano, 13
Castro, Victor, 84, 85, 120, 146, 153,
    162, 164, 167, 169
Castro-Alvarado ranch house,
    131–34, 171, 173–75
Castro de Alvarado, Martina (wife),
    67–69, 70, 73, 130, 154, 155, 161,
    162–63, 166, 167
Cerruti, Henry, 155, 157, 158
Chávez, Antonio, 102
Chávez, Victorino, 140
Chevesich, Anna Virginia, 169, 171,
    181
Chico, Mariano, 41–42, 43, 51
Cholo soldiers, 13–14, 45, 92, 93,
    97, 99–106
Coeyo, Juan, 149
Colonization, 16, 22, 36, 37, 38,
    185n.10
Colton, Walter, 127, 128
*Columbia* (ship), 89, 128
*Congress* (ship), 123
*Constante* (ship), 16
Convict settlers, 16, 22, 45
Cooper, John (Juan) Rogers, 18, 39,
    67, 85, 138, 145, 165
Coppinger, John, 48, 49
Crime, 14, 34, 97, 99
*Criollos*, 4
Cruz, Doña (mistress of Gov.
    Chico), 42, 43
*Curaçao* (ship), 83
Customs duties, 15, 51, 63, 65, 76,
    99–100
*Cyane* (ship), 93, 117, 123

*Danaïde* (ship), 83
Dances, 14, 17–20, 27, 30, 41, 49, 62, 88–89, 95–96, 117–18, 126, 151. *See also* Fiestas
Davis, William Heath, 34, 176
Del Valle, Ignacio, 57
*Diputación* (territorial legislature), 15–16, 21, 22, 23, 26, 28, 34, 35, 36, 38, 40, 42, 43, 44, 46, 47, 49, 50, 64, 75, 96, 109, 111,124
*Diseños*, 26, 165
*Don Quixote* (ship), 49, 109
Douglas, James, 89
Duflot de Mofras, Eugène, 90–91
Dupetit–Thouars, Abel, 56
Dupont, Samuel, 117
Durán, Narciso (fray), 17, 31, 32, 42, 52, 60
Dutra de Vargas, Manuel, 74

Echeandía, José María, 20, 23, 24, 26, 28, 29, 35
Education, 8, 63, 66–67, 97, 129, 148, 175, 178
El Cuartel (Monterey), 65, 95
Emeric, Henry, 169
Emeric, Joseph, 166, 169
Escobar, Agustín, 114
Escobar, John, 182
Espejo, Juan N., 33, 139, 176
Estrada, Joaquín, 124
Estrada, Josefa, 63
Estrada, José Ramón, 69
Estrada, Julián, 124
Estrada, Rafael, 39
Estrada, Raymundo, 6, 12, 14, 39
Estrada, Rita, 39
Estudillo, Joaquín, 179
Estudillo, José Joaquín, 14

Farnham, Thomas Jefferson, 82, 176
Fernández de San Vicente, Agustín, 15

Fiestas, 14, 17–20, 25, 41, 49, 62, 70, 75, 125, 137, 158, 163. *See also* Dances; Bullfights
Figueroa, José, 35–40, 161
Fitch, Henry, 24
Flores, José, 123, 125
Forbes, James Alexander, 165
Foreign residents, 16, 42, 46–49, 52, 67, 80, 81, 82, 92, 101, 102, 104, 106, 108, 118, 175
Forrest, French, 83
Fort Ross, Calif., 10, 30, 86, 87
France: interest in Calif., 71–72, 90–91
Franciscans, 3, 4, 5, 17, 22, 23, 28, 31, 76; from Zacatecas, 36–37. *See also* Missions; *names of missionaries*
Frémont, John Charles, 111–12, 114, 118, 119, 120, 122, 126; commandant of Calif., 125; purchase of Rancho Las Mariposas, 127
Fuentes, Josefa, 97

Gantt, John, 105
García Diego y Moreno, Francisco, 97
Garner, William, 48, 80, 81
Gavilán Peak (Frémont Peak), 112, 114, 120
Gillespie, Archibald, 117–18, 125
Gilroy, Calif., 12
Gold, in Calif., 70, 87–88, 127, 135–36, 138
Gomez Farías, Valentín, 37, 41
González, José María de Jesús (fray), 70
González, Rafael, 116
Goodale, David, 139
Graham, Isaac, 46–49, 52, 53, 80, 82, 85, 96, 104
Graham affair, 80–83, 109
Gray, Nicholas, 166
Great Britain: interest in Calif., 91
Guerra, José de la, 78

Guerra, María Teresa de la, 78, 79
Guerra, Pablo de la, 110, 116, 123, 145
Gutiérrez, Cándido, 162
Gutiérrez, Nicolás, 40–41, 43–44, 45, 48, 49

Hapsburg, Maximilian von, 152–53
Haro, Francisco de, 120
Haro, Ramón de, 120
Hartnell, William, 14, 77–78, 112, 116, 135, 136–37
Hepburn, H., 164–65
Herrera, José María, 25
Hide and tallow trade, 15
Híjar, José María, 37, 38
Hinckley, William, 49
Hittell, Theodore H., 158, 169
Howard, William, 127
Hudson's Bay Co., 86, 89
Hunt, Rockwell, 178

Ibarra, Gil, 57
Immigrants, foreign, 63, 92
Indians, 4, 13, 17, 22, 28, 34, 36, 43, 47, 52, 72, 76, 78, 84, 86, 99, 104–7, 131, 135, 140, 145, 146, 158, 175, 176. *See also* Neophytes
Iturbide, Emperor Agustín, 15

Janssens, Agustín, 39, 56
Jimeno Casarín, Manuel, 63, 65, 75, 78, 84, 96
Jones, Thomas ap Catesby, 93, 95, 96
José el Cantor (singing master), 7

Kearny, Stephen W., 127
Kostromitinov, Peter, 30

Laguna Seca, 103
Land grants, 22, 26, 28, 29, 36, 37, 54, 61, 63, 67, 72, 74, 76, 83, 86, 87, 91, 104–5, 142–45, 164, 179
Laplace, Cyrille Pierre, 71, 72

Larkin, Thomas Oliver, 67, 94, 99, 101, 111, 112, 115, 127, 176
*L'Artemise* (ship), 71, 72
Leese, Jacob, 119
*Leonor* (ship), 31
López, Francisco, 87
López de Santa Anna, Antonio, 41, 92, 147
Loreto, Baja California, 5, 20
Los Angeles, Calif., 22, 35, 38, 54, 93, 97, 106, 111, 122, 124; as capital, 41, 52, 75; reconquest, 127; U.S. takeover, 125
Lugo, María Antonia, 6, 14

Madariaga, Bonifacio, 39
Mare Island, 84
Marsh, John, 85, 105
Martinez, Calif., 171, 173
Martínez, Ignacio, 23
Martínez, José, 17
Martínez, Luis (fray), 17, 25
Mason, Richard, 138
Maxwell, Richard T., 93, 95
McKinley, James, 106, 108, 141
Mejía, José, 100
Mellus, Henry, 127
*Memoria del Rey*, 9
Menéndez, José Antonio (fray), 24
*Mestizos*, 4
Mexico: Congress, 16, 37, 41, 52, 64, 84; Constitution of 1824, 16, 17, 41, 45, 50, 53; Constitution of 1836 (Las Siete Leyes), 41, 42, 54, 55; independence of, 14–17, 23, 26, 27; political instability of, 21, 29, 41, 56, 111, 115, 152–53. *See also* Mexico City
Mexico City, 14, 22, 28, 37, 38, 40, 41, 42, 45, 83
Micheltorena, Manuel, 83, 92, 93, 96, 100, 101, 103, 104, 105, 107, 109, 127, 145; capitulation of, 109; description of, 97–99; in Los Angeles, 97

Militia, 51, 53, 58, 79, 101, 104, 112, 120, 122
Missions, 9, 10, 42, 77; administrators of, 29, 30, 76–79; establishment of, 3, 5; San Antonio, 29; San Buenaventura, 57, 108; San Carlos Borromeo (Carmel), 4, 18, 29; San Fernando, 58; San Francisco de Asis (Dolores), 131, 163; San Gabriel, 43; San Jose, 105, 145; San Juan Bautista, 12, 46, 48, 51, 64, 101, 102, 112, 114, 121; San Juan Capistrano, 58, 78; San Luis Obispo, 6, 25, 124; San Luis Rey, 59; San Miguel, 6, 29; San Rafael, 47, 119, 120, 145; Santa Barbara, 40, 52, 106, 107; Santa Clara, 30, 69, 103, 118, 119, 120; Santa Inés, 52, 57, 97, 121; secularization of, 22, 28, 29, 36, 37, 38, 76–79; Soledad, 85
Moerenhaut, Jacques Antoine, 146
Montenegro, Eugenio, 39
Monterey, Calif., 4, 5, 10, 11, 15–18, 20, 21, 25, 34, 38, 39, 41, 42, 46, 55, 56, 62, 64, 99, 111, 125, 126–27; civic improvements of, 65; description of, 4, 14, 90; population of, 4, 39, 90; U.S. takeover (1842), 93–95; — (1846), 121–22. See also Presidios: Monterey
Monterey junta, 115, 118
Muñoz, Juan Antonio, 47
Munrás, Esteban, 46
Musson, Eugene, 164–65

Napa Valley, 47
Neophytes, 3, 22, 29, 30, 36, 43, 78, 84. See also Indians
Nicasio Valley, 145
North-South California rivalry, 35, 41, 51–59, 62, 75, 115

Oakland, Calif., 148, 155, 160, 169
Ortega, Antonia, 12
Ortega, Clara, 12
Ortega, Ignacio, 12, 13
Ortega, José, 12
Ortega, María Gertrudis, 12
Osio, Antonio María, 13, 35, 42, 51–52, 57, 63, 65, 93, 97, 99

Pacheco, Romualdo, 20
Pacheco, Salvio, 153
Padrés, José María, 28–29, 35, 37, 38
Palace Hotel (San Francisco), 154, 171, 173
Palomares, Ignacio, 57
Peninsulares, 4, 23, 37, 40, 45
Pérez, Juan, 135
Pérez Rosales, Vicente, 13
Phelps, William, 88
Pico, Andrés, 57, 62, 104, 142, 145
Pico, Antonio María, 143
Pico, José de Jesús, 36, 41, 48, 102, 124–25
Pico, Pío, 35, 57, 58, 60, 62, 64, 75–76, 106, 108, 145; exile of, 124; governor, 107, 109–12, 114, 115, 117, 118, 120, 122, 124; heads force to overthrow Castro, 118, 122
Pinard, Clemente, 141
Pinedo, Encarnación, 69
Pliego, Rodrigo del, 27–28
Portolá, Gaspar de, 5
Presidios, 3, 4, 16; description of, 4; Monterey, 4, 5, 6, 10, 11, 13, 14, 17, 24–25, 48, 49; sacking of, 11–12; San Diego, 23; San Francisco, 14, 23, 25, 30
Printing, 38, 49, 62, 81, 92
Prudon (Prudhomme), Victor, 53, 63, 79, 115, 116, 119, 187n.17
Pueblos, 3, 16, 22, 28, 29, 35, 38, 65

Railroads, 152
Ramírez, Angel, 39, 46

Ramírez, José, 57
Ranchos: Alisal, 78, 112, 136; Bolsa del Potrero, 85; Cahuenga, 108; Del Rey, Calif., 11, 12; El Alisal, 78, 85, 95, 96, 102, 105, 112, 115, 125, 126, 141; El Sobrante, 162; El Sur, 39, 85, 130; Jamul, 144; Las Flores, 58; Las Mariposas, 100, 127, 130; Los Médanos, 105; Los Ojitos, 74; Milpitas, 133; Nacional, 48; San Leandro, 179; San Lorenzo, 85, 120; San Ramón, 126; San Ysidro, 12; Suscol, 99; Verdugo, 108. See also Rancho San Pablo
Rancho San Pablo, 47, 69, 102, 103, 119, 120, 130, 135, 152, 157, 158, 177; description of, 131–33, 135; lawsuits, 161, 163–67, 177; partition of, 162, 165, 167, 169; title confirmed, 165, 167
Raoul (Alvarado's cook), 74, 188n.16
Rico, Francisco, 103
Ripoll, Antonio (fray), 23
Rivera y Moncada, Fernando, 5
Robinson, Alfred, 82
Rocha, Juan, 52
Rosa, J. (bartender), 149
Rosamel, Joseph, 83
Rufus, Ernest, 105
Ruiz de Burton, María Amparo, 144
Russian American Company, 10, 30, 36, 38, 85, 87

St. Louis (ship), 83
St. Paul's Catholic Church, 153, 155, 160, 169, 171
Salinas, Calif., 11
San Blas, Mexico, 25, 55, 81, 109
Sánchez, Francisco, 116
San Diego, Calif., 3, 20, 23, 24, 35, 54, 92. See also Presidios: San Diego

San Fernando Valley, 58
San Francisco Bay, 23, 30, 36, 69, 72, 91, 131. See also Missions: San Francisco de Asis; Presidios: San Francisco
San Francisco, Calif., 130, 163, 164; population of, 138
San Joaquín Valley, 112
San Jose, 47, 51, 103, 104
San Pablo, Calif., 152, 171
San Pablo Bay, 131, 155
San Pedro, Calif., 109, 123, 125
San Rafael, Calif., 155
Santa Anna. See López de Santa Anna, Antonio
Santa Barbara, Calif., 23, 25, 54, 58, 62, 81, 118. See also Missions: Santa Barbara
Santa Cruz, Calif., 11, 104
Santa Cruz Island, 84, 126
Santa Rosa (ship), 11–12
Santa Rosa Island, 84
Sarría, Vicente (fray), 17, 23
Saunders, John, 164–65
Savannah (ship), 102
Secularization. See Missions: secularization of
Semple, Robert, 127
Serra, Junipero (fray), 5
Sherman, William T., 126
Ships, foreign, 10–11, 15, 23, 49, 56, 88, 89. See also names
Shubrick, William, 127
Simpson, George, 89–90
Skinner, Lucille Alvarado, 133
Sloat, John, 121–22
Soberanes, Feliciano, 85
Soberanes, Mariano de Jesús, 74
Solá, Pablo Vicente, 8–9, 10, 11–12, 16
Solano (Indian chief), 47
Solís, Joaquín, 25
Sonoma, Calif., 38, 46, 47, 57, 58, 59, 102, 118, 119, 121, 145
Sonora, Mexico, 147–48

Spaniards, 3, 4, 5, 17, 23. *See also*
    Peninsulares
Spear, Nathan, 34
Spence, David, 46, 89, 116
Squatters, 142–44, 151
Stearns, Abel, 35
Stockton, Robert F., 122–23
Suárez Real, José, 80
Sutter, John Augustus, 67, 86–87,
    104, 106, 110; captain in militia,
    104–5; capture of, 108
Sutter's Fort, 91, 112, 118–19

Taylor, Alexander Smith, 136
Tedford, Frank I., 173, 181
Tepic, Mexico, 81, 82, 83
Tewksbury, Jacob, 169
Tewksbury, Lucian M., 173, 181
Torre, Joaquín de la, 119
Trade, 10, 15, 22, 42, 51, 57, 72, 89
*Traveller* (ship), 10
Treaties: Guadalupe Hidalgo, 128,
    137; Laguna de Alvirez (Santa
    Teresa), 104, 107; Las Flores, 58;
    San Fernando, 109; Santa Teresa,
    104, 107

United States: Board of Land Com-
    missioners, 142–44, 164–66; Civil
    War, 57, 151–52; interest in Calif.,
    52, 91, 121
*United States* (ship), 93
U.S.-Mexican War, 111, 121–22,
    126, 128

Vallejo de Alvarado, María Josefa, 5,
    6, 11, 14, 39
Vallejo, Encarnación, 18, 166
Vallejo, Ignacio (grandfather), 5–6,
    9, 13, 14

Vallejo, Mariano Guadalupe, 6–9,
    14, 25, 29–31, 35, 38, 42, 46, 47,
    50, 51, 57, 87, 99, 102, 138, 155,
    157, 158; colonel in militia, 101;
    confirmed as *comandante general*,
    61, 75; disbands Sonoma garri-
    son, 103; favors annexation to
    U.S.A., 116–17; library of, 31,
    134; in Monterey, 81; prisoner of
    "Bears," 119, 123; quarrel with
    Alvarado, 59, 177; quarrel with
    Hartnell, 79; reminiscences, 157;
    resigns as *comandante*, 79; in San
    Jose, 91; in Santa Barbara, 62
Vallejo, Platón, 151
Vallejo, Salvador, 58, 102–3, 119
Vanderstice, Henry, 142
Vargas, Juan, 135
Vega, Plácido, 153
*Venus* (ship), 55
Victoria, Manuel, 29, 30, 34–35
*Vincennes* (ship), 91
Vioget, Jean Jacques, 65

Weber, Charles, 104
Weddings, 18–19, 24, 69–70
Wilcox, James, 10
Wilkes, Charles, 91
Wilson, Benjamin (Benito) D., 108
Wilson, John, 164–65
Wood, William, 102
Workman, William, 106

Yerba Buena, Calif., 23, 30, 65, 89,
    103, 118, 121, 130, 157
*Yorktown* (ship), 83

Zamorano, Agustín, 20, 23, 35, 54